ABSOLUTISM AND ITS DISCONTENTS

Absolutism and Its Discontents

State and Society in Seventeenth-Century France and England

Michael S. Kimmel

Transaction Books
New Brunswick (USA) and Oxford (UK)

Library of Congress Catalog Number: 87-19028

ISBN: 0-88738-180-4

Printed in the United States of America

Library of Congress Cataloging in Publication Data

Kimmel, Michael S.
   Absolutism and its discontents.
   Bibliography: p.
   Includes index.
   1. Despotism—France—History—17th Century.
2. Despotism—England—History—17th century.
3. France—Politics and government—17th century.
4. Great Britain—Politics and government—1603–1714.
I. Title.
JC375.K55   1987   321.6'094   87-19028
ISBN 0-88738-180-4

For my mother

Contents

Preface

I first became interested in the phenomenon of revolution when I believed, in the late 1960s, I was involved in making one. By the end of the next decade I had also become interested in revolutions that fail. The durability and adaptability of U.S. political institutions was startling, and I wanted to study how social structures persist, as well as how they are transformed. My inquiries led me away from contemporary issues, to the era of revolutionary upheaval and transformation of seventeenth-century Europe—the era in which modern economic, social, and political institutions emerged, as did ideological formulae constructed to support them and lend intellectual coherence.

As I explored the secondary literatures on the social organization of early modern Europe, and combed the historiography of seventeenth-century revolution, I became frustrated with earlier sociological explanations. Sociological models of revolution and particularistic historical accounts of specific events seemed equally hard-pressed, although for antithetical reasons, to explain both the causes of revolution throughout Europe and the divergent outcomes of those revolutionary upheavals. In particular I was disappointed that the role of the state in revolution and the relationship between state and society seemed so often misunderstood.

During the course of my empirical research for this book, I became more convinced that history and sociology are necessary complements. Without good sociology, history can degenerate into the *histoire événementielle* against which Fernand Braudel so eloquently argued. And an ahistorical sociology is an impoverished sociology, a sociology condemned to either grand theory or abstracted empiricism, against which C. Wright Mills once railed. In this book I have tried to use the historical record to generate sociological explanations—as opposed to setting up a theoretical model for which empirical evidence is then discovered—and then modified these explanations by confronting again the historical materials.

As will be evident in the pages that follow, I did not come to my

ix

conclusions all by myself, meditating in some sheltered glade. Ideas do not drop from the sky; they come from people, and many people have helped me work out the ideas of this study, either directly or indirectly. I have been inspired by, and have wrestled with, the work of a number of social scientists who have worked with historical materials, such as Perry Anderson, Barrington Moore, Theda Skocpol, Neil Smelser, Charles Tilly, and Immanuel Wallerstein, in addition to a group of young scholars, such as Ron Aminzade, Victoria Bonnell, Craig Calhoun, Wally Goldfrank, and Jeff Paige. In addition, historians such as Richard Bonney, Christopher Hill, Lloyd Moote, Lawrence Stone, and David Underdown evidenced a deep sensitivity to the sociological reasoning that was vitally important to my work.

This book had its origins as a Ph.D. dissertation in sociology at the University of California at Berkeley, where I was fortunate to have several of these scholars as teachers and advisers. Victoria Bonnell's research on skilled workers before the Russian Revolution and Lynn Hunt's work on the relationship among local politics, industrial organization, and revolutionary experience in late-eighteenth-century France are models of meticulous and engaged scholarship. Bill Kornhauser's theoretical insistence of the importance of politics helped to ground my ideas. Each of them offered valuable criticisms and support.

Neil Smelser was an exemplary chairman of that dissertation committee. His comments on various drafts were invariably helpful, challenging my perspective, pushing me to see issues from new angles, to say more in a less unwieldy way—and always responding quickly with a balance of encouragement and criticism that I have found all too rare in the academy.

Many other friends and colleagues—both in the United States and abroad—have added comments, criticisms, and companionship at various stages, among them Rod Aya, Thomas Barnes, Gérard and Irène Besson, Harry Bredemeier, Philippe Djeddah, Bill Domhoff, Jacqueline Dumas, Wally Goldfrank, Jerry Himmelstein, Keith Luria, David Plotke, Julia Sokoloff, Louise Tilly, Ann and Jef Verschueren, Laurie Wermuth, and Philippe Uninsky. The staff of the Bibliothèque Mazarine was especially helpful, as was William Kellaway, who expedited my work at the Institute for Historical Research and the British Museum. Fellowship support from the Institute of International Studies and the Chancellor's Patent Fund, both at Berkeley, permitted me to travel abroad, and a Summer Faculty Fellowship from Rutgers University facilitated one of the revisions. I am also grateful to the late Julia Cameron, a fine research assistant and a good friend.

Since I completed my graduate career and as the manuscript has undergone successive revisions, several scholars have been particularly generous of their time and intellectual energy in working with me, especially in that I have not formally been their student or colleague. Scott McNall, Theda Skocpol, and Chuck Tilly have all offered searching criticisms of the manuscript and valuable publishing advice, and helped sustain a vision of intellectual community. At Rutgers University I was fortunate to work with Irving Louis Horowitz, who has been an exemplary colleague, a trusted editor and publisher, a demanding and gracious "boss" at *Society* magazine, and a valued friend. His insistence in posing the most difficult moral and intellectual questions, and following a rigorous social scientific route to often unpopular positions has been very important to me.

Finally, I am grateful to my family and my friends for their love and support. Several friends—Angela Aidala, Claire August, Martin Duberman, Kate Ellis, John Gagnon, Cathy Greenblat, Martin Levine, and Mary Morris—did not contribute directly to this project but have been so emotionally and professionally supportive that to fail to acknowledge them would make the entire enterprise seem incomplete. And Iona Mara-Drita has not "cheerfully prepared the index," "graciously typed the manuscript," nor "relieved me of mundane household tasks while I pursued the rigorous life of the mind"—or any of the other things that one often reads in prefaces of books by male authors. For that, and many other things, I thank her.

Throughout my life my family has encouraged and sustained me, and I am lucky that both my parents and my sister, and my stepfamily, have given me such a circle of intimate support. It is with admiration, gratitude, and love that I dedicate this book to my mother, whose combination of personal and professional growth has been an inspiration.

—May, 1987
New York City

1

Toward a Historical Sociology of Revolution in Early Modern Europe

What causes revolution? Why do some revolutions succeed and some fail? This book addresses these questions by developing a comparative historical approach to the sociological study of two contemporaneous revolutions in seventeenth-century Europe: the English Revolution, 1640–1660, and the Revolts of the Fronde in France, 1648–1653. The English Revolution succeeded, laying the foundation for liberal capitalist industrialization and formal democracy, and the Fronde failed, collapsing into internecine squabbling among nobles and easily suppressed revolts of other social groups, whose disorganization supported Bourbon absolutism until 1789. A close sociological comparison will allow me to explore both the questions of the causes of revolution and their outcomes. Simply put, specifying the similarities in the antecedents of revolution in both countries may help in explicating the causes, and identifying the differences between the two revolutions may suggest some of the factors that yield different revolutionary outcomes.

In this work I will argue that revolutions are caused by long-run structural changes, especially in the relationship between state and society, and that revolutions are made by political coalitions that come to oppose state fiscal policies, the programs initiated by the state to overcome domestic obstacles to the achievement of aggressive foreign policy objectives.[1] Different revolutionary outcomes themselves depend upon the relationship between political power and capital, the character and composition of the organized opposition that forms the revolutionary coalition, the regional forms of economic organization that experience state initiatives differently, and the effective mobilization of an oppositional ideology

1

that can sustain revolutionary coalitions that are composed of disparate and often competing groups.

Revolution in the Sociological Imagination

The problem of revolution has always been at the center of sociological inquiry.[2] For theorists whose work stresses social order and coherence, revolutions provide a negative case, and specifying the dynamics of revolution can, by negation, inform the student of the dynamics that create social order. More immediately, theorists who focus on questions of conflict and domination find in revolution the apotheosis of social struggle that defines everyday life. Many of the classical sociological theorists—Marx, Tocqueville, Durkheim, and Weber—lived during eras of revolutionary upheaval (the first two witnessed and wrote about the events of 1848; the latter two observed the Russian Revolution, republican efforts in China, and aborted efforts in Germany) and were preoccupied with both the causes and consequences of revolution.

For Marx, revolution was the pivotal historical moment, the cataclysmic break that marked historical epochs from one another. Revolution was the historical outcome of the conflict between two contending classes, each of which was organized by its relationship to the means of production. Tocqueville, by contrast, stressed more political and ideological forces in his analysis, suggesting that the French Revolution was precipitated by the hereditary aristocracy's abandonment of its traditional function as the guarantor of individual liberty against the political despotism of absolute rule, and by the expectations set in motion by a despotic king's belated efforts at reform. Weber's analysis of the revolutionary potential of charismatic authority—its ability to revolutionize people "from within" and its revolutionary break with the inherited traditional system of domination—added a social psychology of motivation to his pessimistic analysis that revolutions historically consolidate bureaucratic political power and enhance state control over the economy rather than result in human liberation. Finally, Durkheim cast revolution as the negative cause of social order, when solidary bonds rupture and allow challenges by disaffected groups that are no longer sufficiently integrated and regulated by social norms.

Contemporary sociological theorists have been equally interested in the problem of revolution. Some have focused on individual cognitive orientations of the participants in revolutionary social movements to understand their occurrence, assuming that explaining the participants' motivations would also explain the phenomenon itself. (See, for example, Davies, 1962; Olson, 1965; Gamson and Fireman, 1979; especially Gurr, 1971,

1978.) By stressing the cognitive orientations of individual participants, this social-psychological model also tends to cast the state as the passive distributor of resources and not as a contender in the struggle for political power, or, indeed, as the creator of its own political opposition. Other theorists have followed the structural functionalist perspective of Talcott Parsons, which emphasizes how revolutions disequilibrate an otherwise homeostatic social system, and how they arise from "social disturbances of societal equilibrium" (Johnson, 1966: xiii; see also Parsons, 1955; Johnson, 1965; Smelser, 1965). Revolutions, in this model, stem from breakdowns in an otherwise functional social system, a disruption of the value consensus that underlies all social and political institutions. But, such an overvaluation of cultural values at the expense of social structural variables leads this school to identify political legitimacy with political power, no matter how it is exercised and constituted; Johnson (1965: 28) for example, writes that "power and authority . . . both refer to relationships of legitimacy" without considering issues of coercion and domination inherent in any polity. Both social psychological and functionalist perspectives place undue emphasis on the motivations of individual participants, so that the interrelationships among structural forces is secondary to voluntaristic notions of individual mobilization.

Several recent sociological studies of revolution have returned to structural variables to explain revolutions. Some, like Wallerstein and Polanyi, have rediscovered the revolutionary potential of the market to motivate specific social groups to reorient their economic behavior, which then leads to confrontations with entrenched political elites and state power (Wallerstein, 1974, 1979, 1980, and Polanyi, 1957; see also Block and Somers, 1984; Kimmel, 1977, 1982; Ragin and Chirot, 1984). In Wallerstein's world-system scheme, revolutions are the result of economically mobilized classes' struggle with existing political institutions and entrenched elites who seek to block or control the new classes' increased participation in the expanding capitalist world-economy.[3] Here, the state is reduced to a by-product of the positioning of economically mobilized classes in the world-economy; Wallerstein (1972: 101) asserts that his analysis demonstrates "how the economic development of particular states in modern times *is and has been a function of* their role in a world-economy, and how the political development within such states have *reflected* the pressures that *derive from the consequences* for various groups of the condition of this world-economy at a given time" (emphasis added).

Others writers follow the more traditional Marxist emphasis on class struggle at the level of production, and employ Lenin's understanding— "the passing of state power from one class to another is the first, the main, the basic principle of a revolution'' (Lenin, 1929: 119)—in their analysis of revolution. (See, for example, Brenner, 1975; Moore, 1966; see also Smith, 1984.) Here, revolutions appear to be based on a metaphor of the boxing match: two fully mobilized classes get into the ring and slug it out, and the winner of that battle wins the crown, state power. Moore, for example, although not as crudely deterministic as this metaphor would suggest, examines the political outcomes that result from the relations between agricultural producers and landlords; especially for early capitalist development, he argues, this class conflict resulted in a specific state form. Unfortunately, such a causal sequence seriously undervalues the autonomy of the state in determining and structuring its own opposition, and it is ill-equipped to explain the divergent outcomes of revolutions in early modern France and England.

Some contemporary sociologists take the state seriously as an autonomous institution and as an analytic variable, exploring the specifically political sociology of revolution, and, in that sense, provide the point of departure for this work. Skocpol, for example, argues that successful social revolution depends on the collapse of the old regime state (due to increased international pressures, both economic and military) and class struggle between agricultural classes, and the eventual reconstitution of political power by new elites. Old regime states collapse, she argues (1979: 285), because

> imperial states became caught in cross pressures between intensified military competition or intrusions from abroad and constraints imposed on monarchical responses by the existing agrarian class structures and political institutions . . . their existing structures made it impossible for them to meet the particular international military exigencies that each had to face.

According to Skocpol, political crisis and the collapse of the old regime state serve as the political moment of revolution, but a successful social revolution requires also the violent clash between the peasantry and landlords, the classic agricultural class struggle of Marxist theory. Such a model suggests a metaphor: the old regime state is seen as analogous to a structurally unsound bridge; cracked and already weak, the bridge collapses under the additional pressure of a heavier weight. In the resulting power vacuum, a group of new engineers builds a more structurally sound bridge that will be more resistant to environmental erosion and able to accommodate additional weight.

Despite some important shortcomings in Skocpol's work (Himmelstein and Kimmel, 1981), her analysis of the collapse of the old regime state shaped not by class struggle but by relations between the state and the dominant class and with other states is essential for the analysis of revolution in mid-seventeenth-century France and England. Each of these old regime states collapsed, although the French state was able to reconstitute itself more assertively than before. The English case emerges as a successful political revolution, and the failure of the lower classes, in both rural and urban areas, insured that the social revolution would not succeed. However, the major weakness in Skocpol's analysis springs from her resolute antivoluntarism. She ignores how human beings, thinking and acting (however haphazardly) in concert, are the mediating links between structural conditions and social outcomes. Structural conditions do not magically yield political outcomes; they do so only to the extent that they determine human options, ideas, and actions, placing limits and defining a range of possibilities. People may not make history "just as they please," as Marx reminded us, but they do "make history."

Here the work of Charles Tilly has been exemplary (see, for example, Tilly, 1973, 1975, 1978, 1979, 1984, 1985, 1986; see also Hunt, 1984). Tilly explicitly rejects social psychological or systems theories of revolution while retaining a balanced interest between structural causes and the mobilization of revolutionary coalitions. He writes (1973: 447):

> Despite the many recent attempts to psychologize the study of revolution by introducing ideas of anxiety, alienation, rising expectations, and the like, and to sociologize it by employing notions of disequilibrium, role conflict, structural strain, and so on, the factors which hold up under close scrutiny are, on the whole, political ones. The structure of power, alternative conceptions of justice, the organization of coercion, the conduct of war, the formation of coalitions, the legitimacy of the state—these traditional concerns of political thought provide the main guides to the explanation of revolution.

To Tilly (1973: 443) revolution is the crisis-level expression of political struggle that occurs all the time, but a crisis because it allows the formation of "coalitions between polity members and revolutionary challengers." A revolution is here analogous to the child's game of "king of the hill," in which contenders for state power battle it out with one another and with the state, and the group on top at any moment can mobilize a larger share of resources with which to do battle. Although Tilly's theoretical work suggests how revolutionary coalitions are formed, his empirical studies of political struggle in France have emphasized how military expenditures propel state actions that, in turn, provoke opposition (see especially Tilly, 1986).

Tilly and Skocpol turn our attention to the state as the explicit object of analysis; other structural arguments reintroduce class struggle and orientation toward an international context as key variables in the study of revolution. In this work I have attempted to bring these three structural themes—international context, class relations at the level of production, and political relationships—through an analysis of fiscal crisis of the old regime state. Fiscal crisis is the "tendency," as O'Connor writes (1973: 2), "for governmental expenditures to outrace revenues." State efforts to resolve this fiscal crisis lead the state to encroach on the traditional privileges of traditional elites, whose withdrawal of financial support begins the process of elite resistance to the state, a withdrawal that signals the beginnings of a revolutionary situation in which more than one socially mobilized group makes a claim for political power. Revolutions begin because the state is unable to balance itself between international pressures (military and economic) and domestic social arrangements (agrarian class relations) and pursue its foreign policy without domestic opposition. I have thus chosen to join the comparative historical sociology of revolution at the moment of state collapse, and attempt then to read backward to understand the ways in which increased international pressure exacerbated traditional domestic struggles, and how efforts by the state to mobilize domestic resources so as to pursue its foreign policy objectives more vigorously set various corporate groups against it.

The fiscal crisis of the old regime state provides the analytic linchpin in a theoretical model of the causes of revolution; it is the "middle-range" variable between the long-range structural shifts that set forces in motion and the proximate immediate triggers of the revolt itself.[4] An analysis of the fiscal crisis of the state allows us to view the state at the moment of collapse and the development of a revolutionary coalition that will contend for political power. The crisis is not the long-run cause of the English Revolution and the Fronde because, as Moore notes (1966: 244), "financial difficulties are no more than symptoms of deeper causes," but the crisis empirically links these deeper causes: the international economic and political context of national development, the structure of the state, and the constitution of the political nation. Fiscal crisis is the moment of conjuncture, when these tensions become sharpened into a situation demanding resolution, in which the legitimacy of the regime is itself questioned. "The public finances are one of the best starting points for an investigation of society," observed Schumpeter (1954: 7). "The spirit of a people, its cultural level, its social structure, the deeds of its policy may prepare—all this and more is written in its fiscal history. . . . He who knows how to listen to the message here discerns the thunder of world history more clearly than anywhere else." By beginning our discussion with the fiscal crisis, we can then more precisely describe the elements that hold a revolutionary coalition together, that enable the coalition to sustain its challenge. Thus, I will set ideological and cultural variables in context of the unfolding revolutionary drama; revolutionary ideas do not cause revolutions, but they may sustain a revolutionary coalition.

Adequate sociological analysis of revolution needs to be both comparative and historical, and this work will compare two historical cases of revolution in mid-seventeenth-century Europe to suggest some of the reasons that revolutions occur and why some succeed and some fail. After all, as Tocqueville reminds us (1970: 111), "Whoever studies and looks only at France will never understand anything . . . of the French Revolution." And, Hintze argues (1975: 23), "You can compare in order to find something general that underlies the things that are compared, and you can compare in order to grasp more clearly the singularity of the thing that is compared, and to distinguish it from others. The sociologist does the former; the historian the latter." The burden, however, on the historical sociologist is in some ways to do both. In the study that follows I hope to suggest some of the general causes of revolution by developing a sociologically informed empirical comparison of the causes of revolution in mid-seventeenth-century France and England, that is, by describing the common elements in the preconditions of revolution and the trajectories taken by coalitions of revolutionary opposition. I also hope to identify some of the reasons that the constituent elements in that coalition in England allowed that revolution to succeed, and why all other efforts at revolution in mid-seventeenth-century Europe failed. Perhaps this second discussion of the specific circumstances that allowed the English revolution to succeed will yield some suggestions about the possibilities of success in revolutionary efforts in general.

In the remainder of this chapter, I will suggest some of the lines of argument that this book will follow. First, I will describe the character of the "crisis" of the seventeenth century, and the nature of the response to that crisis by both the French and English monarchies, specifically, the development of absolutism as a political doctrine and set of institutional innovations designed to facilitate increased autonomous participation in the international arena. I will highlight some of the areas that our comparative and historical inquiry will cover, and also suggest some of the themes that I will use to explain the different outcomes of revolutionary upheaval.

The Crisis of the Seventeenth Century

For many years historians considered the seventeenth century as the "splendid century," *le grand siècle*. Even contemporaries saw it as the "age of magnificence." The reign of Louis XIV in France provided the symbolic capstone of the "golden century" of European finery; his elegance and civility permeated all aspects of society from diplomatic finesse to architectural filigree. It was the watershed era, sandwiched between the bloody Wars of Religion and economic upheavals of the sixteenth century, and the "dark satanic mills" that marked eighteenth-century industrialization.[5]

History is rewritten by each generation; immediate circumstances sensitize the researcher to problems that earlier may have been overlooked. In a sense we rewrite the history we need, seeking in our work those developments and processes that may illuminate our present situation. By the mid-1950s it became clear that the seventeenth century was not splendid at all but, rather, a century of crisis, "when everything was in conflict, and nothing suggests an age of resolution, serenity and order" (Methevier, 1977: 64).[6] In the middle of the century the opulent facade of courtly brilliance was punctured by the outbreak of revolution throughout Europe. The English Revolution is best known and most studied, for it was the only successful revolution of the era. The English Revolution was triggered in part by revolts in Scotland and Ireland. In 1640 Catalonia and Portugal revolted against Castilian domination; in 1641 Andalusia also rebelled. Six years later violent struggles in Naples and Palermo shook the weakened Spanish monarchy again. In France the members of Parliament and the high nobility attempted to thwart royal encroachments during the revolts of the Fronde, 1648–52. In 1650 a palace revolt in the Netherlands displaced the *stadholderate*. The Ukraine was shattered by revolt from 1648 to 1654. The century was also marked by numerous popular uprisings—peasant rebellions, municipal revolts, millenarian movements—that may have been isolated and disconnected from one another but together brand the era as exceptionally contentious. "These are days of shaking," exclaimed Jeremiah Whittaker to the English House of Commons in 1643, "and this shaking is universal" (in Parker and Smith, 1978: 2).

What was the nature of this crisis?[7] Some writers have stressed the demographic dimensions, conditioned by climatological and material forces; Hobsbawm (1954) subsumes these under a more general crisis of the economy as a whole. Agricultural production was inelastic, provoking an "agricultural revolution in reverse" (Braudel, 1975: 427; see also Richet, 1968; Le Roy Ladurie, 1975; Brenner, 1976), which meant famine, dearth, epidemic, and a chronic shortage of labor. Trade stagnated, and new investments were diverted away from productive outlets (Romano, 1978). Brenner (1976: 73) declared the seventeenth century "a crisis of actual scarcity, typical of precapitalist modes of production, and reflecting directly their inability to develop the productive forces."

More important, however, the crisis was a political crisis, a crisis in the relationship between state and society, between the perceived imperatives of kingship and the social sources of political legitimacy.[8] Centralizing monarchies, whose centripetal programs sought to bring greater portions of economic and social activity under their control, squared off against centrifugal social organizations, in which political and economic power was parceled out among several corporate groups, each of which jealously guarded its privileges. Kings and their councillors faced a troublesome paradox: to conduct their foreign policy effectively (which meant, specifically, to participate in the Thirty Years War and compete economically), they would have to concentrate political power at the center, but by doing so, they would risk domestic revolt against the abridgment of those privileges that were the traditional foundations of the monarchy.

This was a risk taken by many monarchies during the course of the century, and absolutism was the ideological justification for the transformation of traditional social arrangements. Most specifically, Spain, England, and France witnessed royal efforts at absolutism, each of which met with differing forms of resistance and each of which produced different results. Justified by a doctrine of "reason of state," the absolute monarchy sought to gain more effective political control over corporate social groups, over provincial and municipal affairs, and over commerce and trade, all to gain a more secure financial basis for an aggressive foreign policy that would be unfettered by domestic opposition.

The Problem of the Absolutist State

What was the absolutist state? Was it an element of feudal reaction, designed to repress rebellious lower classes and contain capitalist development, or an engine of precisely that capitalist development, clearing out residual vestiges of feudalism from economic control? Or was it a neutral arbiter in class struggle, without class character itself? These questions express the arguments of a number of prominent historians and sociologists, many of whom use Marx and Engels as reference points.

For their parts, though, Marx and Engels provide an ambiguous and shifting portrait of absolutism; at times they seem to characterize it in each of the above ways. For example, in *Anti-Dühring* Engels appears to argue that the absolutist state is a feudal state when he writes (1971: 115) that the "mighty [sixteenth-century] revolution in the economic conditions of society . . . *was not followed* by any immediate corresponding change in its political structure. The state order *remained feudal* while society became more and more bourgeois" (emphasis added). But, in *The Origins of the Family, Private Property and the State* Engels suggests (1970: 157) that there are periods when the "warring classes are so nearly equal in forces that the state power, as apparent mediator, acquires for the moment, a certain independence in relation to both. This applies to the absolute monarchy . . . which balances the nobility and the bourgeoisie against one another." Marx himself seems to suggest a third position in the first volume of *Capital,* writing (1967: 751) that capitalists "all employ the power of the state, the concentrated and organized force of society, to hasten, hothouse fashion, the process of transformation of the feudal mode of production into the capitalist mode, and to shorten the transition."

These three passages, all apparently presenting a different theoretical argument, indicate the difficulties in understanding the role of the state in an era of transition. The absolutist state, historically, seems both to hasten and delay capitalist development; it appears to orchestrate class struggle between nobility and bourgeoisie from above while remaining a part of that struggle and a partisan of each side.

The theoretical imprecision and ambivalance that were evident in Marx's and Engels's writings are even more evident today as a number of eminent historians and sociologists continue the debate over the class character of the absolutist state. One group argues that absolutism was a feudal state, designed to perpetuate and strengthen the feudal class society. Hill (1967), Porchnev (1963), and Lublinskaya (1967), among others, agree with Molnar, who writes (1965: 156) that "all the forms of absolutism in Europe served the interests of the nobility or proprietors and expressed the political rule upon the other classes."

Anderson's impressive *The Lineages of the Absolutist State* is the most fully developed argument of the position, suggesting that absolutism was a political response to feudal crisis and the disappearance of serfdom. Feudalism could be reestablished and consolidated from above through the displacement of power upward and outside the hierarchy of "parcellized" sovereignty into a centralized form. The monarchy, no longer constrained by feudal obligations, developed standing armies, national taxation, and permanent bureaucracies, and codified law and diplomacy (Anderson, 1974: 29–37). Absolutism served the interests of the nobility by securing feudal relations of production in an era of commutation of labor services and the appearance of commodity relations. The simultaneous revival of Roman law gave juridical expression to this political power, and secured the right to private property, which buttressed feudal landownership in an transitional era. The absolutist state thus preserved feudal relations by incorporating the bourgeoisie through the sale of offices, and protected the aristocracy from challenge by an emergent bourgeoisie; absolutism was "a redeployed and recharged apparatus of feudal domination designed to clamp the peasant masses back into their traditional social position. . . . It was never an arbiter between the aristocracy and the bourgeoisie, still less an instrument of the nascent bourgeoisie against the aristocracy: it was the political carapace of a threatened nobility" (Anderson, 1974: 18).

To other writers, the absolutist state was neither feudal nor capitalist. According to Roland Mousnier (1971: 236), for example, absolute monarchy was independent of social class:

> By dividing functions between two classes, but reserving the most important of them to the lesser class, the bourgeoisie, and systematically raising up this class and counterposing it to the other, stronger class, the King brought the class struggle to a point of equilibrium between classes, which ensured his personal power, and, in the government and the state, unity, order, and hierarchy.

The absolutist state arose, Mousnier contends, as the bourgeoisie rose; the state, therefore, increased its power commensurately to insure social order and neutralize class conflict, which it did by incorporating the bourgeoisie into the state by the sale of offices. The monarchy, in its drive to raise funds for war and to suppress peasant revolts "finds its ally in the bourgeoisie" (Chabod, 1964: 35). In turn the state aided the bourgeoisie through monopolies, privileges, and tax farming. The state needed the bourgeoisie for revenues as much as the bourgeoisie needed the state for protection. Eventually, the state's balancing act was disrupted as the bourgeoisie pushed through reforms that limited royal power and rearranged the class composition of the state, resulting in parliamentary monarchy.

Finally, another group of contemporary authors argues that the absolutist state was the first capitalist state. Kevder (1978: 14) insists that the "ascendent fraction of capital has to depend on state power in order to increase its share of the surplus." Wallerstein's position (1974, 1979, 1980) is somewhat similar; he argues that the capitalist world-economy emerged in the mid-sixteenth century, and consolidated itself politically during the seventeenth century, through the absolute monarchy. In a conciliatory tone he writes (1980: 32) that he could "accept Anderson's entire statement [quoted above] if the adjective 'feudal' were dropped," which is analogous to accepting Marx's epigrammatic synopsis of history as the history of class struggles only if the adjective *class* were dropped. Wallerstein asserts that a bifurcated nobility—old feudal magnates with regional power bases and lesser nobility commercializing their agricultural holdings—pressures the monarchy to consolidate its power, moving territorially against the feudal barons and in tandem with the gentry to participate in the burgeoning capitalist world-economy.

Poulantzas (1975: 168) also stresses the capitalist elements in absolutism that "impregnate" the state. In eras of transition, he notes, social fragments are dislodged from synchronicity with the relations of production. The state operates not within the existing mode of production but to produce the new mode. Thus, the absolute monarchy serves primitive capitalist accumulation; for example, in the expropriating of small land-owners' property, financing of industrialization, attacking of seigneurial power, and breaking down of internal trade barriers—all of which can be accomplished only by a state that is capitalist in nature. The absolutist state moved against a nobility at a time when it cannot rely on the bourgeoisie to achieve capitalist dominance.

Each of these positions is suggestive and captures a partial truth, but none fully encompasses the empirical-historical complexity of absolutism. The first position underscores the identity of class and state; the last position, of state and international economy; and the middle position denies class character entirely. In Anderson's scheme the absolutist state emerges to protect a system of parcellized sovereignties at the moment they have disappeared historically. Further, though absolutism also facilitates the transition to capitalism, Anderson assumes a tidy unity between class and state; he argues tautologically that the nobility controls the state and therefore is the politically dominant class, and that this political dominance ensures its economic dominance, preserving the feudal mode of production overall. Finally, although Anderson argues that the absolutist state was an effort to clamp the peasant masses back into their traditional social position, he underestimates the extent to which state policies also were, intentionally or not, agents of the disaggregation of the moral economy of the traditional village, disrupting the specific combination of hierarchy and coherence that defined traditional village life in early modern Europe.

Mousnier's conception, though, is far more problematic, asserting that the state is divorced from social classes, and can create national unity by neutralizing class conflict. In effect, absolutism generates class struggle by raising the bourgeoisie to political power, but it does so for its own ends. Venality of office encouraged the bourgeoisie to shed its class character, becoming preoccupied with noble status. However, the equilibrium noted by Mousnier is not static but reveals a crisis in hegemony in which neither class is capable of gaining the dominant position. The state presides over the resulting vacuum and intervenes to reorganize power blocs, but it is not a neutral bystander in the process.

Finally, the arguments of Wallerstein and Poulantzas are also problematic. Poulantzas posits a transitional state but then imputes a class character, placing the state as a deus ex machina to complete the transition to capitalism. The state does not correspond to economic relations, and can therefore transform dominant relations of production. This requires some teleological acrobatics: because the transition is essential and the existing system will not accomplish it, a new form must be found that will complete what is theoretically necessary. Thus, the absolutist state is introduced from outside the social formation, an argument that transforms an inherent dynamic of social change into a matter of systemic necessity devoid of dynamics.

This debate raises some thorny questions for social scientists and historians concerned with the relationships between socially privileged groups and political power. If the absolutist state was feudal, why did the monarchy continue to abridge those groups' traditional privileges and allow broad economic latitude to merchants? If it was a capitalist state, why did the monarchy also shore up the aristocracy and constrain specific mercantile activities? In this book I will develop an argument about the structural sources of the absolutist state's ambivalence toward traditional social classes. Absolutism is here understood as a contradictory effort: designed to preserve and consolidate the power of a feudal ruling class, it also undermined that class and helped prepare the way for capitalist development. Its attempt to unify the nation ended up setting almost everyone in opposition to it (Kossman, 1964: 260; Molnar, 1965: 162). Breaking through the inelastic domestic social relations that constrained its aggressive foreign policy initiatives, the absolute monarchy also eroded the social foundations of its legitimacy, and presented the opportunity for revolutionary challenges.

Absolutism was a transitional social formation, the political form of the transition from feudalism to capitalism. This economic transition from one mode of production to another did not, and could not, happen entirely at the level of production, despite the assertions of orthodox Marxist theory, but required a political vehicle, both to sweep aside many of the intransigent feudal obstacles to capitalist development and to facilitate the more rapid development of nascent capitalist forces. (As we will see, the coincidence of the interests of capitalist industrialization with the imperatives of state building was neither intentional nor inevitable.) Absolutism accepted its political charge to protect the traditional feudal order, but its mission was contradicted by its effect: the pressing to opposition of many of the constitutive elements of that system.

Absolutist monarchies were innovative monarchies, developing institutional mechanisms by which to concentrate political power, ensure domestic order, and pursue their ambitious foreign policy objectives in the name of "reason of state." All had inherited medieval political institutions that were inadequate to meet the increased political and financial needs that were engendered by the drive to participate more actively in the international arena. The possibilities offered by the expanding international

market and the omnipresent possibility of war, even when there was no
overt war, fueled this drive for increased revenues. It was war, or the
threat of war, that was, perhaps, the single most important pressure on the
monarchy, pressing kings to innovate so as to raise enough revenues to
support armies that could sustain increasingly costly war efforts. Absolutism "pioneered the first professional army," but "with the rise of professional armies under royal control numbering hundreds of thousands of
men, the problem of providing money for their maintenance grew apace"
(Anderson, 1974: 29; Wolf, 1961: 429). The achievement of foreign policy
objectives was predicated upon the dramatic growth in the size and
equipment of the army, and the development of an army was predicated
on the capacity of the government to support it. As Hintze notes (1975:
201):

> Maintenance of the army became the chief task of the state's financial adminis-
> tration. This in turn led to unprecedented extension of the tax burden and
> consequently to a peculiar economic system that aimed at increasing the stock
> of ready money and at the same time fostering and stimulating production
> artificially, especially in industry.

Another administrative innovation was the development of a centralized
administrative bureaucracy, both in response to the need for revenues,
which were provided by the sale of offices, and the extension of political
control over the entire national territory. "The development of military
and political power and constant military preparedness were possible only
on the basis of a larger, centrally ruled and administrative territory"
(Hintze, 1975: 174).

Finally, the absolutist state was innovative in the development of new
methods of taxation, largely in response to the new fiscal demands of
contemporary warfare (Ardant, 1975; Tilly, 1975: 54). The drive for taxation was so overwhelming that kings were pressed to promote new economic relationships; because "taxation requires a certain economic structure, developed economic exchange, active commerce, and the division of
labor, it behooves the state, and [it] is in fact vital . . . to bring its powers
to bear upon that structure and to shape it into a structure better able to
support taxation" (Ardant, 1975: 196).

These innovations indicate the institutional response to the persistent
fiscal crisis that characterized the history of the absolutist state. The
state's resources were stretched by the economic possibilities of a burgeoning capitalist market and the demands of war; any state that did not
keep pace was faced with the uncertain and unhappy future of clientage to
a more powerful state. Domestic class relations that characterized tradi-

tional social structure proscribed the types of activities that the state might initiate to increase its share (Skocpol and Trimberger, 1978: 104; Ritter, 1964: 21). The fiscal crisis of the absolutist state was located in the state's insufficient fiscal resources to pursue the economic and political objectives that seemed integral to its economic growth. Any solution to the fiscal crisis engendered a crisis of legitimacy as traditional social arrangements were abridged to garner greater shares of the nation's wealth. In this sense we see that the term *absolute* describes not a political reality but a tendency; efforts to build absolute monarchies met with different obstacles, but nowhere was royal power truly absolute. The fiscal crisis of the absolute monarchy is both an indication of its efforts and a signal of its institutional limits. "Nothing so clearly indicates the limits of royal power," writes Bouwsma (1961: 233) "as the fact that governments were perennially in financial trouble, unable to tap the wealth of those most able to pay, and likely to stir up a costly revolt whenever they attempted to develop an adequate income." The absolute state was "increasingly obliged to employ fiscal means of power, to drain the taxable resources of their subjects" in whatever ways it could, including the promotion of capitalist trade:

> The more money proved itself indispensable to monarchical governments as a means of power, the greater became the influence of the middle class and particularly of the capitalists. The state's own resources—the income from the royal demesne and regalia—were as inadequate to the financial needs of the modern state as was the income from papal property to tremendous cost of centralized administration in the late medieval church. [Ritter, 1964: 21].

The bulk of this book is a discussion of how the French and the English monarchies attempted to resolve the fiscal crisis that each faced, and how their solutions set various social groups in opposition against them. In each case the separate opposition of each distinct group was brought together into a political coalition, which culminated in a profound revolutionary challenge to the old regime. In France efforts to circumvent fiscal constraints on an expansionist international policy led successive monarchs and their advisers to adopt policies that abridged the traditional privileges of the hereditary aristocracy and clergy (who developed various strategies of resistance to royal absolutist efforts, including withdrawal of support and the failure to punish vigorously other rebels); to move against the increasingly important judges in the sovereign courts, as well as other venal officeholders (who responded with a pompous assertion of their privileges to limit absolute monarchy with their approval of royal policies); to attempt to abrogate the traditional autonomy of the outlying *pays d'état* (which witnessed profound popular uprisings during the thirty years before the Fronde); and to squeeze further the peasantry to pay greater shares of existing taxes as well as to pay newer ones. In each case fiscal expedients designed to increase the royal share of the nation's wealth prompted murmurings of political opposition, which coalesced during the minority of Louis XIV into a political coalition of revolutionary opposition. When the regency of the queen mother and her adviser, Cardinal Mazarin, was faced with a bankruptcy in late 1647, and the state treasury collapsed, these disparate groups joined together and presented the monarchy with the most serious political challenge in its history, and the most serious threat to royal initiatives until 1789.

We shall observe a similar process of political opposition forming to state fiscal policies in England. Royal initiatives to conduct an independent foreign policy without parliamentary consent, and royalty's effort to bypass Parliament in the raising of revenues alienated privileged groups, who used Parliament as a mouthpiece to voice their discontent. These were joined by religious radicals who were angered at Stuart moves toward autonomous religious policies, which discounted or excluded the many radical religious sects that had begun to spring up around the country. The opposition voiced by religious dissidents, urban merchants, and rural landowners galvanized lower-middle-class people in the cities, who pressed the revolutionaries to advance far more sweeping changes than the moderate reformers in Parliament had ever envisioned.

Thus, the fiscal crisis that precipitated both the English Revolution and the Fronde pitted similar states against similar forces of opposition, drawn from roughly similar groups. The early demands of the rebels were similar, as were the original concessions from the crown. Both the English Revolution and the Fronde were political revolutions, efforts to transform the structure of the state and its relationship to society. Each began making significant strides toward this end, expressed in the Treaty of Reuil in 1649, and Charles's reluctant acceptance of the Petition of Right and the trials of Strafford and Laud. Modest reformist movements were the outgrowth of political opposition from a fraction of the ruling class for the preservation of traditional privileges.

Many of the similarities end at this point. The triumph of the New Model Army and the execution of the king were far cries from even the most extreme demands of the seventeenth-century French rebels. The English Civil War galvanized lower-class opposition into a movement that portended social revolution; the success of the reformist political revolution depended upon the defeat of both the monarchy and this lower-class revolutionary force. In France, by contrast, the reformist political revolution rippled upward through the social hierarchy, for the call to revolutionary change was heeded not by the lower classes but by the aristocracy and the clergy. The political revolution failed in France, in part because of the absence of a social revolutionary push, which, as in England, might have pushed for further structural reforms and served as the rallying point for the consolidation of the new regime. The English Revolution was a successful political revolution built upon a failed social revolution; the Fronde was a failed political revolution that degenerated into factional conflict among nobles.[9] Koenigsberger (1971: 284–85) offers a panorama of the results of these revolutions:

> The results of the revolutions were . . . very varied. The basic class structure of European society remained intact, was indeed confirmed. The genuinely popular and democratic movements were everywhere defeated. The privileged classes remained privileged. But within this very broad framework there appeared enormous differences. France, Spain and the newly independent Portugal confirmed the absolutism of their monarchies, the special position of the Catholic Church in their social and intellectual life, and to a rather more varying degree, the preponderance of their nobilities. In both Denmark and Sweden, the monarchies were soon to establish their royal absolutism by coups d'état at the expense of the nobility. In Poland, on the other hand, the monarchy had finally lost in its struggle with the magnates, and the king had finally become a kind of Venetian doge in an aristocratic republic whose nobility was more rapacious and autocratic than the absolute monarchies of western Europe. The greatest transformations occurred in the United Provinces and in England. There, compromise solutions were found: mixed constitutions, the emancipation of intellectual life from clerical control and the development of open and flexible, even though highly differentiated, social structures. These were differences which were to determine the course of European history for the next hundred and fifty years.

Explaining Divergent Revolutionary Outcomes

How can we explain the different outcomes of these two revolutionary events, especially because they both proceeded from such similar causes? Here, I believe, one must return to structural factors, especially the relationship between the state and capital and the organization and composition of the revolutionary coalition, as well as those nonstructural forces that provided the political coalitions with enough ideological unity to sustain their revolutionary challenge. In particular, we will need to specify the strength of the state and its relationship to various social groups that were bidding for economic maneuverability. State strength indicates the ability of a state to pursue both foreign and domestic objectives despite opposition; for early modern European states, it is a function of

1. the level of bureaucratization;
2. the relationship between the crown and representative institutions;

3. the relationship between the state and the military;
4. the relative strength of foreign competition; and
5. the relative strength of domestic opponents.

States are strong to the extent that they can overcome domestic opposition to their policies and to the extent that they can achieve their foreign policy objectives despite international competition.

One helpful way to conceptualize these variables that determine state strength is the term *relative backwardness*. Relative backwardness has been used by social scientists to explain the differing lineup of economic, political, and social forces that emerge in the process of social change. It emphasizes that one nation may be lagging behind the development of another, but also stresses that this backwardness is only relative to more advanced nations. The nation that is relatively backward may experience increased pressure to catch up with the most advanced countries, but may also benefit from the "demonstration effect," the ability to use the more advanced country as a developmental model. Thus, relative backwardness may be a mixed blessing: increased international pressure may result in more internally repressive policies, while technological borrowing and developmental models allow the relatively backward nation the opportunity to articulate its goals clearly and avoid costly mistakes.

Although relative backwardness has been used to understand national development, it also makes sense to use the term sectorially. A sectorial analysis of relative backwardness provides additional insight into the era of the nation-state's formation, in which there was no truly advanced nation in comparison to others but, rather, a series of developmental strategies in different geographical locations. I will argue that the English monarchy was relatively backward in comparison with the French monarchy, and that the French economy was relatively backward compared with the English economy. The English monarchy maintained neither a paid bureaucracy under central political control nor a standing army; the crown maintained no independent fiscal base and was dependent for revenues on the consent of Parliament. Credit to finance royal policies was therefore difficult to obtain. Compare this with the French crown, whose massive bureaucracy and well-organized standing armies gave it the ability to pursue its objectives internationally and subdue its own domestic discontents. Royal efforts to control trade and to generate an independent fiscal base were more successful than in England, especially in the absence of a national representative institution to which the crown was beholden for supply.

The relative strength of a monarchy should not, however, be confused with the strength of a state. Monarchies consist of the king, the royal family, and the immediate circle of councillors who directly influence policy-making. States, on the other hand, add to the monarchy those political institutions that compose the entire policy-making apparatus. In France state and monarchy were nearly coterminous; kings did not need to consult any but their councillors to develop policy, and all potentially representative institutions existed only by the pleasure of the king. (Thus, Louis XIV would be able to equate his person with the boundaries of the state.) In this configuration, though, the strength of the monarchy indicated the corresponding weakness of the state because royal power was based upon the exclusion of oppositional forces in representative institutions. The clear disjunction between the English monarchy and the English state—the crown's inability to eliminate social barriers to unbridled political power—indicates the overall strength of the state. Thus, it should be clear that the English monarchy was relatively backward compared to the French monarchy.

The French economy was relatively backward compared to the English economy. In France agrarian class relations preserved the traditional privileges of the hereditary nobility over the peasants. These seigneurs had relatively few incentives to innovate, and agricultural production was often stagnant. Agricultural development did not mean transformation, as it did in England, but diversification to take advantage of regional needs; as the authors of *Maison Rustique* put it in 1600 (cited in Thirsk, 1980: 633), "A good farmer will make profit from everything, and there is not (as we say) so much as the garlic and onion which he will not raise again by selling them at fairs most fitting for their time and season, and so help himself thereof and fill his purse with money." English landlords, by contrast, lived not so much off rents from peasants but from the sale of agricultural commodities: "The growth of commerce in the towns during the 16th and 17th centuries had created in the countryside a market for agricultural products, thereby setting in motion a process leading toward commercial and capitalist agriculture in the countryside itself" (Moore, 1966: 14).

Further, within any country we can observe the dissynchronous development of state and society. In this context it will be apparent that the English monarchy was also relatively backward compared with the English economy, and that the French economy lagged behind both the English economy and the French polity. The reorientation of English agricultural society brought commercially mobilized classes into conflict with political elites; the French commercially minded groups were often absorbed into the state through venality of office. A similar difference emerges between France and England when we turn to industry and commerce, where by 1630 "France was clearly outdistanced by England" (Crouzet, 1966: 258).

Poor circulation of currency and a poorly organized credit system kept France behind, while the English crown offered economic incentives for increased production, such as monopoly protection or tax exemptions. The relative backwardness of French industry and trade increased throughout the century, especially in such vital industries as salt, glass, shipbuilding, and coal production (Nef, 1936a, 1936b; see also Lublinskaya, 1967: 329).[10] In England the merchant class was a strong and vital commercial class, economically independent of the crown and tied to a strong center of activity in London; unlike their French counterparts, merchants "did not retire to the country; neither did they dissociate themselves from city affairs" (Lang, 1974: 47). The economic developments they portended "could not be absorbed within the old regime," which was the ultimate cause of the English Revolution (Hill, 1975: 281). French merchants were lured, pressured, forced, and encouraged to divert productive capital into the state sector, to transform resources into unproductive political capital. Venality of office, taxation, and state credit schemes incorporated the French commercial class into the political programs of the monarchy.

The dynamic tension between state and society pivots on four issues: the preservation of property relations; the maintenance of order and stability; the military resources of the state; and resources from taxation. All four of these issues were confronted by different lineups of forces in seventeenth-century France and England, and these differences in the relationship between state and society proved to be extremely important in the ways that the revolutions unfolded. The impulse for change in the relationship between state and society came from the crown in France and from mobilizing social forces in England. The English crown tried to retard the development of strong independent class forces in the countryside; the rural seigneurs attempted to block state initiatives in France. Both efforts failed in the revolutions of the mid-seventeenth century.

Such a structural comparison will allow us to avoid the problems that have often been offered for the differences between revolutionary outcomes. It is not that France and England evidenced such radically different levels of productivity, or population development, or even commercial development; these aggregate developments were more similar than different. It is in the structural organization of the societies that the small differences in aggregate output or level of commercialization become enlarged so as to be decisive. These structural differences were insufficient to determine whether or not England or France experienced revolutionary challenges in the mid-seventeenth century, for they each did experience those challenges, but they helped to give those challenges different shapes and different trajectories, which were, themselves, decisive in structuring the different outcomes of those revolutionary movements. Through the remainder of this book, as we explore the structural developments first in France and then in England, we can therefore remain mindful of masterful French historian Marc Bloch's caution about the comparative method; we may "learn not to attach too much importance to local pseudo-causes; at the same time . . . learn to become sensitive to specific differences" (1967: 73).

Appendix to Chapter 1:
State Centralization and Revolts of the Periphery in Spain

Although this work will concentrate on an empirical comparison of the relationship among economy, society, and the state in seventeenth-century England and France, such comparative historical sociology can be strengthened by a brief comparative reference to the other great geopolitical power of the era, Spain, and the succession of revolutionary upheavals faced by the Castilian monarchy in the mid-seventeenth century. Here we may observe a similar trajectory for early modern state builders, as well as the different routes taken by opponents to absolutism. We can observe all the various elements that will come into play throughout the book, noting the different lineup of class forces in each revolt against Castilian domination.

Early modern Spain presents a tragic paradox. Perhaps the strongest and wealthiest monarchy, Spain also proved to be the least capable of imposing its will on either military competitors or autonomous groups and provinces within its jurisdiction. Constant international conflict and domestic discontent provoked persistent fiscal crises throughout the sixteenth and seventeenth centuries; the solutions sought by the Spanish crown brought continued resistance and revolt. Early modern Spanish history is a record of the "struggle between center and periphery, between a regalist, bureaucratic, legalistic, nationalistic, and relatively illiberal Castilian center and a cosmopolitan, outward looking, trading, industrious and relatively liberal periphery" (Veliz, 1980: 90). The monarchy's attempts to dominate and incorporate this periphery undermined the state at its center, and it was surpassed by later, more durable absolutisms.

The early union of the crowns of Castile and Aragon by the marriage of Ferdinand and Isabella in 1469 began a period of internal consolidation of Spanish royal power, as Castile assumed the leadership of the new Spain. Fiscal reorganization and more efficient administration allowed an increase in royal revenues from 900,000 ducats in 1474 to 26 million ducats only thirty years later. The development of municipal administrative officers, the *corregidores,* bypassed the Cortes, which vied for local administrative control with the crown. The reconquest of Granada in 1492 ended any threat the Moslems might have posed.

By the turn of the sixteenth century, this early centralization provided the foundation for expansionist foreign policy in both the Old World and the New. "God has set you on the path toward a world monarchy," the grand chancellor told Charles V in 1519 (cited in Koenigsberger, 1971: 2). The "nascent world-economy seemed as though it might become another imperium" (Wallerstein, 1974: 170). In fact, it was the failure of Spain to achieve a world empire (and its ability to prevent the Ottoman Empire from achieving it) that created the political balance of power that allowed the capitalist world-economy to develop in the sixteenth century. It is this failure that must be explained.

The consolidation of Castilian domination and its attempts at imperial expansion ran into domestic opposition almost immediately. In 1520 a popular revolt against fiscal exactions by the corregidores in Castile was coupled with political opposition from the Cortes, the administrative powers of which had been undercut (Elliot, 1977: 151). What began as a united resistance in defense of traditional liberties became, however, a social revolution in 1521, a revolt of the common people against not only royal officials but also, as they put it, "against grandees, *caballeros*, and other enemies of the realm" (cited in Elliot, 1977: 154). That same year the lower classes in Valencia revolted against the nobility because the latter was protecting the Moors, who worked noble lands and paid higher seigneurial dues than did the Catholics. The Germania rebels proclaimed the abolition of all private property, which served to unite the rebels as well as alienate their wealthy supporters.

The suppression of these two revolts seemed to have strengthened the crown. In Castile the Cortes was reduced to subservience, becoming a "pliable instrument" of royal will, and was forced to grant supply before airing grievances (Koenigsberger, 1971a: 190). In Valencia local autonomy was curtailed and the province offered no further threat to royal centralization. In each revolt, however, the crown was forced to rely on the help of the local nobility in suppressing the rebels. As a result, these locally based grandees were able to retain a large measure of autonomous political and financial power; the aristocracy in Castile was able to contract out of its financial obligations to the state and its empire.

It was on the basis of this shaky domestic foundation that Philip II embarked on a foreign policy that was "the most expensive and ambitious known since the days of ancient Rome" (Davies, 1961: 265). By 1540 Spain had gained control over half the people in the Western Hemisphere (Chaunu, 1959: 148). The desire to increase Spanish dominance in Europe and to interfere in France and England was tempered by the persistent

Turkish threat and domestic discontent. Spain had become a "dynastic state enmeshed in the struggle for hegemony on the European continent" (de Vries, 1976: 116).

Domestically, Philip constructed an elaborate absolutism, based on "centralization, repression, and assertion of the supremacy of the crown" and composed of consultative councils and a royal bureaucracy ensuring that "every decision, great or small, rested with the king" (Clarke, 1904: 352; Davies, 1961: 126). Although the Castilian monarchs did not encounter the same level of institutional resistance to the implementation of absolute rule as in other countries, they did face an array of internal forces of opposition: the fabulous wealth of the clergy, the independence of an opulent aristocracy, disgruntled lower classes, unincorporated religious groups (Jews, Moslems), disobedience of royal officials, and outlying provinces and conquered territories that yearned for regional autonomy (Veliz, 1980: 23).

The combination of these international pressures and domestic structural constraints began to undermine the Spanish world empire almost as soon as it was begun. Fiscal crisis in 1557 forced Philip to declare bankruptcy, ending the possibility of world conquest (Wallerstein, 1974: 181; Wallerstein, 1979: 26). Domestically, Spanish absolutism faced a "crisis of insubordination" in the late 1550s as "waves of discontent and disaffection" spread throughout the country (Braudel, 1975: 957). But for slightly more than a century after 1557, the Spanish state struggled to hold onto its empire, centralize its political administration, and reconquer Europe.

The crown first turned to Castile, the traditional base of the monarchy. Throughout the 1560s Philip increased the fiscal pressure through extra-parliamentary taxation, sale of offices, declarations of royal monopolies on imported commodities such as mercury and salt, new export duties on Spanish wool, forced loans, and the seizure of imported bullion (Elliot, 1963: 197–99; Davies, 1961: 180). Although revenues squeezed from "unhappy Castile" increased sharply—from 2.75 million ducats in 1551 to 4.75 million ducats in 1562 and 5.25 million in 1573—the immense burden of debt plagued Philip, who again declared bankruptcy in 1560 and 1675 (Davies, 1961: 180; Braudel, 1975: 897).

In addition to squeezing Castile for state revenues, Philip relied on two traditionally lucrative resources: the Spanish possessions in the New World and the Netherlands. Conflicts between the States General in the Netherlands and the Spanish crown often centered on taxation issues; the "crushing burden of taxation on the provinces" led the States General to question "the conduct of the government's foreign policy" (Koenigsberger, 1971a: 154, 136). Taxation policies designed to raise royal revenues

and offset the fiscal crisis provoked a crisis of legitimacy over the continued Spanish control of the Netherlands. By 1568 maintaining the power of
the Duke of Alba and his administration was actually costing the Spanish
crown more than the Netherlands were providing for the royal treasury.
No longer could Philip dream of a "river of silver" blowing from Antwerp
to Madrid; instead he borrowed £ 80,000 in Genoa to pay the troops in the
Netherlands, which was seized at sea by Elizabethan pirates to help the
English queen raise revenues herself.

Philip resolved to raise revenues in the Netherlands that would both
support the army and replenish the flow of tribute to Castile. In 1569 he
introduced the *alcabala,* a 1 percent tax on all real property, along with a
10 percent tax on all movable merchandise sold or bought in the provinces,
hoping to make the governor independent of the States General (Davies,
1961: 163). These new financial burdens, however, produced increased
resistance, for the Dutch were "more unwilling than ever to grant the
king's financial demands," and ushered in an era of protracted struggle
between the crown and the Dutch provinces, the Netherlands revolt, that
"bundle of local reactions against the policies of a centralizing and alien
government" (Koenigsberger, 1971a: 135; Wernham, 1980: 49).

The revolt of the Netherlands dampened Castilian jubilance after the
victory over the Turks at Lepanto in 1571, and the cost of the war came to
over 4 million ducats a year (Braudel, 1975: 841). In 1575 debts to foreign
bankers totaled over 37.5 million ducats, and the king declared bankruptcy, which led to financial chaos in the banking centers, which, in turn,
disrupted the complicated credit structure on which the transfer of money
from Spain and Italy to the Netherlands depended. Unpaid Dutch armies
mutinied, refusing to repress William of Orange's rebels. The "king's
authority in the Netherlands collapsed with the collapse of his finances,"
and the success of the revolt of the Netherlands followed from the failure
of the crown to pay its troops (Koenigsberger, 1971b: 139).

Throughout the sixteenth century, however, the crown was buoyed by
the remarkable flow of gold and silver bullion from its mines in the New
World. Inflows of bullion, which reached a crest of 35.2 million ducats in
1581–85 and 42.2 million in 1591–95, allowed an "extraordinary financial
flexibility" to the crown that militated against structural reforms or social
transformation (Anderson, 1974: 72). As Sir Roger Williams wrote of the
Spanish king, "His treasure comes unto him as our salads to us; when we
eat all, we fetch more out of our gardens. So doth he fetch his treasure out
of the ground after spending all that is coined" (cited in Wernham, 1980:
25). The remarkable influx of bullion led to a rapid inflationary spiral;
prices were higher in Spain than elsewhere in Europe. Spain became a
profitable place to sell, but Europeans were not disposed to buy there

because of the high prices, which encouraged extravagant court and aristocratic consumption while inhibiting the growth of a local bourgeoisie (Braudel, 1975: 825).

Spanish agriculture remained relatively backward, "inadequate to meet the nation's needs" (de Vries, 1976: 48). Royal control of grain prices made peasant commodity production unprofitable, and Spain often relied on imports of food from the Baltic. The production of wool, long the mainstay of the Castilian economy, also inhibited peasant agricultural production. Through the royal monopoly called the *mesta*, nobles retained the rights to run their sheep over the entire province, trampling down cornfields, breaking fences, and spoiling cultivated land, which gave added meaning to Thomas More's comments about enclosure for commercialization of agriculture while it simultaneously "precluded viable peasant farming" (de Vries, 1976: 50; see also Anderson, 1974: 72; Koenigsberger, 1971b: 40).

Originally, high-quality Spanish wool brought high prices in the international market, although "the dark side of the flourishing Spanish wool exports to Flanders was an impoverished Spanish peasant unable to buy the manufactures of his urban industries" (Koenigsberger, 1971b: 40). Prices doubled between 1550 and 1600, and Spanish wool was gradually priced out of the market, further crippling industrial development as it had damaged agricultural development.

The inflows of gold and silver resulted, therefore, in economic stagnation and a decline of Spanish competitiveness in industry and agriculture. The wealth of the crown was illusory, based on consumption rather than productive capacity. Martín González de Cellorigo brilliantly characterized the problem in 1600, arguing that the disproportion between expenditure and investment was the cause of persistent fiscal crisis, and he urged an increase in national productive capacity rather than in the stock of precious metals. "Money is not true wealth," he wrote (cited in Elliot, 1977: 313), suggesting that surplus wealth was unproductively invested, "dissipated on thin air . . . instead of being expended on things that yield profits and attract riches from outside to augment the riches within." Thus, he concluded, "There is no money, gold or silver in Spain because there is so much; and it is not rich because of all its riches."

The last two decades of the century witnessed a continual inability to pursue foreign policy objectives for lack of funds. The defeat of the Armada in 1588 cost 10 million ducats; the subsequent rehabilitation of the navy cost 8 million more (Davies, 1961: 222). Plans for intervention in French religious wars were scrapped, and rebellion broke out in Aragon in 1591. Philip again declared bankruptcy in 1596, finally ending his imperial ambitions (Elliot, 1977: 283). His death in 1598 left a debt calculated at 100 million ducats, the payment of interest on which consumed two-thirds of all royal revenues (Davies, 1961: 223; Koenigsberger, 1971b: 207).

The crown never fully recovered from its financial collapse in the last few years of the century. Just as expenditures rose, the supply of bullion began to fall precipitously, "partly because of diminishing production, partly because the colonies were becoming increasingly independent" (Cipolla, 1976: 235). The Venetian ambassador noted that the bullion "does on Spain as rain does on a roof—it pours on her and it flows away" (cited in Cipolla, 1976: 235). To offset this shrinking supply of gold, Philip III and his minister, the duke of Lerma, resorted to desperate fiscal expedients. Debasing the coinage by increasing copper coins in circulation drove gold and silver into hiding rather than added to royal revenues. Lerma also sold offices, extorted money from municipalities, and encouraged corruption. The increased tax burden fell even more heavily on the peasantry, whose mules and carts were often seized to pay royal taxes. This led to widespread rural depopulation, noted by a consul to the Royal Council in 1619, who remarked that rather than "wondering at the depopulation of villages and farms, the wonder is that any of them remain" (cited in Davies, 1957: 100). Expenditures in 1608 reached 7.3 million ducats and in 1615 topped 9 million, although revenues remained at roughly 5.5 million (Elliot, 1963: 113). The crown "staggered from inflation to deflation of the coinage and thence renewed bankruptcies" (Koenigsberger, 1971b: 207).

The loss of the Netherlands and the precipitous decline in bullion could not be offset by the annexation of Portugal in 1580, and the coming of the Thirty Years War in the second decade of the seventeenth century led the crown to search again for revenues. Reliance on Castile was now impossible, because, as the president of the Council of Finance wrote in 1616, it had been "drained of men and resources; and to ruin it, and to try to squeeze out of it what is simply not there in order to make ourselves important in Germany—this is a policy which in all conscience cannot be carried out (cited in Elliot, 1963: 188). The beginning of the reign of Philip IV, and his minister, the count of Olivares, changed the relations between Castile and the other provinces, especially Portugal and Catalonia; it was a "transition from neglect to intervention, from an excessive degree of indifference to an excessive degree of interest" in their affairs (Elliot, 1974: 117).

Olivares was an active and energetic reformer who proposed royal policies that would maximize potential resources for war while simultaneously unifying the country under centralized bureaucratic control and eliminating pockets of social and political autonomy and potential resistance. At the same time as he sought to mobilize the nation's resources for war, Olivares faced the "exhauston of Castile's reserves of manpower and money" (Elliot, 1963: 491). Instead of "growing rich on the profits of empire," Castile had impoverished itself "in the defense of its own possessions" and had increased resistance to taxation from a depopulated, plague-ridden province (Elliot, 1963: 184). Olivares was thus pressed to look elsewhere for increased revenues to participate in the Thirty Years War. Such fiscal expedients as state loans, government bonds like the *juros,* and debasement of the coinage were temporary yet insufficient (de Vries, 1976: 221). Olivares realized that "if he were to mobilize the Monarchy for a supreme military effort, he somehow had to undermine the laws and liberties which preserved the autonomous status of the various provinces and shielded them from the heavy demands for taxes and soldiers which were regularly imposed upon Castile" (Elliot, 1974: 118). As he wrote to the king (cited in Davies, 1957: 14):

> You should not be content to be the King of Portugal, of Aragon, and of Valencia, and Count of Barcelona; but you should direct all your work and thought, with the most experienced and secret advice, to reduce these realms which make up Spain to the same order and legal system as Castile. If your Majesty succeeds in this you will be the most powerful prince in the world.

Such strong efforts at state centralization and the abridgment of autonomous political privileges were bound to provoke resistance. The revolt of the Basque province in 1631–32 presaged larger, more sustained opposition (Davies, 1957: 24). The escalation of the war with the entry of France in 1635 brought additional fiscal pressure to both states. The Spanish crown's income for that year was but half the 11 million ducats already promised (Elliot, 1963: 307). By 1640, "short of money, short of ships, short of men, [Olivares] was straining every nerve to mobilize his country more effectively for war" (Elliot, 1963: 402). He resolved to raise revenues from Catalonia and Portugal—the former because of its strategic military importance, the latter because of the wealth of its upper classes, and both because of their relative autonomy from fiscal contributions to the Castilian crown.

As fiscal exactions became more and more severe, the ruling class in Catalonia became increasingly alienated from Madrid and obdurately refused to support the war effort. Olivares had written that "the Catalans in their present condition are not useful to the monarchy, and are not serving in person or with their possessions" (cited in Elliot, 1963: 388). Local ruling-class resistance to the central government's fiscal exactions led to the collapse of royal power in the province. In Catalonia, though, the collapse of central government also allowed the expression of class-based hostility from rural lower classes, provoked by the increased tax burden and the forced billeting of royal troops living off the Catalan countryside (Elliot, 1974: 128). Ruling-class resistance to the state had given way to a social revolution of the poor against the rich. The social revolution, though, forced the leaders of the political resistance from the upper class, the Diputas, "into deciding whether they would take command of events or be commanded by them" (Elliot, 1974: 122). The threat of revolt from below brought a momentary rapprochement between the ruling class and the crown as they joined together to suppress the lower-class rebels.

The revolt of the Catalans was an attempt at political and social revolution; the revolt of Portugal six months later was more a coup d'état. Although the Portuguese ruling class had originally been aided by the union with Castile, it now felt itself restrained by continued association with a declining military power and espoused national independence as its goal. New fiscal expedients by the crown brought together the Portuguese upper classes in political opposition to Spanish domination, but their distances from the fighting did not place such a severe burden on the lower classes, which remained relatively docile. The Portuguese political revolt succeeded in the absence of attempted social revolution, and the unity of the country's ruling class allowed it to replace Spanish rule with its own.

In the Spanish possessions in southern Italy, Naples, and Sicily, the ruling classes did not follow their Portuguese and Catalan colleagues into political revolt, for they "lacked the communal spirit and institutional defenses" enjoyed by the others and were thus "unable to protect themselves from fiscal demands of the crown" (Elliot, 1974: 124). In 1625 the Venetian secretary in Naples wrote, "No business is being transacted in this city, as there is little credit or money" (cited in Koenigsberger, 1971a: 105). Castilian viceroys and local aristocrats worked together in passing this tax burden on to the lower classes in the countryside. In 1647 rising food prices, forced higher by dearth and taxation, inflamed preexisting social and economic hostilities against the Spanish crown. The result was massive popular revolt, which was suppressed by the royal government with support from the local elite, against which the revolt was primarily directed.

In 1640 the social revolution in Catalonia prevented the success of the political revolution, as nobles and crown rallied to suppress popular revolt. In Portugal the absence of social revolution allowed the nationalist ruling class to replace Spanish domination. In Naples and Sicily the popular revolt was easily isolated and suppressed by a concerted royal and aristocratic effort. In each case, the continued power of the Castilian monarchy was shaken and the social foundations of Spanish absolutism exposed as structurally unsound. As Anderson (1974: 81) notes, "Spain had expanded too fast, too early, because of its overseas fortune, without ever having completed its metropolitan foundations." The strain of war had brought Olivares "into constitutional experiments which entailed a radical reorganization of the country's administrative structure, and he lacked both the military and economic resources, and the prestige that would have been conferred by foreign victories, to carry these experiments through to success" (Elliot, 1977: 373).

Persistent fiscal crisis forced the Spanish crown to search for revenues, moving against those groups, both in the Castilian center and in the provincial peripheries, whose continued support would have been vital for the successful implementation of Castilian foreign policies. In 1659 the Treaty of the Pyrénées with France reduced Spain to a second-rate Continental power, confirming what Sir Arthur Hopton, writing home to England in 1640, had observed eighteen years earlier (cited in Elliot, 1974: 109): "I am induced to think that the greatness of this monarchy is near to an end."

Notes

1. This would also suggest a response to H. G. Koenigsberger's caution (1972: 398) that "any general hypothesis about the nature of revolution in Early Modern Europe must be based on comparative studies, both of societies in which such revolutions occurred and in which they did not occur." Those societies in which revolutions did not occur may not have pursued such aggressive foreign policies because they either lacked the ambitions or the resources to pursue them. Further, those states that did not face serious domestic constraints on the foreign policy objectives that they did have would have also been unlikely to experience revolutionary challenges.
2. The question of how sociology has explored the problem of revolution is nicely laid out in Goldstone, 1986. See also my review of Goldstone in *Contemporary Sociology*, 1987. I explore the question of revolution in "The Problem of Revolution in Contemporary Sociological Theory" in *International Journal of Comparative Sociology* (forthcoming 1988) and especially in *Revolution in the Sociological Imagination* (Cambridge: Polity Press/Basil Blackwell, forthcoming 1988).
3. Such an argument is almost directly opposite of the one I have employed in this work. Though I agree with Wallerstein's reliance on structural variables, I propose a contrary causal sequence, in which state activity in the international context is constrained by traditional domestic arrangements, and state initiatives to mobilize domestic resources sets political opposition in motion. Thus, the economic breakthrough of a capitalist class does not cause the revolution in my view, as it clearly does in Wallerstein's analysis, but is instead the outcome of revolution, the result of the clash between state and social groups.
4. Stone makes a distinction among three temporal levels of analysis that is important to us here: long-run structural "preconditions"; the shorter-run

events, "precipitants," that set these forces in motion; and the "triggers," those immediate historical events that ignite the conflict (Stone, 1974).

5. See, for example, Lewis, 1964; Ashley, 1967, 1970; Whitehead, 1968; and Saint-Simon, 1963. In 1876 Alfred Magné (1876: 13) urged his colleagues to

> open their eyes and become inspired by these great examples who made, in their time, the reign of Louis XIV splendid without equal. Literature, conversation, and fine arts, diplomacy, the army and navy and naval administration would find in the past century the most beautiful and the best; commerce and industry fully prosperous, already rivalled . . . the riches and the power of the country in its foreign relations and its intellectual works were preponderant in Europe. At home, modern times inspired a public spirit, and the old world, transformed itself, morality flourished; above all, one works, organizes and marches next to the giants towards French unity that they began to construct: this is a great page in our history!

Much of the present work suggests the fallacies contained in Magné's effusive defense of the seventeenth century.

6. The literature on the crisis of the seventeenth century is enormous, beginning with Hobsbawm's controversial thesis. Mousnier opens his history of the sixteenth and seventeenth centuries (1954: 143) with the following preface:

> The 17th century was a time of crisis which affected all Mankind. . . . The crisis was permanent with, so to say, violent shifts in intensity. The contradictory tendencies had coexisted for a long time, entangled with each other, by turns amalgamating and combating, and there is no easy way of discerning their limits nor the date at which their relationships changed. Not only did these tendencies coexist at the same time throughout Europe, but even in the same social group, even in the same man, they were present and divisive. The state, the social group and the individual were all struggling ceaselessly to restore in their environment and in themselves order and unity.

Aston (1964) and Coveny (1977) reproduce the most important of these works, especially as they regard France and England.

7. Some recent authors have demurred at the label of crisis. Not a crisis in the system, Wallerstein (1980: 33, 18) argues, but "a period of consolidation," an economic contraction that "occurred within a functioning ongoing capitalist world-economy." (Schoffer [1964: 104] anticipates Wallerstein's argument, describing a "period of solidifying and organizing.") Wallerstein points to the areas of expansion in the seventeenth century—urban industry, population, money supply, and the number of marginal entrepreneurs—to demonstrate the stabilization upon which further expansion could be predicated. Mobilized classes in core states, he asserts, organized political power to enhance their position in a contracting market; other nations experienced increased economic hardship. Mercantilism helped some countries weather the storm, and provided increased potential for the plunder of the periphery. I disagree that the seventeenth century was the moment of the consolidation of the capitalist world-economy, for economic changes occurred within a feudal, seigneurial, and absolutist framework. Even if it was a moment of consolidation of the economy *as a whole,* it was no less a moment of crisis for the individual societies that attempted to negotiate their way to a better position in the international economy and geopolitical arena.

8. The literature on the political crisis is also large and varied, beginning with Trevor-Roper's original critique of Hobsbawm's thesis (Aston, 1964). Koenigsberger (1971: 283) called it a "genuine crisis of societies and their political constitutions," and Salmon (1967: 27–28) labeled it a "general crisis in government and society caused by the challenge of the Crown to the holders of venal offices." Rabb (1975: 60) agrees that the growth of royal bureaucracies is central to the crisis, noting that "common to every kingdom, principality and republic were certain essential changes in the institutions and aims of politics, many of which aroused fierce opposition. The all pervasive issue was the increase in central governmental power, exemplified by the growth of bureaucracies." As a political crisis, Shennan adds (1976: 100), it arose "out of the burgeoning power of the princes which brought to a head the question of where ultimate power lay and what sovereignty meant in terms of political action."

9. The only attempt at a social revolution in mid-seventeenth-century France, the Ormée in Bordeaux, was easily suppressed, especially in the absence of expected aid from the English.

10. Lublinskaya notes that "it was very characteristic of France at that time that the general backwardness of its manufactures as compared with Holland or England was intensified, beginning with the decade after 1610, by the subjection of French trade and industry to the interests of English and Dutch merchants and manufacturers. . . . France was not only in an unequal position as compared with her northern neighbors, she was the only one of these countries which in a given period experienced serious difficulties in this respect."

2

The Absolutist Impulse in France

Ready money is at a premium these days.
—Athos,
in *The Three Musketeers*

Early modern France was a remarkably wealthy nation, rich in natural resources, fertile soil, extensive forests, and ample natural waterways. The nation presented a strong international image through its large and powerful army, and a thriving commercial population trading from its port cities. A haughty and wealthy nobility constructed palatial chateaux in the countryside and lived as elegantly as any in the world. A grand and glorious monarchy surrounded itself with many of the world's treasures, living in sumptuous, licentiously ornate opulence.

Yet, France was also a very poor country. Natural resources remained untapped, the agricultural heartland produced barely enough to sustain its population, who frequently hovered precariously close to starvation. Epidemics and crop failures were almost annual events, and over 80 percent of the population was chronically undernourished. The army—unpaid, hungry, and brutally treated—was frequently mutinous. Commerce was crippled by political intervention and insecurity of investment. The nobility was as arrogant as it was economically unimportant, and as wealthy as it managed to be by siphoning off the nation's wealth. Behind the precise hedges surrounding the formal gardens of the Tuileries, the mighty French monarchy tottered like a house of cards. The royal treasury was usually empty, and the government hovered perpetually on the verge of bankruptcy. Expedients devised to raise sorely needed cash were successful only in the short run, and undercut the opportunity for political, economic, and social reforms that were necessary to reorganize the nation's finances.

A persistent fiscal crisis plagued old regime France. Half of all tax revenues were consumed by "the system of prestige spending" and the other half was devoured by war and the debts incurred by wars, leaving only a "trivial" amount for national investment (Goubert, 1973: 136). But, war only exacerbated a crisis that could not be solved by a simple increase in cash flow.[1] The crisis was structural.

To understand the fiscal crisis of the old regime French state, it will be necessary first to map French social organization in the sixteenth and seventeenth centuries, and to describe the traditional fiscal structure of the old regime. Then I shall turn to the new pressures and new opportunities provided by the expansion of both the arena and stakes of military competition and war and the international economy, which set the crown searching for mechanisms to boost its resources. Finally, I shall describe the development of absolutism, especially under Louis XIII and his first minister, Cardinal Richelieu, as a method of meeting fiscal demands without generating structural reform. In this sense Richelieu's absolutism was an administrative revolution without commensurate social reform.

French Society before the Seventeenth Century

Seventeenth-century France was an agricultural nation; agriculture was by far the most important source of wealth. Most of the overwhelmingly (roughly 85 percent) rural population lived in small villages of between 300 and 900 residents. Agricultural production was organized around three areas: the *domaine proche,* the immediate domain of the local lord; the *domaine utile* or *censive,* which surrounded the domaine proche and was leased to the peasants but over which the lord retained certain rights; and the common lands—meadows, heaths, forests, pasture lands—over which the peasants maintained rights. To Le Roy Ladurie (1976: 291) agriculture in the old regime was marked by a contradiction between "the dynamic elasticity of the population" and the "stubborn inelasticity of agricultural production."

Agricultural techniques varied widely and continually adapted to changing conditions (Jacquart, 1973: 175). Different forms of farming corresponded to different geographic regions, each of which manifested different relations between landlords and peasants. In the west and also in the south the *bocage* system was composed of scattered settlements of individual plots marked by hedgerows, in which multiple or extended families would provide for their own needs using a two-crop rotation. The cereal-growing region in the north, on the other hand, used a three-field rotation in open fields; nuclear families clustered in traditional villages, collectively setting harvest dates and allowing gleaning rights to vagabonds and beg-

The French provinces at the time of Richelieu and Mazarin

(Stippled areas are those with provincial estates in 1661 and after)

Source: Robin Briggs, *Early Modern France, 1560–1715* (New York: Oxford University Press, 1977).

gars. Producing for commercial markets, these individual peasant families were "semiproletarianized," yet their reliance on community-based decision making maintained a collective identity.[2]

The proximity to subsistence at the village level had several interrelated consequences. First, the population had few defenses against demographic or climatological variations; crop failures, meager harvests, too much rain, epidemic threatened village existence. A low level of peasant ownership and lack of capital and mechanical aids meant that 75 percent of French peasants were cultivating insufficient land to provide the essentials of life (Jacquart, 1974: 165). Increased fiscal burdens, either from the monarchy or the nobility, meant additional pressures; faced with the choice, many peasants preferred, as Balzac wrote, "more wheat and fewer laurels."

The village was the social and administrative unit toward which most French people were oriented; the "elementary cell" was largely self-contained, autonomous and isolated (Zagorin, 1982: 86). Regions were organized as agglomerations of separate villages; these in turn were organized neither into an integrated formal unit like England nor a loosely bound confederation of independent principalities like the Germanic states. The centrally located *pays d'élections* had been part of the royal domain since the Capetians, but the geographically peripheral *pays d'état* had only recently been added to the realm. One-third of the kingdom, the pays d'état contributed only 10 percent of its revenues because as a result of their incorporation, they had been granted certain rights and autonomous privileges, such as retention of local estates and parliaments, control over taxation—including rights to levy and collect taxes, reduction of some taxes, and exemption from other odious taxes—and looser controls over urban trade. In the pays d'état, provincial estates protected provincial liberties and opposed fiscal impositions by the crown, and they also were a regional political backbone of the seigneurial system, championing the interests of the owners of large holdings in determining provincial fiscal and administrative policies (Beik, 1985: 160).

The political administration of the seigneurial system expressed the contradiction that lay at the heart of the feudal mode of production, between "the centralizing tendencies of a situation where power was locally grounded in land and authority was exercised through the innate preeminence of individuals or groups, on the one hand, and the necessity for higher coordination inherent in such a system of personal authority on the other" (Beik, 1985: 337). Royal power was never absolute, and even the absolutism of Richelieu and Mazarin expressed only a tendency to concentrate political power at the top, not its success. And, even absolutism depended on popular support, on the contract between king and subjects. In the sixteenth century, as political theorist Jean Bodin understood it, the political contract required an intimate union between the ruler and the ruled, an emotional attachment of the population to the person of the king, and not to any abstract entity called the state. In this sense the moral and emotional foundations of the contract between king and people were crucial elements in the maintenance of political stability, implying a set of rights and obligations for both parties. Failure to adhere to these rules was a serious breach of that intimate union, and cause for restitutive action. For the popular forces, that meant the rejection of royal initiatives *in the name of* continued loyalty to the king. The most common cry of the popular rebellions was "Long live the king without [the offending tax, or tax collector, or policy]!" This suggests that the monarchy may have been very strong, while the supporting state apparatus was big, bulky, but ultimately weak.

While agrarian France suffered from its precarious proximity to subsistence crisis throughout the old regime, the two great trends of the sixteenth century—the price revolution and the Protestant Reformation—obliquely and indirectly affected life in the peasant village. Although trade expanded in the cities, and agriculture was somewhat commercialized, at least in the north, for most of rural France, the sixteenth century was "not so much a process of real growth, but rather a movement of recovery, within the framework or within the course of a homeostatic system" (Le Roy Ladurie, 1981: 109). To be sure, the waves of natural disasters that struck France in the early seventeenth century as the entire international economy experienced a reversal and contraction—a merciless series of poor harvests, high agricultural prices, scarcity of food, starvation, epidemics—dramatically affected the traditional peasantry. Feillet reported (1886: 24) that in the first decades of the century the plague "exercised its terrible ravages over the entirety of France"; another observer noted that the "misery is so general on all sides and among all sorts of people that unless there is some relaxation the people will be impelled by their powerlessness towards some dangerous solution."[3]

The conservative character of French rural society may have also shielded it from the shakier position of becoming trapped between traditional social forces and forces of modernization. The peasants "were not crushed by the traditional forces of oppression," writes Le Roy Ladurie (1981: 112), for the clergy and the nobility exercised some moderation, taking only 20 percent of the villagers' land. "Modernity more perhaps than tradition caused the peasant to suffer." As a result, the agrarian component of the crisis of the seventeenth century did not utterly destroy rural society; "the tragedy was not the collapse, but only the inelasticity and rigidity of agricultural production; not its decline but its failure to grow significantly" (Le Roy Ladurie, 1974: 147).

The fragility of peasant life also made old regime France vulnerable to popular uprisings, which reached a crescendo in the twenty-five years before the Fronde but also had a long history. Earlier revolts, such as the waves of fourteenth-century uprisings, coincided with demographic crises and religious movements, and often evidenced a millenarian character (Mollat and Wolff, 1973, 1976; Brucker, 1968; Bercé, 1974). From the mid-sixteenth century, popular uprisings appeared to spring more from a

crosscutting coalitional defense of local autonomy than the more sponta-
neously isolated earlier revolts. The Croquants that swept through southern France in the 1590s, for example, fused class-based hostility with
antimonarchical and anticlerical sentiments. These peasant uprisings accomplished what the Wars of Religion could not; the threat from below
had unified the factious nobility with the monarchy, for the nobles "ultimately preferred royal authority to social anarchy" (Salmon, 1978: 291).
And the urban revolts, such as in Romans in 1580, indicated the ways in
which festivals of symbolic inversion, such as Carnival, resulted in the
expression of a menacing radicalism. In his elegant history of this revolt
Le Roy Ladurie underscores the class conflict that characterized many
revolts, even those against royal fiscal policy. Here, when new taxes were
introduced and the local nobles claimed their traditional exemptions, the
urban lower classes were furious because the entire burden would fall on
their shoulders. "You thieves," shouted one rebel from the gallows (in Le
Roy Ladurie, 1980a: 168), "you're the ones who should pay the town's
debts, all you'd have to do would be to shell out the town's money that
you made off with." Another rebel, anticipating later Marxist ideas by
more than 250 years, understood the link between nobility and wealth,
when he commented (in Le Roy Ladurie, 1980a: 346) that "the rich are
the ones who become nobles. Freedom from taxes is an exemption of
wealth, not nobility." In Dauphine, at least, rebels were not necessarily
backward-looking, atavistic fanatics; they "were not really for maintaining
the status quo or returning to a utopian past. They were reformers, and at
times revolutionaries" (Le Roy Ladurie, 1980a: 43).

The inelasticity of agricultural production had a dramatic impact on the
aristocracy as well. Although the peasants hovered precariously at the
level of subsistence, their survival often threatened by the slightest varia-
tion in climate, harvest, or disease,[4] the aristocracy, standing at the top of
rural social organization, was also experiencing serious difficulties. Noble
status depended upon the hereditary honor of social rank, a position that
could not be bought, earned, or learned, but could only be manifest.
Traditionally based upon the relationship to military force, the high nobility, the noblesse d'épée, was originally the feudal retainers whose military
support made the reign of any particular king possible. Nobility had also
come to be more than a relationship to production as the owners of the
manorial estates, and a military relationship to kingship; it was also an
attitude, a style of life, a status group. La Rogue (1735) defined nobility as

a quality which makes generous whomever possess it and which privilege
disposes the soul toward worthy things. It is the virtue of a man's ancestors that
confer this excellent imprint of nobility. There is in the seed I know not what

power or principle which transmits and continues the inclinations of fathers among their descendents. And everyone who issues from great and illustrious personages feels increasingly at the bottom of his heart a certain impulse that urges him to imitate them, while their memory incites him to seek glory and great deeds.

The price revolution of the sixteenth century adversely affected noble incomes, for nobility was a fixed status in a world of economic and social transformation. Prohibited from *dérogance*—the debasement of their status by "any activity aimed at making money, especially trade" (Mousnier, 1980: 132)—and living on fixed incomes based on predetermined shares of peasant output, the nobility was poorly positioned to take advantage of the sixteenth-century price revolution.[5] The "crisis of the nobility" in sixteenth- and early-seventeenth-century France consisted of this economic decline, an erosion of privileged social status—exemption from royal taxation, for example—by the incursion into noble ranks of urban merchants who had purchased noble titles, and by their profligate consumerism, the flamboyant luxury that marked the aristocratic life-style and consumed enormous portions of declining noble fortunes; it was "the progressive dispossession of a ruling class" (Mandrou, 1976: 107). The contraction of wealth based on land in an era of inflation drove many nobles to the cities, away from what one Parisian merchant called "the desolation of the countryside" (in Mousnier, 1980: 182). Finally, and perhaps most importantly, the nobles were decreasingly central to the royal war effort, so that "what remained of their military role was practically the relics—trophies in chateaux, tales and legends of ancestral battles, glorious genealogies, and even the sense of personal honor" (Bitten, 1974: 2).[6]

The erosion of noble status also precipitated a crisis of confidence among the traditional ruling class; the comte de Cramail addressed the king in 1626, complaining that the nobility "finds itself in the most pitiable state of all time. It is crushed by poverty, robbed of virtue by its idleness, made almost desperate by oppression" (cited in Adam, 1972: 5). A pamphlet by a nobleman during the Fronde described a nobility that by midcentury had "grown old in harness, dying in their houses without reward, constrained to crush the innocent and plunder the peasant in order to live according to their rank and quality" (cited in Deyon, 1964: 346).

Rural life was relatively static in old regime France, and production inelastic, growing only very slowly, and within the constraints of traditional class relations. Similarly, urban life, while developing, was also contained within the shell of traditional relationships. Urban merchants strove to maximize the variety of their investments and their profits, but often were lured away from productive investment by the need to exempt their fortunes from taxation, which could be accomplished only by becoming ennobled.[7] Though their wealth continued to grow throughout the sixteenth and seventeenth centuries, the rate of increase was constrained by the siphoning off of increased amounts by the monarchy in the form of taxes, by France's decreasing position relative to other trading countries, especially England and the Netherlands, and by the lack of incentives to increase domestic production.

A new layer of French society, the venal officers (who are described in more detail below), had developed between the urban merchants and the hereditary nobility. Having purchased noble titles, this *noblesse de robe* had acquired positions in the royal courts and as royal administrators; noble status conferred exemption from taxation and other privileges associated with nobility. Although venality of offices had almost as long a history as the French monarchy, the early seventeenth century witnessed a sharp increase in their numbers, especially after 1604, when a relatively modest payment to the royal treasury called the *paulette* allowed the venal office to be inherited by the possessor's heirs.

Finally, there was the Catholic clergy, suspended over the entire social structure, the First Estate of the realm. The church, from archbishops to parish *curés*, retained the privileges of corporate autonomy and tax exemption. The bloody Wars of Religion that had raged throughout the sixteenth century had even more firmly entrenched the Counter-Reformation, and solidified the Catholic clergy's dominant position. And, although the Edict of Nantes in 1598 did not completely satisfy the Catholic clergy and its noble allies, the Catholic League, because it granted autonomy to Protestants in towns and cities in which they already lived, also confirmed the irrevocable Catholic foundation of the French monarchy.

As France entered the seventeenth century, then, it was a country rich in potential and constrained by its traditional arrangements, "thick with inert obstacles to effective centralised rule" (Lloyd, 1983: 170). The ranks of those who were traditionally immune to royal initiatives, especially royal fiscal initiatives—the Catholic clergy, the high nobility, the traditionally autonomous towns, and the outlying provinces—were now joined by recently ennobled former merchants and the Protestants, who were to be left alone in their cities. Only the peasants remained unprotected as the fiscal foundation of the monarchy, and, as we have seen, their position was precarious enough to prevent the monarchy from squeezing them too vigorously. "The fundamental financial problem of the French monarchy was the inefficiency of its revenue raising system . . . [which] resulted from a tax base that was too narrow combined with an ineffective machinery for the collection of taxes'' (Bonney, 1981: 272). What sorts of resources did the French crown have at its disposal?

State Finances in Old Regime France

There was hardly a time when the French monarchy was not plagued by fiscal crisis; from its founding by Hugh Capet in 982 until the collapse of the Bourbon monarchy in 1789, the crown was engaged in a relentless search for increased revenues.[8] Royal revenues consisted of both ordinary and extraordinary receipts. Ordinary revenues derived from the revenues of the royal domain, that share of the nation that belonged to the crown under its seigneurial regime, much as the receipts of any feudal manor would accrue to the manor's seigneurial lord. Most Frenchmen "thought that the state should meet its ordinary expenses out of the revenue from the royal domain. Resort to taxation should be had only exceptionally" (Mousnier, 1980: 730). These revenues were themselves split into two forms of tax revenues, depending upon what was being taxed: either a person or land (direct taxation) or the production, distribution, or consumption of a commodity (indirect taxation). The chief direct tax was the *taille,* both the *taille personnelle,* which was levied on individuals after an estimation of their wealth, and the *taille réelle,* which was levied on a fixed estimate of the value of a piece of property. The taille personnelle was the predominant form in the north and was variable; the taille réelle was levied mostly in the pays d'état, in the municipalities of Grenoble, Aix, Montpellier, Toulouse, and Montauban. Collection of the two forms of taille varied as well: either the estates or the parliaments (or both) in the pays d'état voted to collect their tailles réelles, and hired local agents to collect it; the taille personnelle was administered in Paris and collected by central agents sent to a municipality.

Direct taxes were supplemented by a series of indirect taxes, which allowed the crown a great deal more flexibility. The *aides* were a sales tax, imposed on goods sold within the kingdom. Among the most important of these were the *octrois* and the *droits d'entrée* collected by royal agents in major towns and cities. (The aides were not at all uniformly administered throughout the realm, and many municipalities retained the rights to collect the octrois and the droits d'entrée.) The *gabelles* were taxes on consumption of salt, an essential commodity to all social groups; this tax carried an exemption for all regions that produced the salt. There were also numerous *traites* or customs duties levied on goods or merchandise leaving the realm entirely or moving from one province to another. Finally, the provincial assemblies in the pays d'état were also often forced to vote gifts to the king in return for his respect of provincial autonomy.

Tax collection was mired in an administrative machinery that was so dense and complex that often there was "no way of knowing precisely what was happening to the royal finances at any given point" (Dent, 1974: 31). This administrative inefficiency was compounded by the collection strategies adopted by the *surintendant des finances* who oversaw collection. Most taxes were collected by an intermediary group of tax farmers, private individuals who had purchased the right to collect taxes by paying the state some lesser proportion of the amount that was anticipated by collection. And, each municipality maintained a fiscal administration, in which *receveurs particuliers* would collect local taxes, deduct expenses incurred in collection and wages, and send the rest to the *receveur général* in each *généralité;* these in turn deducted regional expenses and sent the remainder to the central treasury, the Trésor de l'Epargne, where they would be added to the monies paid already by the tax farmers. As a result, the productivity of indirect taxes "was much less impressive than the burden on the community which it represented, since their collection was farmed out and a great deal of the actual income from them remained in the hands of the tax farmers" (Beloff, 1961: 75).

Even in peacetime ordinary revenues were insufficient, for interest on loans and bonds, wages of royal officials, and maintenance of a standing army were all paid from these funds. The French were not "geared to providing an adequate supply of cash to the government" because they perceived every innovation as an "extortion" (Sturdy, 1965: 571; Mousnier, 1980: 730). These ordinary revenues were supplemented by a series of *extraordinaires,* fiscal expedients designed to answer immediate needs but upon which the crown came increasingly to rely. Perhaps the most important of these was the venality of offices itself, which brought the crown immediate windfalls as merchants raced to exempt themselves and their families from taxation, but which cost the crown dearly in the loss of future taxes. Other fiscal expedients included the *rentes sur l'Hôtel de Ville,* state bonds floated by the crown based on receipts of the municipal government of the city of Paris; *traites,* which were agreements for loans from private individuals; and short-term loans, concluded often with local *financiers.* The crown was also certainly not above committing fraud when no other sources of money were readily available and its credit too weak to obtain funds legitimately (Dent, 1974). Fiscal expedients yielded mixed results, as well; they were, in the words of one seventeenth-century observer (in Saint-Germain, 1950: 30), "a remedy one day for an eternal illness."

State borrowing, the *emprunt,* was certainly the most common form of loans designed to raise immediate revenues without destabilizing traditional social relations. Organizing loans to the state was "the central function of the financial system," the function "about which everything turned in the royal finances. Short term credit was both the thing that kept the state going from day to day and the most profitable field for the development of a financier's resources" (Dent, 1974: 150, 148). One type of loan was the *anticipation,* in which future receipts for various taxes were the guarantor of immediate loans by tax farmers to the crown. Traites were also legion, "furnishing the capital for all new ventures" (Chaleur, 1954: 49). But traites, too, began to yield diminishing returns, and they became "the worst form of public credit" (Chaleur, 1954: 49).

A brief description of the rentes might elucidate the workings of the French fiscal system, and the "bizarre financial insanity" that characterized old regime fiscal administration (Dent, 1974: 50). The rentes were simple loans, "the most ordinary of extraordinary expedients," usually taken at 5.55 percent interest, and repayable over twelve years, when the face value of the rente had been paid (Luthy, 1959, vol. 1: 84; see also Dent, 1974: 47; Schnapper, 1957: 86). A long-term agreement, the rente presupposed a certain level of economic stability and provided the lender (the buyer of the rente) with a stable long-term income and the borrower (the seller of the rente) with large immediate funds. (During periods of inflation, such as the sixteenth century, assuming large loans was profitable, and rentes were particularly advantageous for the seller.) For the crown, the rentes were state bonds, premised on future stable income to the royal treasury; when first introduced, they were sold on future income from the franc-fief, and later on the anticipated income of taxes such as the gabelles, aides, or even the taille.

In the sixteenth century Francis I enlarged the use of rentes as a fiscal expedient, offering them both on his personal income (royal rentes) and on the income of the city of Paris, guaranteed by the Hôtel de Ville (municipal rentes). The latter were especially useful because they placed the financial resources of the entire city administration behind the guarantees of interest payment, and were therefore a far more attractive investment to a potential buyer. In fact, rentes were so attractive that the single largest group of purchasers in the sixteenth century was the magistrates in the Parliament of Paris, who were "capable of using a body which considered itself the highest judicial authority in the kingdom to protect the rentier" (Dent, 1974: 48). Rentes dominated the credit market in the second half of the century, and even the income of the clergy was used to guarantee their repayment (A. N., K 1055, fols. 1–4; see also Dent, 1974: 49; Schnapper, 1957: 155).

Rentes were an extremely popular form of investment in the sixteenth and seventeenth centuries, until the fiscal weakness of the crown was exposed through their poor administration and irregular interest payments.

Even among the nobility, rentes constituted as much as 35 percent of individual fortunes, and after land and offices, they "figured increasingly in marriage contracts and in inventories of estates" (Goubert, 1973: 49; see also Mousnier, 1978: 181). Rentes were also popular among the venal officers, who wanted to use the money to purchase estates in the country-side and begin to live nobly off their investments. Wealthy merchants were also investors in the rentes, and were especially involved in the rentes of the Hôtel de Ville of Paris, seeking a fixed income from which to launch their upward mobility into the nobility. In this way the rentes "served to transfer land and property from the aristocracy to the rising middle classes, and helped eventually to create a new nobility in France" (Kamen, 1977: 177).

The sixteenth century had witnessed a remarkable proliferation of both extraordinary and ordinary mechanisms to increase state revenues, stretching the financial system to its limits. Francis I had reorganized financial administration, and developed a centralized, cash-based system. Whereas finances earlier had been decentralized under the *généraux des finances* and money was raised and spent locally, two edicts in 1523 helped to centralize administration. The Edict of St. Germain-en-Laye created the *trésorier de l'épargne,* who was charged with receiving all extraordinary revenues and using them to build a central cash reserve, and the Edict of Blois extended this to all royal revenues, ordinary as well as extraordinary. But, this could not keep pace with the fiscal crisis; revenues that hovered around 10 million *livres*[9] were barely enough to keep the monarchy afloat, so the king was forced to borrow from bankers in Italy and Antwerp, as well as increase the numbers of rentes and traites offered.[10] The dramatic social changes that characterized the second half of the century, however, stretched the fiscal resources of the crown. The dramatic expansion of international trade, the Wars of Religion, and the secularization of international social relations as a result of the Reforma-tion all put increased fiscal pressure on the monarchy, and when the century ended, the crown was both utterly depleted and faced with perhaps the most intense pressure and the most exciting challenges of its history. In 1572 the crown developed a new layer of venal officers, the *partisans* to administer the rentes, and the income escalated dramatically, from 42,000 livres in 1571 to 533,000 livres in 1572 (Schnapper, 1957: 173). But this change brought new problems, in part because the success of the rentes had come from their reliable administration "by a body relatively inde-pendent from the Crown" (Dent, 1974: 50). Interest payments became irregular and by 1585 were over 4 million livres in arrears (Bonney, 1981: 26), and although disaster could be forestalled by creating new rentes to pay off the interest on the old ones, soon the market began to dry up and purchasers became harder and harder to find (Dent, 1974: 50). The crown then resorted to its other chief expedient, personnel, and in 1594 created a new layer of officers, the *receveurs-payeurs*, to bring in revenues and rationalize the administration of the rentes. By 1597 the rentiers were protesting, claiming that they were "always in pain" (A. N., K 1055). By the turn of the seventeenth century, the relationship between buyer and seller had inverted and the credit market was increasingly a buyer's market; interest rates soared, and the amount in arrears topped 60 million livres (Bonney, 1981: 57). Some rentiers had not received their interest payment in nineteen years, and the poor administration of the rentes indicated a "disorganization of the economy in general and a dread of the future, both traceable to the creation and sale of the rentes" (Schnapper, 1957: 361–62).

Personnel as Policy

Royal finances were also administered by a remarkable number of financial officers, from tax farmers and individual traitants to newly ennobled venal officers who had purchased their title from the crown. These groups were more than fiscal administrators, though; they were themselves often fiscal expedients, for the sale of offices was one of the chief mechanisms that the crown had devised to raise revenues. The proliferation of fiscal and administrative personnel was, itself, a component of royal fiscal policy.

Venality of offices had always served two functions, simultaneously providing revenues to the king and staffing the royal bureaucracy with functionaries more dependent upon royal favors than the hereditary nobility, whose loyalty was questionable and whose own clientage networks and regional or local connections made it less dependent and controllable. The earliest venal officers were those created by Philip Augustus in the early thirteenth century, when he extended the royal domain and required administrative assistance in collecting taxes and adjudicating disputes. The thirty new administrative units were administered by the *bailiffs* in the north and the *seneschals* in the south. His successor, Louis IX (Saint Louis), expanded the *curia regis* into a royal bureaucracy consisting of the Conseil d'Etat (blood relatives of the king who advised him on policy issues), the Chambre des Comptes (which handled financial matters dealing with the royal domain, such as auditing the accounts of the bailiffs and seneschals), and the *parlements* (the sovereign courts that were both the highest appeals courts and bodies that consulted and advised the king on policy matters. Louis's son, Philip IV, extended to the Parliament of Paris in 1302 the right to register all royal edicts, and hence involved it in, at least, the approval of royal policy.

In large part, as we have seen, it was the urban bourgeoisie that "furnished the largest number of officers" to the royal administration, for the members' scramble for noble status and hence tax exemption pressed them to purchase offices (Mousnier, 1948: 17ff.) This "permeation of the central apparatus by the sons of the urban bourgeoisie" indicates to Elias (1982: 187–88) the "close functional interdependence" between the rise of the monarchy and the rise of the bourgeoisie in France. Capitalist development and state building seemed to go hand in hand in Renaissance France, for the monarchy was staffed by loyal and dependent bureaucrats, who assured the royal treasury of steady income, and the officers were granted immunity from taxation and noble status. Unfortunately, this system broke down during the sixteenth century and especially in the seventeenth century, partially from the additional weight of the increasing layers of officers created to raise money, and partly from the contradictions between the needs of state builders to siphon productive capital into state ventures and the conflicting needs of the merchants to invest their capital freely in overseas trade. By the mid-seventeenth century capitalism and state building were no longer mutually reinforcing but were, often, antagonistic and contradictory.

The steady increase in the number of offices contributed to the erosion of their viability for the crown. For one thing, they became almost as costly as they were profitable. Wages that had hovered around 1.2 million livres in 1560 had almost doubled (2.3 million) by 1576, and by 1585 the king paid 5 million livres in wages for offices created that year. "Each creation of offices brought the following year's receipts in to handle the expenses of the previous years" (Mousnier, 1948: 50).[11] And offices were less than completely secure for the officeholder, for whom nobility mattered only if it could be passed on to his children. Before 1604 the reversion of the office to the family was required to take place within forty days of the officer's death, at a time when these legal formalities often took three or four months. Although this resulted in some subtle subterfuges to conceal the death of the officeholder until the paperwork was completed— such as "pickling the corpse like a young pig" (Prestwich, 1957: 119)—it also led a desperate scramble to a more stable mechanism to insure inheritance. The king's offer of the *droit annuel,* a payment equal to one sixty-fourth of the value of the office, permitted the office to revert to the holder's family and remain part of the holder's patrimony, and it also insured regular income from the venal officers, from whom the king believed it would be difficult to raise additional revenues once they had purchased their offices and exempted themselves from taxation. In addition, because the income was regular and predictable, the king could also borrow against it. The droit annuel or paulette (named after Charles Paulet, to whom the first droit annuel was offered) was immensely popular and the prices of offices rose sharply after its institution; for example, the value of the office of parlementaire in the Parliament of Rouen rose sixfold between 1593 and 1622 (Prestwich, 1957: 120; Dewald, 1980: 139).[12]

Obviously, the crown found the sale of offices quite profitable. In addition to the purchase price of the office and the paulette, there were several other sources of income from officeholders. Because the office-holder had purchased the office from a specific king, the *droit de continuer* allowed the officer to retain the office in a new reign while providing the new king with a windfall upon ascension. And politically, the sale of offices "dispersed bureaucratic power" to the benefit of the king, con-structing parallel administrations in the localities that undercut the client-age systems of old noble dynasties (Anderson, 1974: 95). As "the bour-geoisie replaced the nobility in the government of the state," France's state became increasingly "militarized" and the royal administration was increasingly "civilianized" (Swart, 1944: 122; Tilly, 1981: 14). The king counted on a docile and loyal bureaucracy, composed of urban bourgeois, now dependent upon him (Mousnier, 1948: 620; Mandrou, 1965: 52; Tapié, 1973: 55).

But, there were costs. Venality provided short-term profit but retarded capitalist development, luring potential investors away from capitalist ventures and into the state credit sector, for the market for status returned higher social and economic rewards than did capitalist investment in a nation that saw capitalist trade simply as a potential source of royal wealth through customs and duties and other taxes. A good deal of the capital "that might have been invested in branches of industry was used for buying offices" as the officers "became a gigantic organism that took capital from the kingdom and threw it into the royal treasury. They contributed, in this way, to the inability to establish a system of credit" (Swart, 1944: 123; Mousnier, 1948: 385). Porchnev (1978: 124) writes:

> Capital created in the heart of society by productive labor was transferred immediately into credit circulation. Industry and commercial capital was trans-formed immediately into credit capital, removed from capitalist sources and indifferent to modes of production. The tax farmers, the officers and all state creditors . . . gave not the slightest character of capitalism to the seigneurial economy or to the economy of the state.

Venality of office, designed to facilitate the state-building programs of the various Valois and Bourbon kings, also had the effect of retarding capitalist development, and contributed to what Braudel (1973: 68) called the "treason of the bourgeoisie," and to what Porchnev described (1964: 412) as "detouring the bourgeoisie from the revolutionary struggle against feudalism." The bourgeoisie was "feudalized" far more deeply than the monarchy experienced "embourgeoisement," for the bourgeois were only too happy to shed their non-noble pasts and live like the nobility to which they had aspired, purchasing alienated estates and avoiding the degrading "common" forms of capitalist activity no longer appropriate to their status (see also Major, 1962: 123).

Thus, venality of offices captured the contradictory nature of absolutism as a political form designed not only to bring glory to the royal family and hence the nation but also to resolve the persistent fiscal crisis of the old regime. The king became increasingly dependent upon venality, just as the officers were increasingly dependent upon the monarchy. This mutual dependence weakened the autonomous power of the state, even as it increased its autonomy from class domination. And, the dependence of the crown on venality also led to an incessant search for new officers who represented new sources of revenues. In this way venality became its opposite, and "deprived the government of an efficient and reliable body of officials, strengthened the oligarchic tendencies, created a discontented elite, and disrupted the financial system" (Swart, 1944: 123), so that, as Pagès writes (in Brown, 1971: 13), "at the moment royal power triumphed over the last resistance to absolute monarchy, [the kings] set up a new obstacle, which they never succeeded in suppressing entirely."

In all, one could say that venality was "disastrous. The poor recruitment of officers, the temptation and ease of fraud, the abandonment of commerce and industry, the extra expenses on the royal finances by rights and privileges and wages, and the discontent of the nobility, clergy, and part of the Third Estate, were some of the factors that venality caused" (Mousnier, 1948: 404–5). What had facilitated the concentration of royal power over the *grands* and seemed to resolve the crown's fiscal crisis now prevented the monarchy from freeing itself entirely from social contraints and becoming truly absolute (Mousnier, 1948: 623; Mousnier, 1980: 561).

Administrative layering of venal officeholders as a vehicle to resolve fiscal crisis can be illustrated by looking briefly at a few of the different offices created alongside the magistrates in the sovereign courts. The trésoriers and the *élus* were each created to raise more funds by the sale of the position and the increased administrative capability they offered the crown (Bourgneuf, 1745, vol. 1: 43). Created in 1523, the trésoriers were responsible for tax collection within the elections, and the élus were responsible for collection within the parishes. They immediately brought additional revenues to the crown, but they also provoked significant opposition from the magistrates in the sovereign courts, who argued that the venality of the trésoriers' position made them unworthy of entering the chambers of the sovereign courts. Royal support of the trésoriers, however, allowed them to enter the nobility; at Louis XIII's funeral in 1643, for example, the trésoriers wore the same ceremonial robes as the officers in the Chambre des Comptes, and their wives and daughters wore the same dresses as the wives and daughters of the other magistrates. An edict in 1644, reluctantly registered by Parliament, confirmed that the trésoriers had all the rights and privileges of the other magistrates. (Other administrative layers, such as the financiers and the intendants, will be discussed in more detail in the next chapter.)

Trade and War: Magnets and Pressures

Resolution of the Wars of Religion had left France formally unified, and increased the tactical mobility and fiscal resourcefulness of the monarchy, even at the expense of Protestants and Catholic League nobles, for neither group was in a position effectively to challenge royal initiatives toward domestic centralization. By the turn of the seventeenth century the increased economic possibilities of international trade and the pressure of heightened geopolitical competition among early modern states presented the crown with the profound challenge of mobilizing greater revenues both to enhance its trading position and to participate in war. Because revenues were clearly insufficient to generate the necessary resources, the pursuit of an aggressive foreign policy required adjustments of traditional social relations. On the other hand, such adjustments might provoke angry rebellions from those upon whom the monarchy depended for its long-term survival. This conflict, between the centrifugal forces of French society and the centripetal forces of a centralizing monarchy, defined the character of the struggles between state and society throughout the old regime.

France possessed well-developed manufacturing and maintained extensive trade. One observer (cited in Boislisle, 1874, vol. 1: 543) was proud that France

produces in abundance foodstuffs and merchandise which are useful and even indispensable to her neighbors, so that commerce always draws money to the kingdom. . . . Moreover has it not nearly always been estimated that in the return of the fleets from the Indies up to a third has accrued to the French and that much of the remaining ⅔ found its way into the kingdom through the need of other nations for French merchandise?

Impressive gains had been recorded in textiles, "the most important industrial sector"; bleaching, dyeing, finishing, and stockpiling in northern provinces flourished (Goubert, 1970: 56; see also Lacave, 1977). Industrial development was slow, as old industries expanded and new ones were instituted, but without a "sharp break with the past" (Nef, 1936c: 661; see also Richet, 1968). New industries were introduced and the output of old industries increased, but "no wholesale introduction of new manufactures, no unprecedented growth in the volume of salt, glass, ships, coal, iron, metal wares, and building materials, such as led many English traders . . . to hope for a doubling of their business almost every decade" (Nef, 1967: 209).

French trade was relatively backward compared with that of either the English or the Dutch.

> France lagged behind her competitors in respect of all the important indices. The division of labor in France manufacture was at a lower level; the shortage of skilled workers did not allow entrepreneurs an adequate hierarchy of wage levels. State subsidies . . . were casual and sporadic, and small in amount, while accumulation of money was not on a large enough scale; France was excluded from direct plundering of colonies which nourished primitive accumulation in Holland and Spain, and indirectly in England as well. [Lublinskaya, 1960: 144]

French industrial products were comparatively expensive, and lower productive capacity and decreased consumption by workers whose wages could buy less impeded the economic utility of labor-saving devices and other innovations. Antoine de Montchrestien's famous *Traité de l'économie politique,* published in 1615, contained an indictment of French trade, and concluded that France's relative backwardness was substantial and crippling, and that French merchants were at a comparative disadvantage because a weakened central authority could provide neither prestige nor protection. His suggestions included a stronger crown, which could remove obstacles through diplomacy and protectionist measures, such as a ban on imports, and the organization of large-scale trading companies (Montchrestien, 1615, [1889 ed.]).

By the early years of the seventeenth century the gap between France and its rivals was widening considerably.[13] The end of the sixteenth century had witnessed a period of "retrogression" as production declined sharply, and it did not recover beyond slowed growth through the first decades of the seventeenth century (Nef, 1967: 146). In 1596 the citizens of Tours addressed a *cahier de remonstrance* to Henry IV in which they noted that the town lived by silk production. Before the Wars of Religion, there had been 800 master workmen in silk, 6,000 journeymen engaged in labor at silk looms, 300 persons who wound thread, and many others who dyed and dressed the material. They complained that only 200 masters were left, and the amount of silk worked into cloth was about a tenth of what it once had been. These numbers may be tinged with a "medieval statistical fantasy," but they still suggest the extent of industrial decline (Nef, 1967: 146).

Instead of promoting trade, the crown sought to tap it for its own purposes. The relationship between the crown and the bourgeoisie was ambivalent and tense, an "uneasy alliance" based more on mutual dependence than on mutual support and cooperation. The uneasy alliance only partially concealed a fundamental contradiction "between the fiscal interests of the Crown and its desire to stimulate commerce and industry; between its dependence on a hierarchy of officeholders and the need to encourage the merchant community" (Tilly, 1981: 61; Parker, 1980: 93). The king relied on the bourgeoisie to mobilize and advance funds for war making; to generate trade that could produce revenue, and to purchase offices and other privileges that promised the channeling of funds into royal coffers. On the other hand, the king made wars that hampered international trade, seized and taxed accumulated capital, tried to control and regulate economic life, and borrowed too much and too often (Tilly, 1981: 61). For the bourgeoisie, the price of royal protection was extremely high; buying offices, becoming tax farmers, and making loans diverted potentially productive capital away from trade and into the political market, where it was unproductive.

Ultimately, the bourgeoisie was pressured by the crown and lured by the protection and prestige offered by noble status to spend a significant portion of its wealth in the pursuit of venal offices, to parlay capitalist wealth into unproductive capital. Venality of offices deflected the bourgeoisie from acting like capitalists, incorporating bourgeois into the larger "feudal" project of absolutist monarchy.[14] In this sense capitalist development was incompatible with state building in early modern France. The growth of capital may have provided revenues to the crown that were independent of its traditional social foundations, but these revenues were also funneled away from capitalist activity.

If participation in the expanding capitalist market presented the French crown with increased opportunities, the threat of war presented an incessant pressure. War was seen as an integral and inevitable part of the state's functions—"not an optional policy but an organic necessity"—and a mechanism to realize those policies that could not be accomplished through ordinary diplomacy (Kiernan, 1967: 139). Throughout the old regime, France seemed to be constantly at war. The enormous and complicated military machine was insatiable. During peacetime troops needed to be paid regularly and provisions needed to be made for winter quarters. During wartime, when funds were slower in coming for troops supplemented by hired mercenaries, the army was seen by many as a scourge upon the land, marauding through the French countryside like a plague of locusts, devouring everything in sight:[15]

> The expenses were considerable, yet only somewhat effective and hardly ever brought desired results. The soldiers were of dubious valor, and had a detestable reputation, which they deserved. The commanders were generally without energy, and showed only a respect for hierarchy, and even then would place their interests above those of the King. Indiscipline was everywhere, administration was nowhere. The army was not well pleased with the king who paid them badly and didn't feed them. The army resembles more the German tribes who consumed everything in their paths and obeyed only their own chief, who let them pillage and promised them spoils. . . . The King spent a lot, and he did not get very much for his money. [André, 1906: 32].

Successful military competition required enormous sums of money; the search for revenues to make war was a primary impetus to reformist domestic policies adopted by the French state, and to the centralization of political power. "States are warmakers, and wars are statemakers," remarks Tilly (1973: 446), and if absolutist states made wars, wars helped to make absolutism both necessary and possible. For example, mercantilist economic policies "required for the "implementation an expensive navy" (Bier and Grew, 1978: 238). Money remained, of course, "the nerves of war," as Le Bouthellier had remarked, and the French monarchy nervously preoccupied itself with raising funds to defend itself and to participate fully in any war effort.[16] The demands of war heightened royal interest in controlling trade as a source of revenues. As Montchrestien wrote (cited in Tilly, 1986: 121), underscoring the indispensability of trade to a warmaking state,

> It is impossible to make war without arms, to support men without pay, to pay them without tribute, to collect tribute without trade. Thus the exercise of trade, which makes up a large part of political action, has always been pursued by those peoples who flourished in glory and power, and these days more diligently than ever by those who seek strength and growth.

Wars pressed monarchs to embark on increasingly difficult searches for funds, which propelled them to concentrate political power at the center and incorporate any groups or regions whose autonomy constrained military preparations.

The Absolutist Push at the Turn of the Century

In the early part of the seventeenth century a "fragmented, symbolic authority" was confronted with a variety of challenges: "the need to dominate a poor and dissatisfied population; maintenance of at least the principle of law and order with respect to the independently powerful; regulation and jurisdictional conflicts among the different authorities; exorcism of the threat of social insurrection'' (Beik, 1985: 193). The absolute monarchy, designed to meet these challenges, received a strong push then from Henry IV, whose efforts at internal unification and an aggressive foreign policy marked his brief reign. With the help of his finance minister, the Duc de Sully, Henry embarked on an early phase of what we might call an "administrative revolution" in the government. Sully completely overhauled France's financial situation without initiating far-reaching fiscal reforms, largely by subtle financial manipulations.[17] He advocated greater royal control over trade to generate revenues, but Henry demurred, claiming he "would rather fight the King of Spain in three pitched battles than to oppose these lawyers, bankers, clerks, and the other townspeople you intend to regulate" (cited in Palm, 1928: 54). In the guise of supporting advances in trade and commerce, Sully and Henry IV encouraged the development of the guilds, especially because the diploma that conferred the status of master was subject to a tax. During Henry's reign "the number of crafts and trades that were regulated had increased to the detriment of those that were free" (Tapié, 1973: 37).

Sully also used the venal officers as a royal wedge against the hereditary nobility; his invention of the paulette in 1604 was an immediate sensation with Parisian officeholders, for they could, after a payment to the crown, pass their offices on to their heirs. Venal officers were charged with tax collection in the provinces, which angered both peasants and the high nobility. The nobles, using their Catholic zealotry against a king who had betrayed them by protecting the Huguenots, began to oppose Henry's "religious policies, his crippling taxes, and his aggressive wars" (Mousnier, 1948: 49). His assassination in 1610 left a mixed legacy of administrative successes and seething resentments. A depleted treasury, a rebellious nobility angered at the erosion of its prestige, a disgruntled group of urban merchants whose efforts at trade were constantly thwarted and undermined, and a general restlessness among the peasants, who were feeling the increased weight of a monarchy mobilizing for war—these were the disaffections that Henry bequeathed to the queen mother, Marie de Medici, who would rule until her son Louis XIII was of age.

No sooner did the queen come to the throne than she was faced with both domestic and international challenges. Though she had tried to placate the high nobles by increasing their pensions, by 1614 many had left the court and were preparing for civil war (Hayden, 1974). The calling of the Estates-General, which promised victory for the rebellious nobles, concluded with an affirmation of the absolutist project: "It was the three orders of the realm who relinquished all power into the King's hands. They had recourse to royal absolutism and unanimously affirmed the King's undisputed authority. . . . It was the delegates to the Estates-General in 1614 and 1615 who ensured the triumph of royal absolutism in France" (Mousnier, 1970: 280).[18]

But, the most pressing issue for the crown was the possibility of war, and when the Thirty Years War broke out in central Europe, French mobilization was imperative. What had begun as a dynastic, feudal conflict in 1618 ended, thirty years later, as the first "world war" in which political behavior was based less on religious or dynastic motives and more on the calculations of nation states. France's entry into the war in 1635, in fact, signals the transition, for Cardinal Richelieu's calculations were clearly the political tactics of a national leader and not the emotional and ideological impulses of an insulted or threatened feudal dynasty.

Richelieu Comes to Power

Absolutism received its greatest push before the Fronde from Cardinal Richelieu, the architect of royal policies under Louis XIII, whose desperate search for revenues led him to stretch the crown's relationship with each social group to the breaking point. If the king was "a stammering, melancholy, and taciturn hypochondriac," his first minister was a shrewd and measured administrator, coldly systematic and fully consistent (Mousnier, 1984: 9). Richelieu was less concerned with an administrative revolution than in squeezing every *sou* from existing political relations, and his "effectiveness was based not on institutional reorganization but on 'creatures' in key positions who in turn relied on subordinate creatures" (Beik, 1985: 15).[19] Yet, unlike his predecessors, Richelieu was guided by an ideology that was thoroughly secular; *raison d'état* was both the motivation for and the justification of Richelieu's domestic and foreign policies, and was "the most important contribution of Cardinal Richelieu's generation to the growth of political thought in France" (Church, 1972: 11).

Reason of state cast the state as an abstraction, "greater than the sum of the provinces and populations that [were its constituents], possessing interests that outlived its individual rulers and transcended the immediate desires of its subjects," so that for the first time "the force of national authority predominate[d] over local rule"; it was an ideology "predicated upon the partial autonomy of political affairs from theological determinants" (Symcox, 1974: 4; Giesey, 1983: 198; Church, 1972: 91). As an ideology, reason of state allowed a profound—indeed "menacing"—increase in the central power of the crown (Elias, 1982: 180). Richelieu understood that the strength of a state is relational: a state is strong only to the extent that its enemies, foreign and domestic, are weak. A state is strong if it can pursue its interests over and against the interests of potentially oppositional internal and external forces, and if it is unfettered by ideological considerations that constrain its tactical mobility in pursuing those interests. The autonomy of a state is not simply a theoretical given in comparative and historical analysis; it is the outcome of a historical process in which the state comes to be seen as "an objective, identifiable entity, with interests and therefore a morality of its own" (Church, 1972: 350).[20]

State autonomy was vital to Richelieu because France was, as he wrote in his *Testament politique* (1865 ed., vol. 8: 114), threatened by "the unbridled ambition of Spain, the excessive license of the nobility, the lack of soldiers, and the absence of any reserve of savings for the prosecution of war." More was required than rhetorical devices for proposing abstract ideals of government; the task was to "extract those resources without inciting uncontrollable rebellion and without destroying the people's capacity to pay again in the future" (Tilly, 1980: 19). Richelieu's tenure witnessed a virtual administrative revolution without substantive reform; using the "exploitation of the king's right to dispense justice directly," the cardinal-minister developed mechanisms that would allow for increased participation in the international economy and successful competition against military adversaries, and attempted to subordinate potentially rebellious domestic groups that might constrain the *gloire* and the wealth that the crown might obtain (Symcox, 1974; Church, 1972). Richelieu had promised his king (cited in Tapié, 1974: 220), "to employ all my industry and all the authority which it pleased you to grant to ruin the Huguenot party, to abase the pride of the great nobles, and to reduce all your subjects to the obedience that they owe you and to restore your name among foreign nations to the position it should rightly hold." It was a promise he did not break.

The Increased Fiscal Pressure of War

Money, or rather the lack of it, stood in the way of Richelieu's achievement of his goal of European hegemony and domestic supremacy. War preparations "aggravated old problems—especially the problems of finance—and created pressing new needs" (Elliot, 1984: 64). France's entry into the Thirty Years War transformed the nature of the conflict from a dynastic struggle into a world war pursued by states calculating geopolitical strategy. Richelieu entered the war on the side of the Protestant princes who were fighting against the Habsburgs, for defeating geopolitical rivals was more important to the first minister than defending the faith. "Outside our realm," he wrote to the king (Pagès, 1972: 117), "it must be our constant purpose to arrest the course of Spain's progress."

Such a policy was extremely expensive, both financially and politically. The size of the army expanded significantly. Under Henry IV, France maintained a standing army of 12,000 soldiers (Symcox, 1968: 8). By 1635, when France entered the war, the number was 130,000; by 1639 it was over 147,000; and by 1640 it was over 150,000 soldiers and a navy had just been organized (Methevier, 1966: 120). As the numbers grew, so did the amount of money required to sustain them. Military expenses at the beginning of the century had been less than 5 million livres; by the 1620s they amounted to 16 million; in 1635, 33 million livres, and by 1640, over 38 million (B. Maz., A 15939; see also Parker, 1983: 64).[21] The army was the chief expenditure of the monarchy throughout the 1630s (Bonney, 1981: 173).

To pay for these spiraling costs, Richelieu "squeezed, cajoled, and stomped the means of warmaking from a reluctant population," taking whatever he could from wherever and whomever he could (Tilly, 1981: 61). Increases in taxes such as the taille, *taillon, subsistence,* and *étape* were "staggering," and Richelieu doubled the taille personnelle between 1624 and 1636, and more than doubled the gabelles in less than ten years, from 6.65 millions livres in 1632 to 14 million livres in 1641 recorded. But taxes provoked rebellion, as I will discuss below. Sublet de Noyers, the intendant at Amiens charged with tax collection, wrote to Chancellor Seguier, the *surintendant des finances* in 1636 (cited in Burkhardt, 1971, vol. 3: 281):

> In the light of the especial knowledge I have acquired of the extreme poverty of this people, and of the strange inward motions to which their great distress can lead them, I consider it to be in the King's service if his affairs make it necessary to impose this tax, that it should at least be deferred until a more timely season. The mere fear of it has already been enough to bring the town's trade to a halt and has stricken more than 3,000 workmen, some of them being reduced to beggars and death. If I say this, Monseigneur, it is because I have seen it.

Richelieu was forced to rely increasingly on extraordinary fiscal mechanisms, which expanded consistently during the 1620s and 1630s (Parker, 1983: 64; Guery, 1978: 226). Richelieu "borrowed all over Europe at exhorbitant rates in order to pay their armies and their allies" as well as borrowing in myriad forms—sale of offices, tax farms, long-term loans, forced loans from officials—from the French population as well (Goubert, 1970: 33; see also Lublinskaya, 1967: 309).[22] Richelieu was constantly searching for fiscal expedients that might prove capable of generating short-term relief from the plaguing debts brought about by the war effort.

Unwilling to undertake the extensive, modernizing administrative reforms that would transform French social and political relations, Richelieu instead resolved on an incessant series of stopgap measures, designed to shore up the treasury and allow it to hobble from one debt crisis to the next.

No transformation of the whole complex of social and political relations occurred; rather, the relations between each separate group and the crown were stretched and strained to their fullest. In this drive to resolve its endemic fiscal crisis, the monarchy attempted to erode the traditional autonomy of each of the groups upon which its legitimate rule had depended: the high nobility, the Catholic clergy, the venal officeholders in the sovereign courts, the layers of financiers and other officers charged with the collection of taxes, the urban merchants and artisans, and the peasants, upon whose backs the majority of the tax burden fell. And, though Richelieu sought to maintain the separation and to encourage the continued traditional rivalries among many of these groups, the end result of his fiscal policies was greater than the sum of its individual parts. Each of these groups was moved to opposition by his efforts to compromise its traditional autonomy and further subordinate it to royal control. In 1639 Bullion warned Richelieu that "expenditure in cash is up . . . [tax farmers] are abandoning us, and the masses will not pay either the new or the old taxes. We are now at the bottom of the pot . . . and I fear that our foreign war is degenerating into a civil war" (Richelieu, 1853 ed., vol. 6: 608). Indeed it was.

Absolutism was both the cause and the outcome of Richelieu's fiscal policies. Inspired by a doctrine of reason of state that elevated political interests above the interests of any traditionally privileged classes, and that equated state interests with the interests of the crown, Richelieu's ad hoc efforts to generate revenues from every possible source within the old regime had the cumulative effect of a dramatic increase in centralized political control.[23] They also provoked serious opposition, from each group separately and from several short-term coalitions among them. The drive for absolutism had produced its discontents.

Notes

1. Forbonnais noted in 1758 (vol. 1: 10) that "the science of finances doesn't consist simply of levying the necessary money." And Dent notes (1974: 9) that although the revenues of the French crown were eleven times larger in 1661 than they were in 1514, the French fiscal system "staggered from one crisis to another."
2. The phrase is from Parker, 1983: 40. But, see also Brustein, 1985, and Brustein and Levi, 1987, where this difference between a subsistence mode of produc-

tion and a commercial mode of production is elegantly employed to explain the different forms of popular uprisings in early modern Europe. My analysis of the popular uprisings, in chapter 3, follows Brustein's analysis.

3. Cited in Lockyer, 1974: 392. Plague broke out across the north and northeast in the 1630s (Feillet, 1886: 24), and starvation and epidemic were reported throughout the country.

4. The precariousness of survival led Hippolyte Taine to pen his famous description of the peasant: "The French peasant is like a man walking in a lake with water up to his mouth. With the slightest slope in the bed or the slightest wave, he goes under and drowns."

5. This problem was compounded by the differential rate of increase in the prices for agricultural products compared to urban crafts, the latter rising far more quickly than the former. Thus, the nobility was at a disadvantage as producers as well as consumers.

6. The term "crisis of the nobility" is Bitten's (1974), and several writers have also stressed the persistence of noble fortunes and political power well into the seventeenth century. See, for example, Dewald (1980), Harding (1976), and Wood (1980), all of whom stress the overlap between the sword and robe nobility. Dessert (1984) argues that if the nobility had a crisis, it had also recovered enough to become a major creditor of the crown, and was cooperating closely with precisely those venal officeholders that it was supposed to hate. Although all these claims seem accurate, they do not disprove the crisis thesis; in fact, they indirectly support it. Members of the ancient aristocracy would hardly have demeaned themselves to cooperate with, let alone intermarry with, commoners whose chief claim to social status was the amassing of a fortune, unless they were in serious straits.

7. I will return to and further develop this theme below.

8. This section is based largely on Dent, 1974, and Bonney, 1978, 1981, but see also Dessert's recent thesis for another comprehensive, if laborious, account of the fiscal system of the old regime.

9. Reported revenues were (in Forbonnais, 1758, vol. 1: 24–26):

1514	7,650,000 livres
1547	14,044,116 livres
1557	12,098,573 livres
1560	9,104,971 livres
1574	18,628,998 livres

10. In 1523, for example, state receipts totaled 5,155,176 livres and expenditures came to 5,380,269, leaving a shortfall of almost 226,000 livres (*L'Etat des finances pour l'année 1523*, B. N., collection Dupuy, 486, fol. 137–261).

11. The wages paid to individual officeholders, however, were far from overwhelming. In 1560 a councillor in the Parliament of Paris received 600 livres per year, and his counterpart at Bordeaux received 375 livres; in Amiens wages varied between 15 and 100 livres per year.

12. Here is one eyewitness report of the popularity of the paulette from an observer in 1608 (Loyseau, 1640, vol. 2: ch. 10):

I told myself, while you're in Paris, go one evening to the treasurer of the droit annuel to talk with him. I picked a bad time. I found there an enormous group of officers pushing and shoving one another, while the first was delivering his money. . . . I noticed that when possible, these officers marched up to the closest notary to pass their proxies [to pay the paulette].

It seemed to me that they were pretending to walk on thin ice, fearful of making a mistake and thus dying right there in line. . . . But night fell. The receveur des droits closed his door and his register. I heard a general murmur among those who remained lined up to hurry up, and that maybe he would still take their money, just in case they died during the night.

13. Note, for example, the serious decline in the value of the livre turnois in grams of pure silver:

1513	17.96
1521	17.19
1533	16.38
1541	1604
1543	16.62
1549	15.57
1550	15.12
1561	14.27
1573	13.19
1575	11.79
1602	10.98
1636	8.69
1641	8.33
1652	7.65

The simplified and augmented listing is based on Baulant and Meuvret, 1962: 157. See also Hamilton, 1960: 151; Goubert, 1960: 145; Pillorget, 1974: 118, for other assessments of economic decline.

14. Whether the venality of offices promoted the "embourgeoisement" of the monarchy, by bringing to it so many capitalist merchants, or the "feudalization" of the bourgeoisie, by incorporating bourgeois into the state's project, depends upon whether one sees political power as capable of containing economic forces. Mousnier (1948) and Lublinskaya (1967) argue the former position; Parker (1972) and Porchnev (1963) assume the latter. See also Salmon (1967), who mediates the argument but comes down eventually on the feudalization side. Braudel writes that the venality of offices meant the "treason" of the bourgeoisie.

15. Weber (1978, vol. 1: 233) wrote that the use of mercenaries made the French one of the "capitalist armies," for "the provision of administrative means and of the administrative staff itself is appropriated as the object of a profit making enterprise, on the basis of fixed contributions from the ruler's magazines or treasury."

16. Mousnier exaggerates the causal power of warmaking when he calls war "the most potent factor in the transformation that occurred between 1598 and 1789," but not by too much (Mousnier, 1984: xix; see also ibid.: 47, 78). Elliot (1984: 141) notes that the "demands of war provoked an intensive fiscalism, which itself often had strong reformist characteristics because it extended taxation, whether direct or indirect, to regions and social groups which had hitherto been shielded by customary privileges."

17. See Buisseret, 1977: 102 et passim, and also Mousnier, 1971: 185–86. Sir George Carew, James I's ambassador to France, was impressed, writing to his king that although Henry "came to a broken state, and much indebted, yet in a few years he hath gathered more treasure than perchance any other King of Europe possesseth at this day" (cited in Dewald, 1980: 223). Sully, himself,

noted that his master had placed him in office "to increase his revenues and not to deliver justice" (cited in Bonney, 1981: 65).

18. All was not quiet, however, after the defeat of the high nobility in 1614–15. An assembly of the notables in Rouen in 1617 increased noble pressure, but the regent was able to stall effectively implementation of their demands for the abolition of the paulette.

19. Major argues that the real effort to construct an absolutist state came from Marillac, whose policies were rejected for Richelieu's by the king. Marillac promised serious administrative reforms that would "deprive the estates of their traditional role in negotiating, assessing, and collecting taxes." Richelieu, by contrast, "abandoned Marillac's attempt to construct a centralized absolutist state administered by a loyal, non-hereditary, and probably non-venal bureaucracy and reverted to the Renaissance practice of trying to govern through the estates, assemblies of the clergy, and other duly constituted bodies," all of which made Richelieu's administration a "retreat" from absolutism (Major, 1980: 619 et passim). Although Major may overstate the case, it is clear that Richelieu was a traditionalist whose political and administrative innovations were less of the form of relations between king and subjects and more a deepening of royal power within those structures. Of course, as Tilly (1986: 130) notes, "The people who built that increasingly bulky and centralized 17th century state did not seek to create a more efficient government, but to extend their personal power and that of their allies," a purpose at which Richelieu was extremely successful. When he died, he was the richest man in France.

20. This does not mean, of course, that the absolutist project was inconsistent with the maintenance of feudal class rule in the provinces, but merely that it was an expression of an "early modern form of a society of classes." Absolutism was "the political manifestation of a system of domination protecting the interests of a privileged class of officers and landed lords. Strong bonds linked the provincial nobility, the episcopacy, the various corps of officers, and the town oligarchies to the crown and to each other" (Beik, 1985: 335).

21. Richelieu requested the calculations of the organization and expenses of the army, including wages and foodstuffs. In 1638, for example, *Règlement que le Roy veut observer pour les subsistences de ses armées* estimated the total monthly costs of maintaining an army of 140,000 at over 7 million livres (B. Maz., 15939).

22. There is a story, perhaps apocryphal, that illustrates Richelieu's increasing desperation in the search for funds. At the suggestion of his adviser, Father Joseph, Richelieu invited to court a Father du Bois, a defrocked Capuchin monk, who was a known alchemist, and who promised to transmute base metals into gold. He performed an experiment in the king's presence in which two musket balls were turned into an ingot of gold but failed to repeat the experiment. He did perform some other tricks and made profuse excuses for his failures. Eventually, Richelieu lost patience and Father du Bois was condemned to death for counterfeiting coins, practicing magic, and other crimes.

23. Tilly (1986: 83) writes that "the pretensions of absolutism, the growth of the war machine, the rise of the tax farmer, the proliferation of fiscal makeshifts and outbreak of fierce popular rebellion were part and parcel of the same process of statemaking."

3

Absolutism and Its Discontents in France, 1624–1643

The fiscal crisis of the absolutist state in France pressed Cardinal Richelieu and his king to search with increasing desperation for funds to pursue their aggressive foreign policy program and to insure the maintenance of domestic order. Rather than proposing a systematic overhaul of the entire fiscal, and hence political, administration, Richelieu resolved to accomplish his search by piecemeal short-term fiscal expedients. Such expedients could help the monarchy generate sufficient funds but leave in place, indeed reaffirm, the traditional power relations within French society, especially in the countryside, where the monarchy relied upon the hereditary nobility and Catholic clergy to maintain discipline and order and insure a steady stream of tax revenues flowing toward the king's treasury.

Richelieu's version of an administrative revolution—a revolution without reform—may have been designed to leave these traditional class relations intact, but the incremental effect of his reliance on short-term fiscal expedients to resolve the fiscal crisis was the gradual erosion of the legitimacy of his absolutist project. Throughout the second quarter of the seventeenth century, as Richelieu moved in such a contradictory way to raise money and avoid structural transformation, a wide variety of social groups came to oppose these fiscal expedients. And throughout his reign, Louis XIII was faced with growing opposition from the clergy, the high nobility, the layers of venal officeholders in the major cities, municipal oligarchs, Protestants, and the masses of rural peasants, upon whom the growing burden of taxation fell most heavily. In this chapter I will consider the crown's relations with each of these groups in turn, and suggest how the search for fiscal solvency alienated each to the point of rebellion.

Richelieu Confronts the Aristocracy

In the early years of the seventeenth century the nobles had experienced economic decline, in the steady drop in the value of their fixed incomes in an age of inflation, an erosion of their political supremacy and a political chastening at the Estates-General of 1614–15, a loss of social status as the ranks of nobility swelled with newly ennobled venal officeholders, and a gradual diminution of confidence in their ability to command respect as a ruling class. They were "in the most pitable state they had ever known," they complained to the king in a petition in 1627 (cited in Elias, 1982: 195), and were "crushed by poverty . . . rendered vicious by idleness . . . [and] reduced by oppression almost to despair." Yet, the nobility was still strong and belligerent enough to represent a constant threat to the rising bourgeoisie, and haughty enough to pose a threat to the absolutist project.

Though many writers have observed a unified vision motivating Richelieu's policy toward the aristocrats, to subordinate them, "regardless of their place in the social hierarchy, to the interests and powers of the state" (Church, 1961: 270), recent writers have offered a more nuanced view that stresses the contradictory nature of the absolutist effort, and the ambivalent relationship Richelieu maintained with the nobility, a relationship "charged with a tense ambiguity" (Chaunu, 1977: 67). There can be no doubt that Richelieu sought to bring the nobility more directly under royal control, but he also sought "to strengthen the nobility in general" (Ranum, 1963: 199), to reinforce its lagging power in the countryside as a vehicle for maintaining seigneurial class rule in the countryside, "protecting the interests of a privileged class of officers and landed lords" (Beik, 1985: 335). Such reinforcement required a continued maintenance of the patrimonial system of clientage in the countryside as a foundation of noble power (Beik, 1985: 243). Thus, Parker (1983: 89) writes that "the crown's own policies actually extended the scale of privilege and intensified the attachment to patrimonial interests," and Harding notes (1972: 190) that "the construction of the absolutist state coincided with a tightening of the bonds between the old patrimonial elites and the very class of lawyers that were introducing bureaucratic procedures into local government." Royal policy was concerned with both controlling the nobility and sustaining it (Elias, 1982: 194), and Richelieu sought to bring it under royal control socially, to reduce its autonomy and curtail its fiscal privileges, and at the same time to support its dominance at the level of production. For its part, the nobility desired the continuation of class rule in the countryside and was prepared, in large part, to trade off for it. "To attain this serenity the ruling class had to abandon its pretensions to autonomy and place its fate more than ever in the hands of the monarch" (Beik, 1985: 338; see also Koenigsberger, 1955: 350).

Central to Richelieu's policy of social subordination and fiscal manipulation of the nobility was his policy toward the provincial governors. Governorships had been the traditional regional manifestation of noble power; the positions allowed nobles to amass gigantic fortunes while stabilizing their political positions. The governors were the chief military officers of royal troops in the provinces, and they also served as clientage brokers, the central focus of royal patronage, for noble offices in the provinces. The new urban *robins* needed the governor for judicial and financial offices and to ensure their tax exemptions, and the provincial estates and municipal oligarchies required his protection and favors.

Richelieu "felt that the autonomous powers of the provincial governors represented a more pressing danger to the crown than the autonomous powers of the provinces themselves, and decided to make it his first concern to reduce the governors to subservience" (Elliot, 1984: 84). Subservience did not mean obliteration but political subordination, insuring their allegiance in the face of potential provincial opposition from other quarters. To do this, Richelieu and his advisers

> sent provincial and military intendants, military and naval commanders and temporary royal commissioners to assist, restrain and report on the governors. They placed clients in key administrative positions in the provincial government, surrounding the governor much as a pack of dogs would surround a bear. They encouraged traditional rivalries within the provincial administration, hoping that the governors' political enemies, for instance, the Parliament and lieutenant governors would help curb his powers. [Kettering, 1978: 141]

Provincial governors would either conform to royal will or be retired from office; those who refused to obey, who became involved in intrigues or plotted rebellions, were swiftly removed from office and replaced by loyal and obedient servants. Richelieu often ordered the razing of a governor's castle and fortress "to remove all means for revolt and to prevent rebellion by the threat of destroying the property of rebels . . . [or to punish them] in areas where the nobility lent their assistance to revolt or failed to fulfill service owed to the King" (Ranum, 1963: 199). More frequently, governors allied with the crown in the face of popular uprisings in the provinces; the governor of the Bourbonnais, for example, "repeatedly asked Seguier to send *commissaires* to the province to try rebels because the local magistrates would not act against them out of sympathy and fear" (Harding,

1972: 205; see also Porchnev, 1963: Appendix 23, letter of July 21, 1640; Mousnier, 1970, vol. 1: 457–58).

The fortunes of the crown and the governors became increasingly intertwined. By curtailing their powers while simultaneously building up their strictly economic fortunes, the crown persuaded the governors to finance state projects, to become, in effect, state creditors. Many made large loans to the crown, and others brought rentes. In this way provincial governors could augment their incomes through investments in the political market, and thus avoid the dérogance that precluded their activity in the economic marketplace. Yet, there was also serious discontent among the governors because they believed their political incorporation and social subordination contravened the traditional relationship between the king and themselves. Richelieu's policies enjoyed some success; by the time of his death, "the governors hardly intervened at all in administration, and were reserved for questions concerning the troops" (Charmeil, 1964: 355). Only four of the families of the sixteen governors in 1614 retained that traditionally hereditary position when Richelieu died. Many had joined with other nobles in opposing royal policies, some flaunted their noble status in direct violation of royal prohibitions, and still others threw their lot in with popular forces in the provinces who were also disaffected by royal fiscal initiatives.

Richelieu's policies toward the governors were related to, but not identical with, his policies toward the upper nobility in general. It was toward these that Richelieu aimed his most concerted effort to incorporate and undermine their autonomous power and to humble them while simultaneously reaffirming and supporting their continued prestige, provincial power, and military valor (Ranum, 1963: 191). In 1626 he issued an edict banning dueling:

> This crime, which offends gravely against God's majesty and in a detestable form of sacrilege destroys his living, breathing temples, violates the law of nature, which seeks to keep everyone in being, desolates the noble families of our kingdom, and, finally, weakens the state through the loss of the blood of so many *gentilshommes*, who could have used it so much more valuably and honorably for the state's defense and security. Furthermore, contempt is shown to our authority, which is greatly injured by the fact that each private individual not only disposes of his life contrary to our intentions but also presumes to take justice into his own hands and finds satisfaction in shedding the blood of his enemy on the pretext of safeguarding his honor: which honor, however, obliges him above all else to show respect to his sovereign prince and obedience to his laws. [cited in Mousnier, 1980: 140]

Dueling had always been a traditional prerogative of the noblesse d'épée, which derived from their traditionally military position in society as "those who fight"; it was less "an inchoate primitive form of violence [than] a thoroughly articulated code of behavior" (Schneider, 1984: 289). And, though dueling had been a capital offense since 1566 and a crime of *lèse-majesté* since 1576, Richelieu's ban was viewed as far greater than a simple clipping of wings. It was seen as an affront to the idea of nobility itself.[1] In the first three decades of the century the number of duels increased sharply, in part fueled by the inflation of honors that devalued noble status and the loss of a firm identity as military retainers. The nobility evidenced a kind of "dueling mania," which prompted the Venetian ambassador to observe that the "greatest bond between [the nobility] is that of the duel," and the *Mercure François* to observe in 1626 that "duels had become so common among the French nobility that the streets of Paris usually served as the field of combat" (Schneider, 1984: 270, 277, 268).

Richelieu's policy expresses eloquently the contradictory position of the absolute monarchy in relation to its nobility. On the one hand, Richelieu banned dueling to stop the noble bloodletting, to save the nobility from itself. "Let us not be so unnatural as to arm ourselves against ourselves, to defeat ourselves by our own devices," pleaded Savaron (cited in Schneider, 1984: 288). On the other hand, Richelieu sought to deal with pockets of traditional autonomous activity with "uncompromising severity" to insure uniform obedience to the crown (Schneider, 1984: 268). These two themes converged in May 1627 when Henri de Montmorency, the comte de Bouteville, fought a duel with the marquis de Beuvron in the Place Royale, in full view of Richelieu's window—a direct challenge to the cardinal. The young duke's arrest and subsequent execution was extremely controversial, for Henri was the king's cousin. Richelieu later wrote of his difficulties (cited in Tapié, 1974: 164):

> I confess that I was never more torn by conflicting emotions than on this occasion when I could scarcely prevent myself from succumbing to the compassion that was felt for them everywhere. . . . The tears of his wife moved me very deeply . . . but the river of your nobility's blood (which could only be stemmed by the shedding of theirs) gave me the strength to withstand my weaker self and harden Your Majesty's resolve to enforce the sentence for the good of the state, although it is well nigh contrary to the feelings of everyone as well as to my own personal inclinations.

Richelieu made clear that the decimation of noble ranks and the disorder expressed by dueling each contributed to his resolve to enforce the ban; in this way the "interests of the early modern French state and the nobility converged over the duel, and in attempting to rid itself of its violent habits the nobility was not only promoting public order, but also transforming itself" (Schneider, 1984: 288). Although Richelieu reduced the nobility's autonomous sphere of action, the nobility expressed a solidarity based upon rank and its resentment at the intrusion of the newly ennobled. By complying with the ban, the nobility enlarged its "horizontal sense of community, in large part by discarding old notions of rivalry, honor, and the legitimacy of private justice" (Schneider, 1984: 288).

Richelieu's ambivalent policy with the nobility can also be illustrated by two additional policies he developed in the 1630s. First, he embarked on a program to root out all "false nobles," those men who were claiming hereditary noble status to avoid taxation; the *recherche de la noblesse,* instituted in 1634, required that all nobles who claimed hereditary exemptions document their lineage. This not only increased the amount of money brought into the king's treasury but forced the nobility to recognize the king's power to determine the legitimacy of noble claims (Sturdy, 1973: 552). At the same time, though, it also insured that the status of the true hereditary nobility was reaffirmed. Second, the cardinal used courtesy as a means of coercion, as a "device to coerce all the king's subjects to enhanced obedience" (Ranum, 1980: 430). By enforcing the traditional customs of genuflection, hat doffing, reverential speech, lowering of the eyes, obeisance, and assurances of devotion and obedience, Richelieu guaranteed increased obedience to the king as the ultimate temporal power, and therefore subordinated the nobles, who often considered themselves immune from courtesy's demands. But, again, it simultaneously assured the nobles that their courtesy to the king would force the rest of the population to remember to defer to them. Such policies were simultaneously humbling and elevating to the nobles' pride of rank.

Richelieu faced sporadic resistance by the sword nobility throughout his tenure as first minister. Often, as in the Chalais Conspiracy in 1626 and the Day of Dupes in 1629, resistance came in the form of factional court intrigues, with some nobles and their lovers and favorites aligning themselves against royal policies for a variety of more personal reasons. (In the Day of Dupes, even the queen mother cast her lot with the rebels.) Yet, even these minor tempests revealed that some nobles had become "alarmed at [Richelieu's] firm grip on government and strong hold on the King" (Brown, 1972: 47). The Cinq-Mars Conspiracy in 1642 confronted the aging cardinal with his handpicked client, who had become a Spanish agent to wrest Richelieu's cardinal's hat away from him (B. Maz., ms. 2117, fol. 178).

Throughout the 1630s and early 1640s noble opposition looked less like court intrigue and more like support for provincial and local resistance to the absolutist project. For example, in 1632 the duc de Montmorency, the governor of Languedoc, revolted over the cardinal's plan to convert the pays d'état into pays d'élection, and thus make them more vulnerable to royal taxation. Though this policy was eventually abandoned, the revolt was easily suppressed and the duke was captured and tried for treason, and later that year beheaded in Toulouse.

Such a discussion reveals the ambivalence of the absolutist project in regard to the aristocracy. The nobility was considered to be part of the state, and must therefore recognize its subordinate position to the king. If this required moves against particular nobles, then these were taken to preserve the aristocratic foundation of the absolutist state and the dominance of the nobility at the level of production. To Richelieu, the king and his state were both theoretically and practically inseparable, and if nobles "still wrote and spoke of allegiance and love for the person of the King, while admitting rebellious action against his state" then such nobles would need to be better incorporated into the state (Ranum, 1963: 204). Thus, "while the nobility remained the biggest, if not the only political threat to the Crown, they also recognized their dependence on the monarchy for the conservation of their privileged position in the social hierarchy" (Parker, 1967: 78). Nobles' revolt would have to take a different cast, for the political and provincial bases of autonomous political organization had been thwarted while their status was confirmed. The nobility would be forced to seek out new allies if it was seriously to challenge royal power.

Venality and the Costs of Absolutism

Although venality of offices had almost as long a history as the French monarchy, Richelieu turned to it with increasing frequency as a mechanism for generating immediate income to the royal treasury. He was met with increased opposition from those who purchased the offices, as well as those upon whose toes they stepped and upon whose backs they trod in administering the king's justice. In fact, venality of offices proved to be such a contentious expedient that Richelieu abandoned it after France's entry into the Thirty Years War, and its importance as a percentage of total royal revenues declined precipitously. This can be most easily seen in the following chart: Venality accounted for almost 52 percent of all state receipts in 1633; 23 percent the next year; and just over 10 percent in 1642, when the market for offices was "swamped" (Dent, 1974: 60; Mousnier, 1948: 391–92). In 1643 the percentage dropped to below 10 percent for the first time since 1619 as offices that had been created remained unsold.

Why would venal offices be so popular as a fiscal expedient until the mid-1630s and then decline so dramatically as a source of royal revenue?

TABLE III-I: Percentage of State Receipts from Venality of Office in 17th Century France

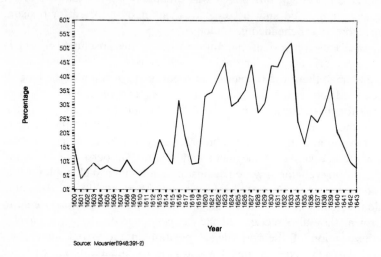

Source: Mousnier(1948:391-2)

For one thing, Richelieu distrusted and disliked venality as a source of royal income, in part because he believed it diluted noble privilege, and more important, because it checked the maneuverability of the crown. In one letter to the king he wrote (in Avenal, 1894: 159–62):

> Your Majesty . . . I urge you to discontinue the *droit annuel,* and to banish the venality of offices, two of the most pernicious challenges to your authority and to the purity of the administration of justice, allow the great number of officers to die quietly, especially those that aren't created by the clamoring of the people. . . . It is essential for the principal laws of the kingdom to refrain from alienating the charges of the Maison de Roi, of war and government, and never again receive a *résignation* from either father or son.

In 1629 he toyed with the idea of refusing to renew the paulette when it expired (Pillorget, 1976: 99).

Richelieu saw venality as dangerous and threatening, "a crime against the establishment of a new republic." But, he continued, "prudence does not permit us to crush it under the foot of the monarchy, since the imperfections have already passed into everyday life and the disorder is already accomplished" (cited in Pagès, 1952: 132); he saw the officers as "a class prejudiced against the State, but nonetheless necessary. This type of officer is an evil who we do not know how to avoid, but we must reduce it to a manageable level" (cited in Porchnev, 1963: 394).

Richelieu resolved upon a two-pronged approach to the venal officeholders, one that expressed the twin imperatives of his administration, that is,
to generate increased revenues and to leave the traditional social organization in place. In regard to the venal officers, he sought to undercut their
administrative powers at both the national and local levels while he
simultaneously used them as state creditors, inducing and forcing them to
invest in the state market of offices and loans. In the early 1630s Richelieu
tried to circumvent the venal officeholders; for example, he attempted to
handpick the judicial commissaires who would preside at political trials, a
function traditionally reserved for the Parliament of Paris. "In crimes of
state," he argued (in Kitchens, 1982: 330), "the King was free to pick
whatever judges he thought appropriate in the prevailing circumstances
and to define the criteria of selection himself." Another means of circumventing venal officers was to multiply the existing number of offices and
create new ones; this would both ensure venal subordination and their
continued contribution to state coffers. Indeed, venal offices might prolif-
erate until they no longer had any meaning or the present officeholders
could be pressured into buying the new ones to protect their original
investments:

> The Crown's creation of new offices threatened the parlementaires with devalu-
> ation of the capital investments in officeholdings and reduced their income from
> office by non-payment of *gages, augmentation des gages,* loss of *épices,*
> disciplinary suspensions, refusal to recognize their exemption from the taxes of
> *franc-fief, amortissement, nouveau enquetes, lods et ventes, taille,* and troop
> billeting. [Kettering, 1978: 231]

In addition, Richelieu tried to undercut the officers by creating new
institutions. For example, in 1635 he announced creation of a new chamber
of the Cour des Aides. The magistrates already seated in the court were
angered, but they were also unable to supply the 1.5 million livres that
they would have needed to purchase all the offices in the new chamber.
They managed to stall registration of the edict, thus effectively blocking
the initiative until 1639, when Richelieu threatened to open a new Cour
des Aides in Lyon, which proved far more threatening to the Parisian
magistrates. They quickly registered the 1635 edict and came up with the
money to purchase the offices. Similarly, he created a semester parliament
in Rouen in 1641, which he was forced to abandon in 1643 because of
popular disturbances (Kettering, 1982: 278).

Richelieu also divided offices in half as a method of squeezing funds
from officeholders, who were exempt from taxation because of their noble
position. An office was to be administered for one semester by the current
holder, and sold to another officer for the second semester. When he

initiated a semester parliament in Aix, the officers complained that the crown had "cut their judicial robes in two" (Kettering, 1982: 278).

After 1635, though, one of Richelieu's chief strategies both to subordinate the venal officers and to raise additional revenues was to add new layers of officers, a strategy that would have the additional benefit of increasing intraofficer competition and rivalry. The utility of older officers, such as the trésoriers and élus, became markedly diminished. As they were accepted into the nobility, they also became entrenched in the local political structure, seeing their fortunes connected more to their position in the election than to the crown. Although servants of the state, the trésoriers' corporate self-image had become that of local men of property and title; tied to their local interests, they often moved to block royal initiatives. By the 1640s they were often "reluctant to call in the troops to enforce the levy of the taille" (Bonney, 1978: 195). As a result, the crown adopted the same policy toward the trésoriers that it had earlier adopted in its dealings with both the noblesse d'épée and the robins, simultaneously inflating their status honor while transferring their administrative powers to yet other layers of officers who would be more dependent and reliable agents of royal policy. In 1645 the crown transferred the collection and administration of the taille from the trésoriers and élus to the intendants, which prompted the trésoriers and élus to throw in their support with the growing number of officers who had been dispossessed of their important tax-collecting privileges and bypassed as state creditors. In so doing, they were welcomed into the growing coalition by the magistrates in the sovereign courts.

Other administrative layers of venal officeholders were added when the revenues brought in by the trésoriers and the élus, either through the sale of the offices themselves or by the collection of taxes in the provinces, was no longer sufficient to permit the crown to limp from one fiscal problem to another. Two additional groups of officers, the financiers in the cities and the intendants in the countryside, were added to the complex administrative and financial bureaucracy already in place. Their initial successes in providing credit and collecting taxes, respectively, generated significant revenues for the crown as well as significant opposition from the other officers whose privileges were abridged as well as those who were forced to pay the taxes. Both the financiers and the intendants proved more reliable than any other venal officers, and their dependence upon the crown for security—either their personal safety in the case of the intendants or the security of their investments in the case of the financiers— kept them exceptionally loyal. (I will discuss the intendants in more detail below.)

The financiers, "one of the most distinctive developments of the 17th century state," were appointed to administer the revenues of the king, were involved at every level of state finance, and were increasingly active in tax farming, purchasing rentes, and other loans (Beik, 1985: 251; see also Dent, 1974; Dessert, 1984). Their rise to prominence as one of Richelieu's and Mazarin's favorite fiscal expedients again illustrates the structural ambivalence of the absolutist strategy of administrative revolution without reform, the absolutist impulse that attempted to mobilize the fiscal resources of the country and centralize political power while freezing traditional social relationships. The position of financier was not an office, which was venal and hereditary, but a commission, subject to the will of the monarch, who could revoke it on a whim. Structurally more dependent upon the state, financiers therefore supported a "strong government, able to pay them the agreed rates of interest on their loans. The strong government that they wanted must also, however, be strongly in need of credit from them" (Dent, 1974: 270–71). An ideal mix would have been, for the financiers, a state strong enough to pay its financial backers and yet weak enough to have a desperate need for their financial support at high rates of interest. This was precisely the situation the financiers found, especially during the administration of Cardinal Richelieu, when the crown became, in Bourgin's words, "a vassal and tributary of the financiers" (B.N., ms. Thoisy 397, fol. 8). Commonly referred to as "parasites" and "harpies" by their adversaries, they were nonetheless indispensable. "The Crown needed them for the credit they could provide and nobles, administrators and magistrates needed them for their dowries that came with the financiers' daughters, and for the way in which the financiers' descendents filled essential posts in the administrative and social governance of France" (Dent, 1974: 242–43).

The financiers did not profit as spectacularly as their adversaries believed, however. As Dessert's massive thesis (1984) shows, the financiers' fortunes were subject to wild swings, especially because most of their investments were short-term and in paper credit, which experienced the most extreme fluctuations during the seventeenth century. Moreover, the financiers' entry into the world of French credit, although seemingly a necessary fiscal expedient, did nothing to further capitalist development in the country. Attached neither to commerce nor industry, they had "little to do with what one might call 'bourgeois capitalist accumulation.' The world of financiers existed apart from commerce and trade" (Dent, 1974: 78); they were what Weber called "political capitalists," whose primary function was to meet the "financial needs of the state as purveyors and by supplying governmental credit" (Weber, 1978, vol. 1: 478).

Financiers concerned themselves primarily with three forms of state credit. First, they lent money for the *comptants*, the secret expenses of the crown that were neither accountable to nor reported by the Chambre des Comptes. Under Henry IV these had been moderate expenses, but they grew rapidly after his death: from less than 3 million livres in 1615 to 48 million in 1643 and almost 59 million in 1646 (see Chaleur, 1954: 32). Second, they were granted the *assignations*, by which a financier "donated" money to the king in return for the privilege of serving as an investor with a writ demanding some payment for some other party. In practice this was really a way for the crown to create tax farmers out of its loan collectors. And, the financiers were used also directly as tax farmers, especially for the *anticipations*, which were fractional amounts of the anticipated revenues expected from a particular tax, which would be paid in advance by the tax collector in return for the right to collect the tax. Often the financiers became, themselves, the brokers for the tax, purchasing the anticipation from the crown, and then reassigning it to another tax collector at a small profit. Anticipations also ballooned during the era before the Fronde. The financiers answered part of the crown's need for resources but, without structural reforms, they perpetuated the centrifugal political administration that haunted state builders in early modern France. As the financiers "came to dominate the financial administration of the state," Dent writes (1974: 20), they also "parcell[ed] it up into private fiefs in a fragmentation of authority redolent more of a low species of bastard feudalism than of an absolutist bureaucracy."

The rise of the financiers in fiscal administration parallels the increased use of rentes as an instrument of royal credit and as a fiscal expedient to solve the crown's fiscal crisis. Rentes were becoming more popular to Richelieu because he could be reasonably certain of finding buyers, for the rentes were guaranteed not on royal income but on the income of the city of Paris or on the income of the clergy, both of which were extremely reliable. Moreover, he did not need anyone's permission, not even their registration by Parliament, in order to create them, which freed his hand administratively as well. No wonder that Richelieu found them so useful during the 1620s, when over 10 million livres in rentes were created and sold (Dent, 1973; Martin and Bezancon, 1957: 26ff.).

Even these rentes were yielding diminishing returns as early as the 1630s. Eight million livres in new rentes, created on the revenues of the taille in 1634, were to be sold at dernier 14 but were actually sold at dernier 2 or 3.[2] "Much of the financial confusion and disorder which lasted until 1661 was a direct consequence of the excessive issue of rentes in 1634," writes Bonney (1981: 168), because they threw the collection mechanisms into disarray and began to erode the fiscal support of the crown by its former creditors. Another 100,000 livres in rentes were offered on the income from the aides in 1636, as well as 400,000 livres on the *Cinq Gross*

Fermes, and 300,000 on the aides in Paris alone. The rentes taken on the Hôtel de Ville of Paris were subdivided into smaller ones to encourage their purchase. In the last years of the decade, the crown had created another 10 million livres worth of rentes, and had found fewer and fewer willing buyers (see Forbonnais, 1758, vol. 2: 40–41). On the issue of rentes in 1639, 600,000 livres' worth remained unsold and were withdrawn because the market was "flooded" (Dent, 1974: 50; see also Bonney, 1981: 166).

Richelieu had held grandiose hopes for the rentes as the solution to his fiscal problems, but the increased difficulty with their administration indicates the progressive erosion of support of the crown by the state's creditors. Caillet (1861: 417) calculated that the cardinal had hoped that the 30 million livres in rentes he created would generate somewhere close to 480 million livres for the royal treasury, if sold at dernier 16. Yet, the rentes lost most of their value, and were eventually sold at dernier 5 or 6, as Forbonnais (1758, vol. 2: 28) describes it:

> This was the origin of the disorder and the confusion that the King introduced in finances from this time until 1660. The prodigious quantity of the rentes created by different ministers, without any title since the Edict of 1634, had begun to enfeeble all the revenues of the state: it became impossible to satisfy all the debts and meet all the payments; and the disorder was augmented by the selling of the rentes at the lowest possible price. The government wanted to turn a profit, and charged a wide variety of traitants with the acquisition and disposition of the rentes. This they did, all right; but they passed by their purchase at dernier 14 or dernier 18 and bought them again at dernier 2 or dernier 3.

The 1634 edict on the rentes had also attempted to undermine the withdrawal of fiscal support by the venal officers who had become rentiers in another way. The noble status of the receveurs and the *payeurs* of the rentes was confirmed, so refusal to purchase rentes was, in effect, denying the request of an equal noble. On the other hand, these offices were not allowed to pay the paulette, which prevented the offices from becoming hereditary, and hence the officers were not quite the equals of the other officers who had become rentiers. Such tactics also played into the crown's strategy of dividing the officers from one another to insure each would continue loyally to serve the royal fiscal efforts. The officers, such as the members of the sovereign courts, were thus thrown into a difficult position: although they had resisted further contributions to the royal treasury and often refused to continue as the state's creditors, they also deeply resented the crown's turning to any other officers for those loans, for they perceived it as an undercutting of their political leverage. They did not want to finance the state, but they certainly did not want anyone else to do so either. This contradictory motivation characterized the responses of the venal officers throughout Richelieu's administration. Often they protested so vigorously against the various initiatives proposed by Richelieu that the king was often forced to abandon certain projects (Ranum, 1963: 14). "We do not only suffer the disgraces of the general misery of the times which make the exercise of our charges perilous," one group of venal officers argued (cited in Porchnev, 1963: 303), "and in the small use in the general ruin of the country, one strives to oust us, the small business and authority which stays with us in the towns without which our subsistence would be shamed and impossible."

By the 1640s resistance by the venal officeholders was often more troublesome than searching for other forms of revenues, and the king had difficulty both in subordinating the officers and in using them as a source of revenues. When Richelieu resolved to increase the taille to raise money in 1641, he was faced with serious opposition from members of the Parliament of Paris, who refused to register the edict, which they believed (correctly) would undercut their pretensions at legislative power. The élus and trésoriers also organized themselves into syndicates for protection, and they began to meet in Paris in October 1641 (Mousnier, 1959: 98). The king forced the registration of the edict in a *lit de justice,* where the king appeared at the Parliament's session and the edict was registered in his presence. (The custom of the lit de justice, in which the king arrived at the session of the sovereign court carried in on a divan, came from a traditional understanding that no one in the realm could deny the king's wishes if he asked them directly in person.) The edict declared that "a monarchial state cannot suffer any hand to be laid upon the sovereign's sceptre or that any share of his authority. The power concentrated in the King's person is the source of the monarchy's glory and greatness and the foundation upon which its conservation rests" (cited in Tapié, 1974: 414). Moreover, the king warned the Parliament, Matthieu Molé, first president of the Parliament, noted (1854, vol. 2: 143–44 [orig. 1664]) that "you are hereby solely to judge between master Peter and master John, and I intend to put you in your place; and if you continue your undertakings, I will cut your nails to the quick."

By the time of the deaths of Richelieu and Louis XIII, the older venal officers, lodged in the sovereign courts and the provincial parliaments, were strongly hostile to the designs of the monarchy and casting about the social structure for allies in a contest with the new regency for lost privileges. Molé enumerated their complaints in a speech in 1647 (cited in Moote, 1972: 153); state crimes, he argued, "included legislation without judicial review; illegal and violent procedure in collection taxes; judgement by royal agencies regardless of the rights of the normal law courts; and actions of the intendants that make them little Kings in the provinces." For these crimes, the monarchy was indicted by the parliamentaires. They were not likely only to join a coalition of political opposition; it was the Parliament of Paris, and later the sovereign courts of the capital city and the other provincial parliaments that provided the leadership in the first wave of revolt in the Fronde.

Pacification of Religious Minorities

Richelieu was faced with two religious groups whose autonomy he sought to curtail and whose resources he required to pursue his foreign policies. The Huguenots constituted a "state within a state," and thus posed a threat to his state-building ambitions; so, also, did the Catholic clergy, whose privileges as the First Estate protected them from any consistent fiscal obligations. Of course, Richelieu did not invent his religious opposition but inherited it from the resolution of the sixteenth-century Wars of Religion. The Edict of Nantes had been Henry IV's attempted mediation between the fanatic Catholic League, who had advocated the annihilation of the Huguenots, and the Huguenots themselves, who had continued autonomy as their goal. He pacified the Protestants with the edict, which allowed their continued autonomy, the "coexistence of a republic with an absolute monarchy," and appeased the Catholics with his conversion and affirmation of the state's resolute Catholicism.

To Richelieu, the problem was more political than it was religious. Autonomous Huguenot organization divided the country ideologically, socially, and geographically, precluding the political unification and subordination that Richelieu sought. In the late sixteenth century the Huguenots had presented a serious ideological threat, "formulating an idea of an inviolable sovereignty that implied the existence of the secular state as an entity distinct from ruler and people," an absolutism without religious foundations (Lloyd, 1983: 155). But, by 1620 French Protestantism was "provincial, conservative, royalist and gallican," and Protestants' struggle was "essentially defensive," seeking "not new gains but to keep what they had against the threat of falling at the mercy of the royal will" (Parker, 1980: 188; Zagorin, 1982, vol. 2: 19; see also ibid., 49). Their prime interests, Parker writes (1978: 22), "lay in defending their privileged position in the social hierarchy, advancing themselves as hereditary office-holders or important landowners, and preserving the ancient fiscal, military and judicial privileges of their particular municipalities. They looked to the King as their immediate superior to protect their liberties and their royalism was deep." Recognizing this, Richelieu saw the Huguenots through the eyes of a political minister not a Catholic priest; it was their organizational autonomy, not their religious heresy, that troubled him. Richelieu supported the idea of religious toleration as "a politically necessary evil . . . demanded by the economic situation," against Marillac, for whom such toleration spelled the "ruin of the state" (Stankiewicz, 1960: 44; Marillac cited in Bonney, 1981: 124).

Huguenots' organizational autonomy did pose a serious threat to France's unconstrained ability to mobilize against the Habsburg threat abroad.[3] Huguenot strongholds overlapped considerably with the pays d'état, whose incorporation would provide more secure borders against the Habsburgs and a more reliable source of revenues. And, many of the nation's wealthiest merchants and financiers were Huguenots, so that, in many eyes, finances "were quite literally in Protestant hands" (Mousnier, 1971: 154).

Richelieu's campaigns against the Huguenots occupied domestic policy through the 1620s, and their resolution made possible his entry into the Thirty Years War in 1635. Earlier setbacks against the Huguenots in Montauban and the Treaty of Montpellier (1622) maintained autonomy and fiscal privilege, while the Peace of Alais, offered to the Huguenots in June 1629, reconfirmed the Edict of Nantes without reconfirming the supplementary articles that guaranteed political and fiscal autonomy. A separate military organization was prohibited, their fortresses were demolished, and religious toleration was reinterpreted to permit Catholic worship in Protestant areas.

Such recasting of the relationship between the crown and religious minorities prompted the revolt of La Rochelle against the decimation of their political liberty. The city was symbolically important to Richelieu, "the Holland of France," and when that city's Protestant oligarchs invited English assistance—the English laid siege to Re, an island off the Rochelais coast—this permitted Richelieu the opportunity to move decisively against the Huguenots, writing that they "must be broken" (Parker, 1980: 33; B. Maz., ms. 2117, fol. 56; Richelieu, cited in Tapié, 1974: 184). The siege of La Rochelle was relatively brief; the reluctance of the English to engage directly with French forces left the Rochelais defenseless, and they surrendered on October 22.[4]

The defeat of the Huguenots was the pivot upon which Richelieu's political project turned. Although expensive—the siege had cost the crown about 40 million livres (Clamageran, 1868: 478; Tilly, 1979: 19)—the royal victory destroyed the Huguenot republic, insured continued Catholic support for the war effort, and would insure that Protestant resources would be at the king's disposal, and that previously autonomous Huguenot merchants were reduced to "equality with the Catholic bourgeoisie"

(Lublinskaya, 1967: 219; see also Parker, 1972: 85–86). Pagès (1972: 117) writes:

> The French monarchy was stronger for external enterprises than ever before. By crushing all resistance, it had no longer to fear occupation for its energies at home, and by its toleration of religion it had rendered itself capable of accepting the service of all its subjects, and it could offer its alliance to Protestant states, without fear of suffering a rebuff.

The pacification of the Huguenots by the Edict of Nantes and the dismantling of their political and economic autonomy through military conquest, symbolized by the successful siege at La Rochelle, transformed the relationship between the French Protestants and the monarchy. Their earlier "autonomy and spirit of urban independence was . . . completely broken" so that after 1630 Protestantism "was no longer a significant factor in the rebellions of the French nobility" (Parker, 1980: 54, 121). Throughout the 1640s, during the Fronde, and beyond, the "spirit of the Huguenots remained dormant until Louis XIV revoked the Edict of Nantes. The triumph of Richelieu was not only that he destroyed the Huguenot physical force, but that he paralyzed their will to resist" (Stankiewicz, 1960: 138). The Huguenots saw their continued privilege of protected worship as dependent upon the crown, and they were thus both too weak and too politically dependent to add their voice to the growing chorus of political opposition that began in Paris and echoed through the nation. What is remarkable about the French Protestants is how loyal they remained throughout the Fronde, and how little influence they exerted on the course of the old regime.

The Crown and the Catholic Clergy

The Catholic clergy was the backbone of the monarchy, the interpreter of the divine law by which the king ruled, and the First Estate of the realm. During the waves of popular uprisings in the 1620s and 1630s, "the clergy found themselves always on the other side of the barricades: the church forcefully preached submission to the authorities, and in particular payment of taxes," even when the aristocracy and venal officers sided occasionally with the rebels (Porchnev, 1963: 308). In the towns the clergy offered sanctuary to the *gabelleurs* and other hated tax collectors pursued by murderous mobs. But if the Catholic clergy appeared to be unambiguous supporters of Richelieu's state-building program, they were also vigorous opponents of several measures he developed to accomplish it. Here, again, Richelieu's initiatives bespoke twin motives of subordination and finance; the clergy, he hoped, would be further incorporated into the body of the state, to which they would contribute larger shares of its finances, and their continued dominance at the top of the social hierarchy would be confirmed.

Some measures were purely symbolic, designed to undercut clerical allegiance to the pope as a possible basis for resistance to the king. For example, in 1625 the Assembly of the Clergy was pressed by Richelieu to recognize "that over and above the universal consent given by peoples and nations, the Prophets announce, the Apostles confirm and the Martyrs declare that Kings are ordained of God and not only that, but that they are indeed Gods." It was one thing to confirm the divine right of kings, and quite another to assert the actual divinity of a king, but this was a precursor to the subordination of clerical autonomy to the absolutist project.

This was, in turn, often simply the mechanism by which Richelieu expected to tap into clerical wealth. Although the clergy asserted its traditional exemptions and privileges from taxation—the people contribute to the state with their goods, the nobility with their blood, and the clergy with its prayers—Richelieu saw fiscal relief in the fabulous wealth of the church. He demanded funds to pursue the siege at La Rochelle, "as it is a war of religion in which the assembly has a notable interest," he argued (cited in Parker, 1980: 136), "His Majesty wishes to be assisted not only by your prayers and good wishes but by your temporal wealth in proportion to what is necessary."

In 1636 Richelieu commissioned the computation of the church's resources and revenues, in order to submit them to tax assessment, and calculated that its yearly wealth was greater than 104 million livres (B. Maz., ms. 2117, fol. 113). The cardinal believed that "clergy were similar to all others in matters of sovereignty and that ecclesiastical lands might be taxed like all others, for necessities of state" (Lebret, 1689: 24) and argued (Forbonnais, 1758, vol. 2: 39) that

> the needs of the state are very real and pressing, and the pretenses claimed by the Church are individualistic and chimerical: that the King had stopped the enemy troops at the border, that he had prevented them from entering the heart of the nation, and that if he hadn't the Church and the clergy would have been ruined and have to pay, in tribute, about three times as much as he was asking; that he has been the defender of the religion, and that he has brought increases in the wealth of the Church.

The church's response reiterated the history of ecclesiastical exemptions from taxation that established a precedence of privilege; the *Alliance de l'Immunité et Contribution Ecclésiastique* (B. Maz., ms. 2117, fol. 93–109) declares that "necessity may not hold back the law, and that the law specifies exactly what it gives and holds back, the ecclesiastical contribution falls under no law, the Church is obliged to obey the doctrines of canon law . . '. and one may not interfere with those matters that are dedicated and consecrated to the church'' (fol. 109).

Clerical pretenses were ill equipped to thwart Richelieu's fiscal ambitions. He coerced, threatened, expelled uncooperative members, and fined them, extracting 1.3 million livres during the 1630s. In 1641 he demanded voluntary contributions totaling 4 million, and also assessed each clerical rank a fixed percentage of its annual value. Although the Assembly of the Clergy balked at these demands, and several bishops refused to agree to any contributions to the royal treasury, Richelieu had established his claims to a share of ecclesiastical wealth (Michaud, 1977: 154). However, even as most local prelates continued to support the crown, the Catholic clergy was no longer among the state's most ardent supporters. Its opposition was weak, and drawn entirely from within a support of the ideology of absolutism; only the Huguenots might have generated a religious ideology of opposition that might have sustained a political rebellion. And the Huguenots had already reconciled themselves to royal domination and depended on royal protection from Catholic zealots. Consequently, although religious groups joined the growing chorus of political opposition, their voice was neither strong nor capable of sustaining the sound of revolt.

One key reason for the weakness of the church's support for the dissent has to do with divisions within the church itself, which were reflected in both church doctrine and church organization, and paralleled the conflicts between state centralization and local, provincial autonomy. As the conflicts in seventeenth-century France pitted a centralizing state, promoting national order, against myriad local and regional orders, religion became one of the locations of this conflict, capturing the conflict between national and local identities (Luria, 1977).

After the religious wars had left French Catholicism in a shambles, bishops sought to rebuild the church along more centralized lines, undermining the authority of the local parish curés, and fostering a new respect for, and obedience to, centralized church institutions (Luria, 1977, 1978). Because the bishops considered themselves servants of the king as well as servants of the Lord, their efforts contributed to the absolutist state. ''They were the ecclesiastical equivalents of the intendants. Their concern for greater centralization and conformity in the Catholic community proved an indirect support of the monarchy's own program of centralization'' (Luria, 1977: 4).

The conflict was between national and local allegiances within the church institutions, and about church doctrine and the significance of traditional religious symbols. Local and popular religious celebrations had developed ostentatious local worship services, and beliefs that depended on the mechanical manipulation of divine powers. Local curés stressed secondary altars and manifest saints and mystical interventions. The proponents of clerical centralization emphasized uniformity and the interiorization of religious feeling, and promoted the simplification of worship by abolishing the excesses of popular devotion. Religious authorities undermined local cultural systems, just as secular authorities were attempting to undermine local identities and loyalties. Centralizing reformers emphasized the importance of the central altar, and used the Eucharist as a device to "make local religious worship conform to a uniform ideal and a centralized authority. It provided a central tenet and a rallying point for the reformers' efforts to establish a national religious culture" in a parallel way to the efforts of the king to symbolically fulfill the role of the centerpiece of a unified national culture (Luria, 1977: 37). The Eucharist and the monarch were "the twin symbols of the destruction of local systems of beliefs, values, loyalties and identities" (Luria, 1977: 37).

These tensions between the central church hierarchy and local parish curés paralleled the tensions between the centralizing monarchy and the various sources of local, regional, and social autonomy and privilege. What was at stake was whether or not the national order could come to prevail over the myriad local and regional sources of identity and political, economic, and social organization. When the Fronde erupted, these tensions within the Catholic Church were given expression, and the religious Fronde, which continued to disrupt church policies long after the political revolt had been crushed, was characterized by the rebellion of the local curés against the reforming centralizing forces within the church. When religious issues entered the Fronde, therefore, they did so not because of any inherent doctrinal impulsion to revolt but because of the preexisting organizational (and doctrinal) tensions that already existed within the church. It was not a religious struggle but a political struggle that occasionally took on religious shadings.

The Incorporation of the Provinces

France's patchwork of overlapping jurisdictions and pockets of regional and corporate autonomy also provided a serious roadblock to Richelieu's resolution of fiscal crisis. Potential sources of revenues—from peasant taxation to provincial funds and the proceeds from municipal trade—all went relatively untapped, and the autonomous pays d'état, which were, with several exceptions, clustered at the two frontiers with the Habsburgs, rendered France more vulnerable in the war effort. For fiscal and military reasons, Richelieu resolved to incorporate these provinces, to tap their resources, and subordinate them to the interests of the state as he defined them; it was clear to Richelieu that "if all France had been pays d'état the Thirty Years War could not have been won" (Bonney, 1978: 443). Of course, Richelieu's policy was marked by the same contradiction that marked his entire absolutist project: the twin drives to resolve the fiscal crisis by generating revenues from previously autonomous social groups while simultaneously upholding the traditional social relations that characterized France's seigneurial and monarchical system. For his efforts, Richelieu was met with the most serious opposition he faced; France was "overwhelmed by a paroxysm of agrarian uprisings" as the early seventeenth century became "the classic time of large-scale popular rebellions against taxation" (Zagorin, 1982, vol. 1: 180; Tilly, 1986: 85).

The popular uprisings before the Fronde are among the best-studied and most extensively debated phenomena of the old regime.[5] For Boris Porchnev, the popular uprisings represent the bourgeois revolution that failed, for the venality of offices had "feudalized" the bourgeois, and thus prevented them from acting in their longer-term class interests and joining in, and leading, the class-based and class-conscious coalition that faced the old regime—the king and the nobility—in the countryside. Had not the bourgeois abandoned their class's historic mission, the revolt of the magistrates in the sovereign courts during the Fronde would have been part of a bourgeois and popular coalition against the feudal order, "a general crisis of the feudal absolutist order," not simply a crisis at the "surface of politics" (Porchnev, 1963: 40ff.). This position is opposed by, among others, Roland Mousnier, who understood the popular uprisings as the resistance by localities against the centralizing and war-making state's efforts to maintain an upward spiral of revenues and mechanisms of enforcement as well as encroachments on local autonomy. For him, venality produced the "embourgeoisement of the nobility" as officeholders invaded aristocratic ranks, so that the aristocracy became concerned with finance, tax farms, and adjudication instead of its traditional military function. Thus, the state, the truly progressive force of the era according to Mousnier, was confronted by cross-class fronts of popular forces and nobles, and was thwarted in its efforts to transform a hodgepodge of autonomous regions into a truly national society. Far from rational, the popular uprisings were furious mobs, manipulated by contentious nobles (Mousnier, 1958, 1970a, 1970b).[6]

The origins and trajectory of the popular uprisings reveal the contradictions of the absolutist impulse. Although demographic contraction, the movements of troops, and increased taxation all contributed to the eruption of uprisings, the form of a particular uprising depended upon the regional organization of agricultural production and the relationship of the local elites to the crown (see Brustein, 1985; Brustein and Levi, 1987). Some regions, characterized by a more highly commercialized agriculture, experienced interclass struggle, as in the urban revolts in Bordeaux (1635), Moulins (1640), and Montpellier (1645). The poor people "bear the nobility on our shoulders," noted one pamphlet in 1649, "but we have only to shrug our shoulders to throw them onto the ground" (cited in Kamen, 1971: 384).

In other regions, such as the less commercialized south and west, which were characterized by small-scale, enclosed, subsistence farms, dispersed settlements, and woodlands (Underdown, 1986: 8), the popular uprisings suggest the more common form noted by Zagorin (1982, vol. 1: 215); he writes that the "underlying cause" of agrarian rebellion

> lay in the monarchy's construction of its absolutist rule and the grievances incident thereto: in its thrust toward administrative centralization, in its attack upon surviving forms of autonomism, in its determination to quell intermediate powers, in its ruthless disregard of limits to its authority founded in custom and privilege, and in its unrestrained fiscal demands, enforced by violent military methods of collection.

In these cases the agents of absolutism met a united front, drawn from a cross-section of class forces. "The state became the target in subsistence regions where the lack of markets made the raising of tax revenues particularly difficult and where subsistence classes were not dependent on the state for markets and, therefore, had little incentive to cooperate with the state" (Brustein, 1985: 462). Such a form was far more common, given the preponderance of subsistence farming in the seventeenth century, and the village community as "the main locus of rural solidarity and the chief repository of rights under which rural people had a strong investment" (Tilly, 1978: 233; see also Bercé, 1974). Such a local character to these cross-class fronts against royal taxation also rendered the revolt vulnerable, for "lacking large scale organizational bases for collective action, peasant uprisings tend to be confined to single villages and therefore readily repressed. Unless a coercive crisis undermines the capacity of the state to contain these uprisings, rebellions remain isolated *jacqueries*"— which was precisely their outcome.

In most popular uprisings, regardless of the mode of agricultural production in the region and the resulting infusion of class struggle between owners and producers in the more commercialized areas, the chief targets of the revolt were the crown's representatives in the region, most often the tax collectors. The French, Le Roy Ladurie writes (1974: 152–53), "confined themselves to fighting the tax-collector, whereas the real sources of their difficulties lay in the social organization itself." The antifiscal nature of the revolts joins both class-based hostilities with class fronts against a centralizing monarch, and brings together the various groups and institutions, such as the provincial estates and parliaments, whose traditional autonomy and privilege had been eroded by the absolutist drive for revenues. In most cases the popular uprisings were tax revolts, whether against seigneurial taxation or against royal taxation.[7] This was a matter of great concern for Richelieu because these taxes were seen as so necessary to the escalation of the war effort. Imagine Richelieu's chagrin when he read a letter in 1639 from Claude de Bullion (cited in Ranum, 1963: 143) reporting that "the people will not pay either the new or the old taxes. We are now scraping the barrel, and I fear that our foreign war is degenerating into a civil war."

Provincial opposition to absolutism took two forms, regardless of the overlay of class conflict on the opposition to state building, and each of these forms was really resistance against innovations that abridged traditional arrangements and were initiated from the capital. The first of these was, of course, the popular wrath unleashed by new taxes, fiscal innovations designed to augment the already crushing burden of taxation placed upon the locality. (As we have suggested, the form of resistance to these fiscal innovations varied by the regional mode of production, which determined, in large part, the distribution of the burden through the region.) Rebels "were not looking for reform," writes Rudé (1980: 63), "but for a return to the good old customs existing before the days they began to be harassed by *gabelleurs* and other rapacious officials." Thus, the moment of rebellion was "the establishment of a new jurisdiction, the registration of a new law or the coercion of a new officer" (Bercé, 1974: 177). The imposition of a new gabelle was seen as a "veritable declaration of war," a "fiscal inquisition," and the cause for the slaughter of the tax collector (Feillet, 1862: 67), as in 1636, when the peasants of Saintonge complained of the "despair and extreme poverty in which our province now finds themselves because of the great tax assessments and the new burdens that they have imposed upon us and invented in this reign" (cited in Tilly, 1978: 233).

The popular rebellions were not only essentially defenses of the local community against the fiscal innovations of the absolute monarchy but defenses against innovative efforts to transform the nature of public administration in these regions, uprisings against the new personnel charged with carrying out the centralization of the state. In particular, popular uprisings were directed at the intendants, an "essential instrument of absolutism," the lever that was "designed to administer and reform the domestic fiscal system, to discipline it and subordinate social and domestic tensions to the larger foreign policy war effort" (Mousnier, 1970: 8; Bonney, 1978: 449).[8]

Originally conceived as a royal instrument to undercut the autonomous provincial powers of the aristocracy, to procure and administer the armies during the Wars of Religion, and to "accelerate the flow of resources to the central government," the intendant was recruited from a national pool and had no ties to the locality to which he was sent (Tilly, 1981: 205). According to one contemporary commission (cited in Brown, 1971: 76), the intendants were

> not only to perform the function of *intendant de justice* in the provincial capitals, which serves their vanity better than the public good, but to go everywhere in their provinces investigating the ways of the officials, learning how the nobles behave, putting a stop to all kinds of disorder and especially the acts of those who, being powerful and rich, oppress the feeble and poor subjects of the King.

The intendants' flexibility was first recognized under Sully, and their "functions became more numerous and varied"; under Richelieu they became the chief weapon against domestic opposition to the war effort (Permezel, 1935: 18). "Both in their political role of suppressing revolts and in their financial role of collecting taxes, the intendants were indispensable, and it is difficult to imagine the two peace settlements of Westphalia and the Pyrénées being achieved on such advantageous terms for France without them" (Bonney, 1978: 443). Some recent research indicates that the assumed opposition between governors and intendants is exaggerated, and that the two often worked well together, but there was also a good deal of tension between the two, and greater tension still between the intendants and the robins and the municipal oligarchs.[9]

Richelieu both greatly increased the number of intendants sent to the provinces—surpassing in the years 1630–43 the entire number of intendants created in the seventy years previous (120)—and enlarged their administrative functions. They were charged with the levying of forced loans (1637), the *subsistence* (1638), the *taxe des aises* (1638), the sales tax (*sol pour livre*, 1641), and eventually the administration and collection of the taille (1642). Consequently, the intendants became the symbol of the oppression of the localities by the absolutist policies of Cardinal Richelieu. The "initial attack on the intendants came from those financial officials whose interests had suffered most from their administration," because the élus and the trésoriers, as well as the magistrates in the sovereign courts, perceived the gradual erosion of their local power and privilege, high social standing, and the wealth that derived from their offices (Bonney, 1978: 190). "If these dangerous innovations continue, and are authorized," one élu complained in 1642 (cited in Brown, 1971: 99), "nothing will remain of our offices but the vain name of the magistrate." The arrival of the intendant, in fact, brought together previously antagonistic layers of venal officeholders, such as the élus and trésoriers on the one hand, and the judges in the parliaments on the other hand, whose overlapping jurisdictions had earlier sustained the provincial disharmony upon which state centralization depended.

But more than the opposition of the officers, the transfer of tax administration to the intendants provoked anger from those who would be forced to pay. Richelieu "regarded taxation as both a mechanism for supporting the royal establishment and as a means of discipline" (Church, 1961: 270). And, the intendant brought good news and bad news to the peasants: "positive in that a reduction of the amount to be paid was possible if the intendant considered that the parish was doing its best; negative in that the ultimate recourse for the intendant was to billet troops in the parish if it persisted in its refusal to cooperate" (Bonney, 1978: 190). But in the majority, the intendant brought bad news to the peasantry: increased taxation with a more reliable and efficient mechanism to extract the heavier tax burden. To the peasants, the intendants were "an army of taxation" (Berce, 1974: 118).

Provincial Resistance to Absolutism

The confluence of provincial opposition to Richelieu's efforts at state building is most understandable as a defensive resistance to the disruptive intrusion of centralized political administration and, to a lesser extent, the reorganization of peasant life by the introduction of market incentives in agricultural production. This royal effort, supported by an "alliance of intendants, governors, Parisian bankers, and local financiers, many of whom were loyal enforcers of unpopular royal policies, seemed like a decisive wedge driven into the province's ability to manage its own affairs" (Beik, 1985: 257). These efforts "to seize peasant labor, commodities and capital" by ruthless profiteers and royal agents "violated peasant rights, jeopardized the interests of other parties in peasant production, and threatened the ability of the peasants to survive as peasants" (Tilly, 1980: 44). That antifiscal agrarian rebellion often, in some regions, took on a hue of class struggle in addition ought not to surprise us, for the state-building efforts of absolutist kings were, in part, efforts to sustain the seigneurial system of manorial peasant production while bringing the entire nation under more reliable royal administrative control. Increased taxation combined with other fiscal maneuvers by the crown, which also articulated with loss of local autonomy, economic hardship, rural jealousy of the cities, and peasant opposition to local elites in generating an extremely volatile countryside (see for example Collins and Arthur, 1982). This process can best be grasped by examining briefly a few of the most important popular uprisings during Richelieu's administration.

From 1624, when Richelieu entered the king's service, to 1635, when France entered the Thirty Years War, popular uprisings were more often urban municipal revolts than regional agrarian rebellions. In these centers for production and trade, Richelieu's fiscal expedients included the introduction of new taxes, especially upon commodities that had earlier been exempt, and the dispatch of new tax officials to administer taxes already in place more systematically. Such efforts provoked sharp opposition. In 1630, for example, revolts broke out in Dijon (the Lanterlu revolt), Caen, and twice in Angers; and in 1631 revolts were reported in Paris, Bordeaux, Poitiers, Marseilles, Orleans, and Aix. In wealthy towns, with strong merchant communities and often the seat of a provincial parliament, urban bourgeois and robe nobility were joined by, and occasionally attacked by, a large number of urban lower-class and petit bourgeois elements. Government interference in the trade and manufacture often provoked urban revolt, as in Laval in 1628, when the crown abridged traditional municipal exemptions from taxation, or in 1634, when the Bordelais received word that this salt-rich region would thenceforth be subject to the collection of the gabelle and a new tax on wine (Porchnev, 1972: 171; Bercé, 1974: 302). The introduction of a new tax on the export of finished products prompted revolts in Lyon in 1630, 1632, 1633, and 1642, during which the offices of the customs officials were plundered. The introduction of the gabelle in Rennes in 1636 met with rebellion as well, as city folk shouted, "Long live the King without the gabelle!" and "Let us kill the commissioner and all have a piece of him!" (cited in Shennan, 1975: 49–50). And in Agen in 1635, the arrival of new tax officials in the city provoked a violent revolt; "Your Majesty's officials have been murdered; between 30 and 40 soldiers in the new regiments have also been killed," the intendant dutifully reported to the king (cited in Burkhardt, 1971, vol. 2: 284–85). "The fact that the native troops are loath to proceed against their fellow countrymen gives great cause for concern."

The Cascevoux revolt in Aix in 1630 provides a useful example of urban insurrection.[10] Aix was a wealthy regional center, with a well-developed market, artisanal production, merchants, a parliament; it was the nodal point in the entire Midi. Serious demographic crises—famine, epidemic, and dearth—were exacerbated by heavier fiscal demands from the crown, such as increasing the taillon and the gabelle, creating a large number of venal offices, and revealing plans to transform Provence into a pay d'élection (Kettering, 1978: 63; Porchnev, 1972: 156; Pillorget, 1975: 317–20).

The demands threw together previously antagonistic groups, uniting virtually the entire province against the royal initiatives. When the newly appointed intendant arrived in the city in September, he was greeted by an angry mob of persons wearing small bells on white ribbons (lending the revolt its name) and shouting, "Vive le Roy! Fuero elus et larrons!" (Long live the king! Out with tax officials and robbers!) (see Grimaldi and Gaufridy, 1870: 107). What began as a "spontaneous popular protest against royal taxation" threatened to expand into a full-scale revolt against the absolute monarchy (Kettering, 1978: 180); cries of "Down with the new taxes!" easily became "Down with taxes altogether!" (Pillorget, 1975: 76). The fury of the mob ultimately disintegrated the municipal interclass alliance against royal fiscal initiatives; although the parliamentaires used the opportunity to register their grievances with the crown, they also sought to contain popular rage and protect their own property and privileges. Their "fear of the poor people is so great," one contemporary observed (cited in Pillorget, 1975: 119), "that the city of Aix is deprived of its most notable citizens." Richelieu's compromise on a few fiscal edicts was enough to bring these rebellious judges back into the royal fold, which, of course, isolated the refractory lower classes and made royal suppression relatively easy. This use of a few token capitulations to drive a wedge into the rebellious coalition, and regain the allegiance of the venal officers, was a common strategy for Richelieu, although it had its less sanguine side, setting in motion the possibility of an opposition "party" of disgruntled parliamentaires and merchants that could join with popular forces against royal efforts.[11]

The municipal revolt in 1635–36 in Amiens,[12] a highly developed wool and textile manufacturing city, also illustrates how antifiscal revolt could assuage class-based hostility and forge an alliance of different urban classes. As in other cases, a severe demographic crisis (in this case an outbreak of plague) and other problems, such as currency depreciation and unemployment, aggravated longer-run structural problems, such as the erosion of traditional privileges, and increased the general tension about the possibility of Spanish invasion (Gallet, 1975: 137). Against this backdrop, Richelieu's insistence on increasing the tax on finished woolen and linen cloth, the sol pour livre of 5 percent, was seen as a citywide provocation. When negotiations between de Bullion, Richelieu's secretary of state, and municipal oligarchs and merchants broke down late in the year, and Richelieu was intransigent in regard to collecting, a revolt of the merchants ignited a full-scale revolt of the wool carders and artisans. "We have neither work nor bread," they declared (cited in Gallet, 1975: 148), "we prefer to die." A letter sent to the duke of Chaulnes (cited in Gallet, 1975: 147) warned ominously of the growing alliance between merchants and artisans: "The bourgeoisie has been called to arms; there is no one here yet; we fear that the evil is becoming great." Richelieu's capitulation to the demands of the rebels in 1636, the removal of the sol pour livre and the return to Paris of its collectors, indicates how effective, and how threatening, was this interclass alliance against fiscal expedients.

Urban revolts predominated before 1635; serious rural uprisings proliferated after France's entry into the war. To be sure there had been serious rural uprisings before 1635, especially in the southwestern provinces of Languedoc, Perigord, Acquitaine, and Gascony. But after 1635, royal fiscal and military pressure on these outlying provinces increased, especially as troops moved openly to those provinces that border on Spain. An earlier plan to transform the pays d'état into pays d'élection was scrapped as too dangerous, for Richelieu risked full-scale provincial secession, but the fiscal screws were tightened in every way Richelieu and his councillors could imagine (Le Roy Ladurie, 1981: 119; Rudé, 1980: 55).

In 1636 croquant movements were reported in Saintonge, Angoumois, Poitou, Limousin, Gascony, and Perigord; hardly a province between the Loire and the Garonne was not in revolt against "these Parisians, taxfarmers and others, who oppress them with taxes" (Mousnier, 1970: 57–58). In May twelve minor tax collectors were murdered in the village of Saint-Savinen, and in June Richelieu required troops to quiet a revolt in Angoumois in which a rioting mob had ripped a surgeon to pieces, "having mistaken him for a gabelleur," according to one eyewitness (cited in Burkhardt, 1974, vol. 2: 287; see also Porchnev, 1972: 65).

Veritable armies of peasants, frequently spontaneous and only occasionally led by nobles, scoured the countryside in these first years of open war against Spain. The rebels' rage was so intense and terrifying that many nobles made overtures to save themselves, their families, and their property from the fate of that poor surgeon in Angoumois. Rage erupted when new taxes were imposed, old ones were increased, or new agents arrived to collect either. Peasants in Perigord, for example (cited in Mousnier, 1970: 80), sarcastically expressed their frustration at the collapse of trade and the persistence of the tax burden: "Since trade has ceased, since cattle, wine and chestnuts have no longer any outlet beyond our borders, this province has been unable, in order to continue our tax payments, to change stones into bread, or ferrus into silver, or by our ceaseless toil to meet a thousand new charges that were unknown to our fathers." All they wanted, they wrote, was to "abolish these new charges, remove from us these financial officials, make this province a pays d'état" and allow the formation of a peasant syndicate to "convey our grievances to Your Majesty."

Perhaps the most fascinating and frightening popular uprising occurred in Normandy, where the Nu-pieds, "the climax of the pre-Fronde movements," emerged in 1639.[13] Demographic problems—outbreaks of plague and a series of dreadful harvests—increased the pressure on a province that was perhaps the wealthiest in the realm but also the most heavily taxed (Sturdy, 1976: 554–55). During the 1630s sporadic revolts were recorded throughout the province as peasants rebelled against fiscal impositions, and riots in Rouen in 1630 and 1632 found cloth workers furious because of increased importation of English goods; leather tanners opposed new officers; rope and paper makers attacked the office of the tax collector; and playing-card makers rioted against a new tax on finished playing cards (Mousnier, 1970: 93–97).

But, the Nu-pieds were qualitatively different. New taxes, new offices, and the encroachment of the state on provincial liberties had brought together many nobles, priests, and a mass of peasants in the countryside, who joined with many magistrates, merchants, and a large number of laborers, artisans, and urban poor in the Norman cities throughout the summer of 1639—presenting a "front of the province against the state" (Foisil, 1970: 339). A 6,000-person "Army of Suffering" led by the mysterious and pseudonymous Jean Nu-pied was "cheerfully" subsidized by the "entire countryside," complained Chancellor Seguier (cited in Kamen, 1970: 355). "The discontent of the sovereign courts, of the nobility, of the richest of the towns and of the countryside would not have caused any movement," observed Alexandre Bigot de Monville, the president of the Parliament of Rouen (1976: 4). He suggested a more altruistic interpretation. "Those who have honor and property at risk do not easily undertake to disturb the public order, but new taxes affecting the mass of poor people aroused their anger."

The violent suppression of the revolt was extremely costly to the crown, for it consumed a great deal of time, troops, and money. And, resentments smoldered throughout the province for the rest of Richelieu's administration. Moreover, the rebellion of the Nu-pieds presents another important feature of pre-Fronde popular uprisings. The rebels not only had presented the monarchy with the broadest-based coalition of opposition it had yet faced but had sought to transcend their regional base and enlarge the political coalition beyond provincial boundaries. Early in the rebellion the Nu-pieds had appealed directly to the citizens of Paris to "demonstrate your courage in the emergency of the suffering to make with your forces a successful troop" and come to their aid (cited in Porchnev, 1972: 367). Whereas earlier rebellions—both rural and urban—had been easily repressed by Richelieu (despite the costs) because of their geographic isolation and their localism, the Nu-pieds reached out to make alliances.

Suddenly the strictly defensive posture of resistance to encroachments on traditional local privileges had taken a potentially national turn.

We have seen how each of the constituent elements of old regime France was set in motion by royal efforts to resolve the crown's endemic fiscal crisis. Richelieu's military ambitions had been constrained by domestic structural relations that entrenched local privileged groups and maintained exemptions from taxation from precisely those best able to pay. Yet, his efforts to resolve the fiscal crisis were themselves constrained by the twin imperatives of his administration: generating sufficient revenues to pursue the war effort, and maintaining the traditional set of structural relations that defined the old regime. His administrative revolution without structural reform expressed the contradictions of absolutism; it was designed to support the power of those groups he simultaneously was attempting to undermine. Both efforts failed. The funds generated by his incessant string of ad hoc fiscal expedients were scant, and the costs of administration (tax farms, suppressing revolts, paying wages to new officers) consumed a large portion of the potential revenues. These expedients did, however, generate a significant amount of opposition from diverse quarters of the realm, from hereditary nobility and venal officers, from Catholic clergy and Huguenots, from urban merchants and artisans, from rural peasants and the poor city dwellers. While the king and his first minister lived, though, the opposition from these groups remained geographically isolated and socially disparate, and the suppression of pockets of resistance proved relatively easy (if costly). But the deaths of both the king and Richelieu in 1643 provided the occasion for coalition among these groups as a regency government for the eight-year-old Louis XIV attempted to continue the policies of the late cardinal and his king. Against Queen Anne and her minister, Cardinal Mazarin, however, many of the groups joined in a coalition of political opposition to the absolutist initiative of the crown, and led by the Parliament of Paris, presented the old regime monarchy with the most serious threat prior to 1789.

Notes

1. Recall, for example, D'Artagnan in Dumas's *The Three Musketeers,* whose father advises him to "fight at every opportunity, all the more willingly because duels are forbidden and consequently it takes twice as much courage to fight one." Richelieu was reportedly angered by Corneille's play *Le Cid* because it contained a passage praising the courage to duel, and thus made it harder for the cardinal to enforce his ban.
2. The dernier denominations indicate the rate of return to the crown as well as the potential interest rate to the buyer. A rente sold at dernier 14 would yield 14 times the face value of the rente to the crown over the course of its term.

The higher the dernier, the lower the interest rates and the larger the return to the crown over the long term. A reduction from dernier 14 to dernier 2, therefore, indicates that the crown would both be paying larger interest payments and receiving less in return over the lifespan of the rente.

3. If France were to enter the war against the Catholic Habsburgs, moreover, Richelieu was certain to face strong resistance from important Catholic leaders at home, and so his policy against the Huguenots domestically, while subordinate to his desire to pursue a vigorous foreign policy, was also designed to counterbalance Catholic domestic criticism.

4. The siege was particularly brutal, according to witnesses. Food was scarce at best, disease and death daily occurrences. Dog and donkey meat were luxuries, and "grotesque recipes were used, such as pieces of leather boiled in tallow." The inhabitants were "pale, yellow and as emaciated as corpses," and when the king's troops entered the city gates, they had conquered a city "of ghosts, not of people" (Tapié, 1974: 187).

5. The theoretical issues at stake in the debate—the dynamics of the transition from feudalism to capitalism, the utility of Marxian class relations as a means of understanding early modern social movements, the nature of absolutism and the opposition it engendered—make this debate the analog of the "storm over the gentry" that has preoccupied historians of the English Revolution.

6. Porchnev's and Mousnier's works are each marred by telling problems. Porchnev assumes a unity between state and ruling class, even though, as we have seen, the contradictory nature of absolutism, an effort simultaneously to undermine and uphold the seigneurial system, often led the king and his ministers into confrontations with precisely those groups they were committed to support. Absolutist interests are not congruent with seigneurial interests; the relative autonomy of the absolute monarchy is a central theme of the era. Mousnier's problems are far more serious. Although factious nobles may have participated in, and even organized, some of the popular uprisings, this does not stamp them with an indelible noble character or remove the other possible class interpretations of the events. The peasantry was hardly the blind and furious mob that Mousnier's crude psychologism suggests (Mousnier, 1949: 56). In fact, Mousnier seems to want it both ways: a groundswell of seething lower-class passion that was consciously and deliberately manipulated from above. An enormous literature has since commented on this debate, using historical materials further to refine theoretical positions. Salmon (1967) urges more serious treatment of the impact of peasant uprisings from the sixteenth century. Mandrou (1976) and Le Roy Ladurie (1974) each explore peasant psychology. Bercé (1976) stresses the symbolic nature of protest, suggesting how rural unrest often coincided with popular festivals (see also Le Roy Ladurie, 1974: 192–97; 1979). The letters and memoirs of Chancellor Seguier, (B.N., ms. francais, 17367–17412) are a rich source of contemporary reports about the uprisings.

7. Here, incidentally, Porchnev and Mousnier agree. "The primary demand of the insurgent peasants was the diminishing of taxes; their primary practical program the massacre of the tax collectors," a motive that provides a connection between urban and rural movements (Porchnev, 1972: 53, 87). For Mousnier (1970: 310), "the armies . . . were the principal causes of the increased tax burden and brought most ruin to the places through which they passed," and

for Porchnev (1972: 59–60), the army represented an additional burden on an already beleaguered peasantry.

8. Among the voluminous literature on the intendants, the work by Bonney (1978) stands out as the most complete and insightful. Much of the material in this section owes a great deal to Bonney's work.

9. Mousnier writes (1984: 477) that the intendants and the governors "were not opposed but rather complementary. The governor was an agent of the government, the intendant a magistrate with administrative and judicial responsibilities." Harding (1976) notes the extensive ties between governors and the intendants (see also Salmon, 1981: 249); and Beik (1985: 116) argues that the intendants mediated the relations between noble power brokers and the central government, "between a monarchy wanting various things done in the province and a collection of rulers wanting various measures enacted by the monarchy."

10. This discussion of the Cascevoux revolt is based on René Pillorget's massive and impressive work (1975) and Kettering's more focused and analytic work (1978). See also Grimaldi and Gaufridy (1881).

11. One legacy of the Cascevoux is suggested by the minister of finance who in 1639 wrote that he had raised 30 million livres in Aix, largely through the sale of new judicial offices, that 22 million more was required, but he was fearful of the magistrates' possible reactions (Ranum, 1963: 137–39).

12. My account of the revolt in Amiens is based on the works by Gallet (1975), Lecocq (1881), and especially Deyon (1967), as well as accounts by Porchnev and Mousnier.

13. My account of the Nu-pieds is based on Foisil (1970), and her edited collection of the memoirs of the president of the Parliament of Rouen (1976). Bercé (1974) provides an interesting discussion. Flouquet's *Histoire du Parliament de Normandie,* vols. 4–6 (1842), is valuable, as is the diary of M. de Verthamont, which recounts Chancellor Seguier's visit to the province after the rebellion. (published in 1842, the work can be found in the Archives de la Seine-Maritime, B.H.N., 51). I am grateful to Phillipe Uninsky for pointing out this diary, and for his friendship during my sojourn in Rouen.

4

Toward Revolution:
The Formation of a Revolutionary Coalition,
1643–1648

Everything is poor and mean in France at this time. We have a King of 10 years of age who does not know yet what he wishes; we have a queen whom a belated passion renders blind; we have a minister who rules France as he would a vast farm—that is to say, preoccupying himself only with what will bring in gold, and working for it with Italian intrigue and cunning; we have princes who will make a personal and egoistic opposition, who will accomplish nothing except to draw from the hands of Mazarin some ingots of gold, some bribes of power.

—Athos, in *The Three Musketeers*

The most perilous moment for a bad government is when it seeks to mend its ways.

—Tocqueville

Louis XIII's Legacy: War and Insolvency

The reign of Louis XIII had lasted less than thirty years, and yet in that short time had witnessed a dramatic program of bureaucratic centralization; a large number of formerly autonomous regions and municipalities, as well as religious, social, and political groups were brought under royal control. France was vigorously pursuing its objectives in the Thirty Years War, scoring military victories on both of its borders with Habsburg lands. More money had been raised in taxes by Louis XIII than by all his predecessors put together (Bonney, 1981: 188), but the costs of Richelieu's governmental revolution without social reform were great as well. The persistent fiscal crisis that had plagued his administration deepened because Richelieu's efforts at resolution had been only a series of fiscal expedients designed to meet short-term needs and not to answer the longer-term structural problems of fiscal organization. The expedients had also provoked a great deal of opposition from various quarters, and the new regency government in 1643 faced a contentious nobility, a disgruntled Catholic clergy, desperate and frightened Huguenots, a pretentious and furious robe nobility, an overburdened peasantry, merchants who felt themselves shackled to an anachronistic political economy, and regional power brokers whose patronage had been undermined.

In the years between the formation of the regency government and the end of the Thirty Years War, political opposition intensified until events in late 1647 and early 1648 brought many of these groups into a coalition of political opposition. That initial coalition was formed, as revolutionary coalitions often are, of present or potential state creditors, who removed their financial backing of the old regime. The coalition expressed more than the anger of individual corporate groups over the trampling of their privileges; some groups suggested that the authority making fiscal demands had no right to make such demands, that it was, in essence, illegitimate. To be sure, few extended this to include the idea of absolute monarchy itself; in fact, the illegitimacy of the regency of Queen Anne and Cardinal Mazarin was set in contrast to the legitimacy of the minority king, so that the opponents of the cardinal could posture themselves as the true defenders of the monarchy.

Even this concerted challenge to the legitimacy of the regency constituted a bold step in old regime France. In his efforts to raise revenues and subordinate autonomous groups, Richelieu's policies had an effect opposite from that he intended, subtly undermining the seigneurial system of agrarian production and destroying "utterly the political viability of feudalism" that he had worked so hard to sustain (Bridges, 1935: 30). Richelieu had "perverted and reversed the ancient form of government and changed the maxims of legitimate monarchy into those of tyranny," as one pamphlet put it in 1649 (B. Maz., ms. 498, fol. 15). Cardinal de Retz wrote that Richelieu "created, within the most legitimate of monarchies, the most scandalous and dangerous tyranny that any state, perhaps, has ever submitted to" (cited in Keohane, 1980: 225).

If opposition to royal fiscal policies was Richelieu's legacy to Mazarin, then it was Mazarin's desperate search for new revenues that welded the opposition into a fragile coalition. Richelieu had made a revolution possible by setting so many different groups in motion against royal policies—the

Fronde was "the legacy of Richelieu," writes Elliott (1984: 171)—but Mazarin made it probable by bringing those groups together. Part of this is explained by the regency government itself, which carried so much less legitimacy. Part is explained by personality variables. Mazarin was no Richelieu. A foreigner, he was seen as cunning and sly, clever and malicious, incapable of administrating a nation, and "incompetent," as Claude Joly wrote at the time, "in all things but the infamous art of deceit" (1718, vol. 2: 134). One of the rentiers described Mazarin as "the most foul stench of the century" (cited in Mousnier, 1978: 283). But, the largest part of the explanation rests upon structural factors, the inability of the absolutist strategy to resolve its fiscal crisis without undertaking social reforms that would destroy the class-based seigneurial system it was designed to uphold.

Fiscal pressure was unrelenting as Mazarin came to power, especially because the war effort had escalated. The desperate need for military personnel for the war pressed him to sacrifice the vigorous collection of increased taxes (which had required the use of troops to enforce collection and suppress revolt). The French forces scored an impressive victory at Rocroy in 1643, seemingly turning the tide of the war,[1] which allowed Mazarin to consider an invasion of England; he had become frightened of the potential of the Civil War and had resolved to intervene to restore Charles I to the throne (Lossky, 1975: 470; Polisensky, 1978: 172). In fact, Mazarin was so anxious to end the war with the Spanish that he broke a promise not to negotiate without Dutch representatives present. He offered to exchange occupied Catalonia for the freedom of the Spanish Netherlands, and he signed treaties at Munster in 1646 and 1647 that were precursors of the Treaty of Westphalia, which ended the war in 1648 (B. Maz., 16033, fols. 37–50).

The Treaty of Westphalia expresses the transition that the Thirty Years War evidenced, from the last feudal dynastic struggle based on religious motives—a conflict between Protestant states and the Holy Roman Empire—to the first "world war," a battle among sovereign nation-states for Continental, and hence world, hegemony. All contenders for Continental hegemony except France and Spain had been removed, and the threat of a unified Habsburg force was ended. Although this conflict between Spain and France was not finally concluded until 1659, the Treaty of Westphalia marks the beginning of the end of the Spanish Empire in Europe, and the ascendancy of the French in international relations.

Ends of wars are dangerous times for politicians, even those who have won their wars, because the extraordinary fiscal mechanisms that had been used to satisfy emergency needs lose their justification. After the Thirty Years War finances were "in terrible shape," with revenues anticipated already for the next several years, an inability to concoct new fiscal expedients, and returning troops that demanded to be paid (André, 1906: 280).

New Resources for Old Challenges

To deal with the fiscal crisis that he had inherited, Mazarin turned to the methods developed by Richelieu to hold it at bay: short-term expedients. Because they provoked too much opposition, some of Richelieu's policies had to be abandoned, such as the use of the handpicked commissaires in the Chambre de l'Arsenal to hear political trials and thereby undercut the authority of the Parliament of Paris (which made the Chambre de l'Arsenal something like the Star Chamber in England; see Kitchens, 1982).[2] Mazarin also borrowed extensively, from any sources he could find; more money was borrowed during the early years of the regency than at any time in the history of the monarchy (Bonney, 1981: 197). He attempted to raise every tax he could think of, and to float enormous numbers of rentes to be guaranteed on the municipality of Paris or on the income of the clergy. The anticipations, for example, spiraled out of control during the first few years of Mazarin's administration as he literally mortgaged the crown's future financial solvency for immediate return. The estimated tax revenues for 1643 totaled 58 million livres, of which 48 million was "already paid in anticipation" (B.N., ms. Francais, 16423, fol. 9). In 1645 the entire anticipated tax revenues for 1646, 1647, and 1648 had already been spent, and their collection farmed out in anticipations.

Mazarin's efforts to resolve the fiscal crisis met with the same opposition as had Richelieu's efforts. An aristocratic conspiracy, the Cabal des Importants, sought, as La Rochefoucauld put it (1864: 394), to reestablish "the old form of government which Richelieu had begun to destroy"; exposed in September 1643, its noble leaders were arrested and exiled to their country estates. And, Mazarin's efforts in the countryside triggered a new round of popular uprisings. In 1643, for example, uprisings were reported in Poitou, Saintonge, and Angoumois; in all three, tax farmers were mobbed and beaten, and tax records destroyed. In Rouergue the tax collector was murdered and the popular forces vowed to resist all taxation (Degarne, 1962: 7). "Whatever Monsieur de Nouailles may say," they sang in the streets, "we will not pay any tailles, tra-la-la" (B.N., French Ms, 15621, fol. 257). A riot broke out in Marseilles in 1644, prompted by high bread prices, new taxes, and the cardinal's efforts to introduce a highly depreciated coin for urban trade; and a revolt in Languedoc in 1645 was a "straightforward tax rebellion" against the imposition of a tax, the *joyeux avènement*, which was levied for the king's accession (Harding,

1978: 210; see also ibid.: 208). Venal officeholders could everywhere be found joining in the popular uprisings, especially in 1645–46, as a severe fiscal crisis threatened to bankrupt the crown and "tested the ability of provincial groups to take advantage of various related forms of agitation by forming a power bloc strong enough to bargain with a weakened monarchy" (Beik, 1985: 206). In some cases, like Aix and Toulouse, the officers directed the popular uprisings overtly, or at least lent visible leadership (Kettering, 1978: 184; Harding, 1978: 211).

Mazarin's response to the persistence of opposition to royal fiscal policies was as contradictory as the policies themselves. Although he ordered most popular uprisings to be suppressed as gently as possible, so as not to interfere with the population's ability to continue to pay (Mazarin, 1894, vol. 1: 414–14), in Rouergue, the absence of noble participation allowed a swifter and more brutal suppression of the 1643 revolt, which included lodging troops in the houses of the rebels until they had paid their assessed taxes (B.N., ms. Francais, 15261, fol. 247).

Mazarin withdrew from the costly efforts to subdue the outlying provinces and autonomous municipalities, and began to focus on the city of Paris as the chief source of funds to continue the war effort. Louis XIII and Richelieu had provoked only minor disturbances from rentiers and wine merchants in the 1630s, and the city had generally remained quiet because of "his preferential treatment of its inhabitants" (Moote, 1972: 94). Like Richelieu, Mazarin was no financial planner, and was "not interested in fiscal reforms"; his finance minister kept the cardinal perpetually "one jump ahead of disaster" (Wolf, 1961: 34). But, fiscal necessity pressed Mazarin to turn on his capital. He created new officers, and brought in dozens of new financiers, which he hoped would have the dual effect of replenishing the dwindling supply of state creditors and prevent the possibility of an alliance between wealthy bourgeois elements and the venal officers in the Parliament of Paris, upon whom Mazarin could no longer rely for investing in royal bonds or purchasing loans. Mazarin sought to use the financiers in the city as Richelieu had used the intendants in the countryside: a flexible instrument of royal policy and a source of immediate revenues.

Mazarin sought to raise revenues from officers and merchants while he simultaneously sought to control and subordinate them to his will. Because he was interested in trade only "insofar as it brought in revenue," he raised tariffs and imposed new customs and sales taxes, but would not spend anything to provide naval protection for merchants' ships. He transferred the power to negotiate and audit state loans (except the rentes) from the Chambre des Comptes and the Parliament of Paris directly to the financiers (Moote, 1972: 81). These officers were angered by their loss of investment opportunities as their money was increasingly siphoned into less productive state markets, and infuriated by the steady erosion of their juridical and legislative powers. They sought to move against the financiers, "throwing in their lot with the popular revolutionary forces" (Salmon, 1969: 25; see also Kossman, 1954: 34). And the financiers, themselves, were able to dictate much stronger terms of credit, for they understood their increasing value to the royal fisc, often receiving upward of 15 percent in interest (Brown, 1971: 99).

The continued reliance on the financiers to make loans during periods of political crisis increasingly angered the magistrates in the sovereign courts and the trésoriers and élus, whose authority had been undercut. One pamphlet expressing venal officers' anger called the financiers "unnatural, inhuman, and inclined towards the total ruin of the state"; another charged that the financiers

> were men of low origin who made a great deal of money out of the state's financial system; they bought expensive official posts, acquired estates and gave large marriage portions to their children; the financiers formed a conspiracy of thieves united in their aim of destroying a state; they corrupted the rest of society by the scandalous example they gave of high living, which caused less well men to ruin themselves by attempts at emulation. [Dent, 1974: 7]

Rentiers asserted in one political pamphlet that the entire fortune of the state "can today be found in the pockets of the financiers" (A.N., K 1055, fol. 3). Opposition ran high among all the various layers of the venal officeholders, just as opposition also coalesced against the intendants in the provinces. "Possessed of similar titles in the mass to those of the financiers, the magistrates were observing groups of men newer than they rising in one or two generations to status that the forebears of magistrates had attained with some difficulty and have maintained for some considerable time without much further advance" (Dent, 1974: 176). As one contemporary put it (in Maland, 1970: 273), "If a tax farmer fails, the courtiers say of him: he is a bourgeois, a man of no importance, a ruffian; but if he succeeds, they want to marry his daughter."

The remonstrance from the élus to the parliaments in 1643 illustrates the rivalry among officers and the growing opposition to the financiers. Threatened with prosecution by the Chambre de Justice for mismanaging royal funds, the syndicate of élus protested innocence. If the crown seeks to punish someone, they argued, it should punish the financiers, and the fines they sought could not possibly be paid by the élus, who were "too poor." The élus drew a fascinating portrait to justify their poverty: the financier is dressed in velvet, they complain, and an élu can afford but simple cloth. The financier lives in a chateau, a superb townhouse, or country manor surrounded by land, and the élu has a "maisonette" that he often leases from a financier. The royal officer never has enough money to provide for his family, while the financier holds magnificent banquets, displaying his familial acquisitions for all to see, reminding everyone of the recentness of their purchase. The poor élu can claim only what his mother and father have passed on to him, for his sole source of income comes from the commissions and mandates of the king, and he never touches the gold and silver belonging to the state. The financier, on the other hand, always has his hand on royal finances, and is known to have pocketed "large amounts" (in Sheehy, 1977: 407–8). The fractures within the officer corps served the absolutist impulse in its earliest stages, when officers could be set against one another and each could be manipulated for the interests of the crown. When they had outlived their usefulness to the crown, on the other hand, and were discarded, they often found their former enemies to be among their strongest allies. Thus did the élus and the trésoriers throw in their lot with the magistrates in the sovereign courts by the middle years of the 1640s, in opposition to the financiers and the intendants.

A new fiscal expedient, the *toise*, also triggered intensified political opposition from wealthy bourgeois and also venal officers. The toise was a hated tax on houses constructed outside the walls of the city that had originally been put in place because of the extra expense of providing adequate defense of those more vulnerable dwellings. Such a tax was particularly odious to the wealthy merchants and magistrates because they had been the groups that had built houses outside the gates of the city since the end of the sixteenth century, creating in the *faubourgs* the first suburbs of France. Parcelli d'Emery, Mazarin's finance minister, advised that those who did not wish to see their houses torn down pay the toise immediately (Forbonnais, 1758, vol. 2: 77). Riots broke out in 1644 and 1645, when a president of one of the chambers of Parliament was arrested for his opposition to the registration of the edit of the toise (Brown, 1971: 101). Mazarin eventually resorted to a lit de justice[3] to insure the registration of his new fiscal edicts by a recalcitrant Parliament, and even then "there were those who advanced the thesis that a minor King did not have the right to a *lit de justice*, or to impel verification of his edicts by virtue of his absolute power" (Kossman, 1954: 37). At the lit de justice, parliament registered new fiscal edicts calling for creation and sale of new offices, a series of taxes on several previously untaxed crafts, and a tax on alienated domains, all of which were strong setbacks for the city's merchants and crafts corps, who threatened to close up their shops rather than pay the new charges.

Parliament's resistance to the toise, and the merchants' refusal to pay it and other new taxes joined these two previously antagonistic groups in an alliance of state creditors who were withdrawing their fiscal support of the crown. Earlier, Parliament "had come to the aid of the taxpayers of the toise," writes Moote (1972: 104), and now "the tax payers provided Parliament with a victory in defeat, showing by their refusal to pay, that parliamentary review alone could convert the King's will into law." When a new tax on all produce and merchandise entering the city was proposed in October 1646, the parlementaires and the merchants were again visible in opposing it; by August 1647 the edict was still unregistered and parlementaires cried, "Tax the financiers!" in the chambers of the sovereign courts (Forbonnais, 1758, vol. 2: 87; Kossman, 1954: 39). In addition, the effort to impose the franc-fief brought formerly wealthy urban residents deeper into the coalition of opposition. Even on their newly acquired estates, theoretically exempt from taxation, they were finding the long arm of absolutism attempting to rake in some profit. One contemporary complained (Wicquefort, 1648 [1978 ed.]: 45) that he had worked hard all year on his land but one small edict by the king wiped it out in a matter of minutes. The popular classes in the city of Paris also became vigorous opponents of the edicts, and not only because of the fruits and other luxury foods that the magistrates had come to cherish. The cost of living in Paris was significantly higher than elsewhere in France, because food and other commodities had to be imported into the city. Bread, for example, consumed half the daily wages of guild artisans (Moote, 1972: 97).

By 1647 "the financial situation was desperate. Massive new revenues were needed to stave off bankruptcy. Without new revenues, loans from financiers would no longer be forthcoming. Without such loans, the war could not be continued" (Bonney, 1978: 52). The king owed 17 million livres on old debts from the war and Mazarin's attempts to levy a tax on the Six Grands Corps of the city infuriated the merchants once again (Forbonnais, 1758, vol. 2: 90–91). By the end of the year the bankruptcy was evident, and it "paralysed the government without permanently removing the burden of debt" (Bonney, 1981: 205). Mazarin attempted to parlay the bankruptcy into a source of revenues for the crown, largely by playing a combination of the last two fiscal cards he still held: the loyalty of the financiers, who were still willing to purchase rentes, and the ability to commit financial fraud.

The rente crisis of 1647–48 was the last gasp of the crown to retain fiscal solvency, and it precipitated the final withdrawal of all potential state creditors, for even the financiers dared not invest in such an unsettled political climate. The crisis had been well prepared by royal maneuvers with rentes in the last years of Richelieu's administration and especially in the years since the deaths of Richelieu and Louis XIII. Almost 20 million livres in rentes were still outstanding in 1640; royal credit began to sag (Dent, 1974: 50). A new issue of rentes of 1,000 livres in 1641, which in 1634 might have brought in as much as 14,000 livres was selling for a mere 4,000 livres (Bonney, 1981: 166). Instead of the 175 million livres available to the crown in all its rentes, the royal treasury barely had the 20 million it needed to pay the interest on rentes already created. In 1644 Mazarin had sold 3.2 million livres in rentes and also in anticipations of the revenues on the aides from 1645.

Mazarin had profits, not repayment, on his mind. On the eve of 1648 he declared a royal bankruptcy, asserting that he would be unable to pay the interest on the rentes as well as the suspension of the paulette (which would throw all existing offices up for renegotiation with the crown). Omer Talon, the most prominent magistrate in Parliament urged Mazarin to reconsider continuing to meet the interest payments on the rentes because rentes assured the families that had descended from mediocre blood that mobility into the ranks of the nobility was possible. The suppression of the interest caused the ''misery of many whose total goods consists of these little rentes, which they have been left and which they leave to their lines of successors'' (in Martin and Bezancon, 1957: 22). As a result of the suspension of the interest payments on the rentes, the price of rentes declined sharply as rentiers sold off the bonds that would no longer provide interest income, often for about 2 percent of the face value of the rente. Mazarin instructed his own agents to surreptitiously purchase these deflated bonds from their despairing owners at bargain prices. When all but about 10 percent of the rentes had been repurchased by Mazarin's clients, he announced that a miscalculation had led to earlier hasty assessments of the crown's ability to maintain interest payments. The price of the rentes soared predictably, and Mazarin was able to sell the repurchased rentes to the highest bidders at exorbitant profits.

This bit of royal chicanery was the last straw for the rentiers, even the financiers upon whom Mazarin had relied as the chief state creditors in the mid and late 1640s. Financiers now sought allies against the royal fiscal policies and came, naturally, to their earlier enemies, the judges in the sovereign courts and the bourgeoisie of the great urban manufactures. In January 1648 the financiers presented their grievances to the Chambres des Comptes, and sought alliance with the magistrates in the sovereign courts, thus joining the coalition of political opposition against Mazarin.[4]

With the end of the Thirty Years War and the signing of the Treaty of Westphalia, Mazarin's entire fiscal edifice collapsed, as if the end of the war was the signal ''to release those criticisms which had been partly suppressed'' and bring together all the possible elements in a full-scale withdrawal of state creditors.[5] The treasury was bare, the crown was bankrupt. And the coalition of political opposition, welded together by the Parliament of Paris, had become a revolutionary coalition. When the Parliament of Paris invited the magistrates of the other sovereign courts to deliberate jointly, it heralded the beginning of the Fronde, "by far the most serious ordeal the French monarchy ever faced, not only during the seventeenth century, but right down to 1789," and arguably "the greatest anti-fiscal revolution in France's history" (Zagorin, vol. 2: 52, 188). The Arrêt d'Union issued by these magistrates called for sweeping reforms, and "signalled the formation of an extraordinary coalition of judges and officials, high bureaucratic elites and representatives of the robe, in a direct assault upon the monarchy's absolutism" (Zagorin, 1982, vol. 2: 197).

The revolutionary coalition did not have its origins in Paris among the magistrates but in the disparate oppositions that the fiscal policies of Richelieu and Mazarin had engendered. The previous three decades of fiscal expedients and political subordination had culminated in the sovereign courts, for the Fronde was the crest of a long wave of political resentments.[6] But, just as the growing provincial, municipal, and corporate oppositions led to that revolutionary coalition, so, too, did the articulation of the opposition ripple back through the entire countryside, giving those previously dispersed, disorganized, and isolated oppositions the opportunity to organize and join the coalition. At the provincial level, the Fronde was the "fuse for the simultaneous explosion of all the festering grievances, factious animosities, and political resentments incited by the monarchy's absolutist thrust" (Zagorin, 1982, vol. 2: 188); the revolutionary coalition was as much the outcome of the Parisian revolt as the cause. "If there ever was a moment for a regional collaboration in defense of a traditional constitution, this was it. In 1648 conscious efforts were made to draw together" (Beik, 1985: 206).

The governmental revolution designed by Cardinal Richelieu for Louis XIII and inherited and extended by Cardinal Mazarin, administering for the young Louis XIV, had been an effort to resolve a persistent fiscal crisis that plagued the old regime in France. It was a revolution without reform; the state apparatus was perceived to be stronger than any of the forces arrayed against it. But the administrative efforts of these cardinal-ministers had engendered a legitimacy crisis by alienating a large portion of the nation from domestic policies, even when those policies were justified by the war-making needs of an absolutist state. By 1648, without the awe of a majority king and an adroit minister, this legitimacy crisis spilled out of the sovereign courts and into the streets of Paris. When a desperate Cardinal Mazarin, facing a bankrupt treasury, moved to arrest several of the most vociferous and radical parlementaires, the stage was set for the eruption of the Fronde. More than an aristocratic imbroglio, an effete challenge by a pretentious robe nobility, or the last gasp of a sinking peasantry against a centralizing state, the Fronde was all these and more; it was a political revolution, a concerted effort on the part of a revolutionary coalition to alter the structure of the state and the social foundations upon which political power rested.

Notes

1. The glory that Mazarin had hoped for, however, went to the two generals who defeated the "flower of the Spanish infantry" at Rocroy, and who eventually squared off in the Fronde. And, it is a glory that continues to the present. Turenne, first a Frondeur sympathizer and later the commander who laid siege to Paris for Mazarin's troops, is buried at Invalides, in the rotunda of France's most illustrious generals that surrounds the tomb of Napoleon. And though Conde's leadership of the princely Frondeurs precluded his omission from that inner circle (despite his reputation as the most able military leader in the realm), a mural depicting him leading the troops at Rocroy adorns one wall in the Great Hall of Mirrors in the palace at Versailles.
2. Of course, Mazarin "could not erase the memory of its humiliating impact on the court's public functions, jurisdiction, pride, and prestige" (Kitchens, 1982: 347).
3. The lit de justice was a tradition; the king would be carried into the chamber of the Parliament on a cushioned sofa, or "bed," to ensure the registration or verification of his policies. Because Parliament's function was verification and not legislation, its major strategy to increase its political power was to delay registration. The lit de justice circumvented these delays because no one could deny a royal request in the presence of the king.
4. Throughout the Fronde, the issue of the rentes remained central, binding together the various layers of state creditors, even after their earlier antipathies threatened to drive them apart. A rentiers' syndic was established in 1648 to insure regular interest payments during the Fronde, and to coordinate the activities of all rentiers. In *Factum contenant les justes defenses des Rentiers de l'Hôtel de Ville, et des moyens veritables de la sureté de leurs Rentes et de leur conservation* (A.N., K 1055) the rentiers plead their case and present a history of their present woes. Financial maladministration through Mazarin's chicanery and evil favoring of the financiers had brought the country to the brink of ruin, the syndic argued. "It seems everyone has gotten rich off the poor rentiers."
5. Recall here Anatole France's statement that "a people living under the perpetual menace of war and invasion is very easy to govern. It demands no social reforms. It does not haggle over expenditures on armaments and military equipment. It pays without discussion, it ruins itself, and that is an excellent thing for the syndicates of financiers and manufacturers for whom patriotic terrors are an abundant source of gain." Imagine the difficulties of the monarchy when even those manufacturers and financiers find wartime finances no longer

profitable, and prefer to throw in their lot with a growing revolt against the very system that had been so generous to them.

6. Ranum, for example, writes (1968: 201) that the Fronde "consisted of a series of extensive rural rebellions which eventually gained the towns and finally the capital."

5

The Centralizing Impulse in Sixteenth-Century England

> *A monarchy divested of its nobility has no refuge
> under heaven but an army. Wherefore the dissolu-
> tion of this government caused the civil war, not
> the war the dissolution of this government.*
> —James Harrington

> *Property is political power individualised and
> made visible. The destruction of the monarchy
> was only the political expression of an economic
> change which had begun in the reign of Henry
> VII.*
> —R. H. Tawney

Royal absolutism triumphed in seventeenth-century France, and the end of the Fronde heralded the beginning of a long and relatively glorious reign by a succession of pompous and arrogant Bourbons. The Fronde failed to achieve a permanent republican solution or to effect the diminution of royal power. French society remained subordinated to the state, and the state remained dominated by the monarchy and its bureaucracy. Louis XIV glibly asserted that he was the state, and his successors faced sporadic but easily suppressed domestic opposition for over a century.

Not so in England. Just as the Fronde was erupting in France, Charles I was facing a concerted coalition of political opposition. Charles's efforts to centralize and concentrate political power along an absolutist model must be rated among the most dismal failures in English history. His efforts met consistent opposition, and ultimately Charles himself met his death on the execution block at Whitehall. The English regicide was certainly the most extreme and dramatic resolution of the intense conflicts between state and society that characterized the history of early-seventeenth-century Europe. And although a king was eventually restored in England, kingship never again enjoyed the same far-reaching powers nor ever again attempted to encroach on the residual powers and liberties of English society.

The history of the English Revolution has been recited well and often, and it is not my intention to retell it here. Nor do I intend to engage systematically in all the debates that characterize the historiography of the English Revolution. As a historical sociologist, I will focus on the structural relationships—among classes, between classes and the state, between any social group and ideological currents—that established the structural parameters for revolutionary situations, as well as on the shorter-term abridgment of those relationships by a crown desperately and consistently short of funds with which to implement its foreign and domestic policies. I am aware, however, that such sociological attention involves one, perforce, in historiographic debates among students of the English Revolution. Recently, a wave of revisionist historians have rejected historical explanations that have relied on sociological variables, intentionality of the revolutionary actors, Marxist understandings of class relations, and other theoretically informed models. In this reading the English Revolution "was not a world-historically important event requiring a commensurate scale of explanation, but rather represents, at least in origins, a somewhat bloody tiff between a specific monarch and certain factions among his subjects" (Fulbrook, 1982: 252). To focus on immediate and local issues concerning the personality of a particular king and his subjects decomposes the Revolution into a series of skirmishes that bear little or no relation to one another, and that happened, coincidentally, to cluster around particular years.

Three themes stand out in this historical tradition. First, revisionist historians argue that the Revolution was a coincidental set of local reactions, reactions against "insensitive interventionism by central government in the affairs of the shires or boroughs, the imposition of national priorities" (Morrill, 1984: 13). The Civil War, a "tragic but temporary upheaval," was merely "one of a succession of problems to which society at the time was particularly vulnerable" (Everitt, 1969: 26). Local people "were so fully engaged with purely local issues that they seemed to have had little interest in concerns of more far-reaching import" and believed that "the safety of the kingdom . . . was not our work" (Everitt, 1969: 16, 9).

Second, revisionist historians stress psychological variables to explain the behavior of both king and political opponents. Charles was "inaccessible, glacial, self-righteous, deceitful," and parliamentarians were fearful, small-minded conservative localists who believed that the crown had been "persuaded by evil counsellors to invade the liberty and take away the property of the subject" and therefore "believed that they had to look to their own defense, the king having become incapable of discharging his trust." The Civil War "grew out of the policies and out of the particular failings of a particular king" and opposition developed "not because they feared royal tyranny, but because they believed the King had ceased to rule. He had become a zombie" (Morrill, 1984: 11, 13, 15).

A third theme in the revisionist explanation is the causal role of religion in the genesis of opposition to royal policies. To the extent that a national and social cause is posited, it is often the struggle between two institutionalized churches, Anglican and Presbyterian, to distance themselves from Catholicism, and to attract the many Puritan sects that had sprung up around the countryside and the cities. "The civil war was not a clash of social groups: it was the result of incompetent kingship which allowed religious militants to settle their disputes about the nature of the church, and therefore of different concepts of moral order, to fight it out. It was the last and greatest of Europe's Wars of Religion" (Morrill, 1984: 15).

I find the localist, revisionist explanations unsatisfactory and unconvincing, coming "near to proving that the civil war did not happen" (Hill, 1986: 22; see also Morrill, 1980: x). I will argue for a return to structural explanations of revolution in general and the English Revolution in particular. I will argue that the conservative defense of the localities against royal intervention has a structural foundation, deeply rooted in the organization of English society, and that the contrapuntal relationship between the monarchy and the nobility, and the state and agrarian society created deep fissures in traditional English social structure that made revolution possible. Second, I will argue that the personalities of the various actors, no matter how abrasive they may have been, provide perhaps a surface-level immediacy to the struggles that characterize the shorter-term origins of the English Civil War, but that personality variables become operative only within the context of policies that various social groups find particularly heinous. Personality clashes do not cause revolutions, although revolutionary situations—in this case, Charles's efforts to crush traditional privileges and his desperate fiscal expedients created to resolve his fiscal crisis—are facilitated and strengthened by personality clashes, which become a convenient psychological shorthand to explain deeper political differences. "The causes of the civil war must be sought in society, not in individuals" (Hill, 1940: 8). Finally, I will argue that although religious differences play an important role in the generation of ideological opposition to royal policies, the true salience of religious variables comes into play after the revolution is under way, when religious opposition serves to maintain the unity of a revolutionary coalition after economic or political interests have begun to tear the coalition apart.

My structural interpretation does not signal, however, a return to the traditional Whig interpretation of the English Revolution, an interpretation that cast the revolution as a pivotal moment in the heroic march of parliamentary democracy toward its actualization in England. Such interpretations have often suggested that the English Revolution was made possible by the confluence of several structural features of traditional English economy and polity: (1) England is an island, and thus its domestic market was far more unified than that of other countries, and naval issues had traditionally predominated over land issues, and hence there was no standing army, and (2) the structure of government required parliamentary institutions and saw little evidence of the burgeoning administrative bureaucracy that marked France and other nations. The absence of an army or a bureaucracy, the importance of Parliament in consenting to taxation, and the unified home market represent, in these interpretations, a set of exceptional qualities that mark England among all other early modern European nations, and are thus the determinants of its revolution.

These arguments confuse cause with consequence; English exceptionalism cannot explain the causes of the English Revolution precisely because revolution occurred in so many other countries in Europe at the same time. The causes of the English Revolution are to be sought in the structural features that England shared with other European nations, not in those that set England apart. These features may help us later explain why the English Revolution was the single successful revolution among the entire set of seventeenth-century revolutions, even though the features will be important only within larger political-economic contexts. English exceptionalism cannot, however, explain the outbreak of revolution in England.

I will again emphasize the fiscal crisis of the old regime state in England. Like their French counterparts, English kings were constantly in need of revenues, but each one rarely had, as Adam Smith commented, "the immediate means of augmenting his revenue in proportion to the augmentation of his expense." The fiscal crisis of the old regime state in England was intensifed during the sixteenth century as the price revolution increased commercial possibilities but also placed increased financial burdens on those, like kings, who lived on fixed incomes. Foreign wars and domestic rebellions also depleted royal funds and stretched governmental legitimacy to the breaking point. The increasingly desperate search for revenues led the crown to centralize its administration and abridge traditional relationships; the "administrative revolution" of Thomas Cromwell as the minister for Henry VIII presents an interesting parallel to the political centralization of France under Cardinal Richelieu and Louis XIII.

By the turn of the seventeenth century and the death of Queen Elizabeth, the crown was faced with an even more difficult situation as increased economic and military competition from abroad confronted a less popular and less solvent Stuart monarchy. Although James I was at least minimally successful in raising sufficient funds in the 1620s, Charles I, like Cardinal Mazarin, attempted to coerce Parliament into backing him financially, and when it did not, he designed drastic fiscal expedients to raise the needed funds. The expedients had the double impact of alienating large segments of previously loyal political groups, many of whom had served as royal creditors, and further raising the ante for later expedients. A coalition of political opposition began to form among the scattered groups opposed to specific expedients. During the prerogative reign, 1628–40, the severity and frequency of these expedients increased, fusing the opposition into a coalition that questioned far more than the specific policies of an unpopular king. The declarations of war against Scotland in 1640 and against Ireland in 1642 broke the back of the English fiscal system and triggered the outbreak of rebellion and eventually the Civil War.

The fiscal crisis of the old regime English state followed a trajectory similar to that of the crisis in France. In both cases the fiscal crisis was embedded in the structure of class relations and the relationships between classes and the monarchy, and surfaced when pressures from international competition (military and economic) and domestic troubles (demographic, social, and economic tensions) coincided, bringing even greater pressure to bear on the fragile monarchy. The adoption of fiscal expedients to solve these new pressures generated sporadic and disunified opposition at first, but the increased frequency and severity of the expedients began to forge a coalition of opposition that vied with the monarchy for political power.

Traditional English Social Structure

> *Kings rule or barons rule;*
> *We have suffered various oppression,*
> *But mostly we are left to our own devices,*
> *And we are content if we are left alone.*
> —T. S. Eliot,
> *Murder in the Cathedral*

England, like France, was a decidedly agricultural nation before the seventeenth century. A nation of roughly 3 million people in 1540, English rural society was "essentially a federation of gentry-led county units," "a confederation of overlapping communities, politically united only on the

English and Welsh Counties in the Sixteenth and Seventeenth Centuries

7 = Rutland
8 = Huntingdon
9 = Isle of Ely (not county)
10 = Cambridge
11 = Middlesex (with Westminster)

usual occasions when the representatives of these communities were summoned together in Parliament" (Thomas, 1978: 49; Underdown, 1971: 24). In the "field" or "champion" areas of the country, which covered most of the corn- and grass-growing regions of the south and east, the traditional patterns of unenclosed common fields prevailed. Nucleated villages were part of a highly organized manorial economy, tightly bound by church and traditional hierarchies, and English peasants "accepted the established system of society with its hierarchy of authorities and division of class functions, and they had a most pathetic confidence in the Crown" (Tawney, 1912: 339–40; see also Thirsk, 1967; Underdown, 1986: 5). Collective use of common fields allowed, in the champion areas, the development of a strong moral economy, a "feeling of practical proprietorship" and "commonal aspirations" that indicated a strong cooperative spirit; villagers believed that the common fields "belong to their town in a quite effective and intimate manner, that they stint it, turn off intruders, guard it for their descendents, defend it, if need be, with bows and arrows and pikes, and the other agricultural implements of that forceful age" (Tawney, 1912: 246). Despite the traditional class divisions of the manor, then, champion areas evidenced little class conflict, and the lower classes were relatively docile, for the moral economy of the English village provided a coherent, if hierarchical, stability.

The pastoral regions of the north and west of England, by contrast, were dotted by hamlets or single farmsteads having little association with their neighbors. The population was far more sparse, and parishes tended to be larger, with a more marked contrast between rich and poor, and far less direct contact between lords and peasants. Here people engaged in cattle or sheep breeding and fattening, dairying, pig keeping, and horse breeding, for the local arables satisfied local demand without much penetration by the market. As one contemporary summarized the difference (cited in Underdown, 1986: 5):

> Our soil being divided into champaign ground and woodland, the houses of the
> first lie uniformly builded in every town together, with streets and lanes, whereas
> in the woodland country (except here and there in great market towns) they
> stand scattered abroad, each one dwelling in the midst of his own occupying.

The people working these small, enclosed family farms "were likely to be more individualistic, less circumscribed by ancient custom. Lacking strong manorial institutions, the villages were often unable to prevent immigration by outsiders. They thus tended to grow more rapidly than the more controlled arable parishes, and to be more unstable, more vulnerable to high prices in bad harvest years" (Underdown, 1986: 5). The more mobile population was far less difficult to control, so that the woodland areas were rougher, inhabited, as one contemporary put it by "the mean people [who] live lawless, nobody to govern them, they care for nobody, having no dependence on anybody" (cited in Thirsk, 1967: 111).

These regional differences between the traditional moral economy of the English village in the south and east on the one hand, and the scattered individual settlements of the north and west on the other meant that the profound economic and social changes of the sixteenth century would affect England in different ways. Throughout the sixteenth century, the north and west remained, as one contemporary put it, "that dark country, which is the receptacle of all schism and rebellion," and was the locus of the most significant popular uprisings of the century, the Pilgrimage of Grace and Ket's Rebellion (cited in Thirsk, 1967: 112). The enclosures of the common fields, which spread throughout the century, also had dramatically transformed the moral economy of the English village in the fertile farmlands of the south and east, setting in motion processes of social dislocation whose effects were not fully felt until the first half of the seventeenth century.

In addition to the enclosures, other social and demographic changes were being felt in the countryside. The population of England was growing dramatically, nearly doubling between 1540 and 1640. This led to increased pressure on the market because farming techniques developed far more slowly than the population. Prices rose rapidly and wages lagged woefully behind, and the gap between prices and wages increased most dramatically between 1550 and 1650, as chart 5.1 makes clear (see also Hirst, 1986: 2).

The commercialization of agriculture also indicated a shift in the patterns of land ownership. The percentage of land owned by the great landlords remained constant at 15–20 percent between 1436 and 1690; the percentage owned by the gentry increased from 25 percent to nearly 50 percent; and the percentage owned by the yeomen increased from 20 percent to 25–33 percent. The amount of land owned by the church and by the crown declined from 25–35 percent to 5–10 percent as the crown first sold church lands and then its own as fiscal expedients to compensate for deepening fiscal crisis (Mingay, 1976: 59).

These social, demographic, and economic changes were experienced very differently in the various regions of England, and also by the various social classes that composed rural society. At the top of the pyramid were the peers, the hereditary nobility, which included barons, earls, dukes, and viscounts, who numbered roughly 55 in 1603. Unlike their French counterparts, English peers were not exempt from taxation, not barred from marrying commoners, nor were they prohibited from participating in trade. Thus, their "status was empty without money," and most of their

Agricultural Prices and Wage Rates in Southern England, 1450–1650

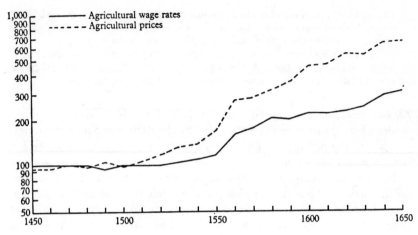

Source: Joan Thirsk, *The Agrarian History of England and Wales, 1500–1640* (Cambridge, 1967), p. 609.

Note: 1450–99 = 100.

revenues developed out of the ancient obligations of the peasantry (Hirst, 1986: 12; see also Smith, 1970: 46). But like their French counterparts, the peers were undergoing important changes in both their economic and social positions, and in their relationship to the crown. Stone's important work on the Elizabethan peerage, *The Crisis of the Aristocracy* (1967), documents a precipitous decline in all aspects of aristocratic life, and especially relative to the gentry. His collective biography of the English ruling class remains unsurpassed; he argues (1972: 29) that

> the aristocracy lost military power, territorial possessions and prestige; that their real income declined sharply under Elizabeth, largely due to conspicuous consumption, but recovered equally strongly in the early seventeenth century, largely due to buoyant land revenues and lavish royal favors.

In England, as in France and Spain, the traditional function of the hereditary nobility had been military, but after the Wars of the Roses, in which the English aristocracy had exercised near-autonomous military power, its military capability declined precipitously. By the sixteenth century the English aristocracy had begun to wane, and it paled in comparison to the bellicose vitality of its French counterpart. Economically, socially, and politically, the English aristocracy was declining. Hill writes (1967: 16):

> The numbers, wealth and political influence of the greater aristocracy had been diminished: by death on the battlefield or the scaffold or by lack of male heirs, by habit of ostentatious living and a traditional reluctance to take part in trade, by the growing expenses of war and its diminishing profitability as the English were expelled from France, by fines and attainders in England, by the secularization of the abbeys and consequent loss of patronage and perquisites.

As one contemporary noted (cited in Hill, 1967: 16), "Although many modern families have been great gainers by the destruction of monasteries, yet the ancient nobility . . . found themselves much impoverished thereby, both in power and profit."

Though the aristocracy's difficulties "were at bottom financial," as landholdings and purchasing power both declined, Stone also enumerates several social factors that led the aristocracy to become "even more obsessed with status than with money" (Stone, 1967: 4, 108). As a status group, its crisis was social:

> The decay of their military power in men, arms, castles, and will to resist; the granting of titles of honor for cash not merit, in too great numbers, and to too unworthy persons; the change in their attitude towards the tenantry from suppliers of manpower to suppliers of rent; the undermining of their electoral influence due to the rise of deeply felt political and religious issues; the increasing preference for extravagant living in the city instead of hospitable living in the countryside; the spread throughout the propertied classes of a bookish education, acquired at school and university, and the demand by the State for an administrative elite of proved competence, irrespective of the claims of rank. . . . [Stone, 1967: 351]

As the nobles declined economically, their efforts to offset their decline and restore their fortunes included squeezing more revenues from their feudal dependents and searching for political offices that might serve as a hedge against economic decline. Thus, Stone suggests, "Their financial recovery was achieved by trading respect and loyalty for cash" (1966: 75–76). In this way, they found a monarchy most obliging to assist them in their efforts to recoup their economic losses through an intensification of status distinctions. Here, as in France, the social buttressing of the aristocracy by the crown indicates a similar royal ambivalence in the relationship of the crown to its ruling class. On the one hand, royal favors affirming status distinctions, and lavish pensions, lucrative tax farms, and the granting of monopolies allowed peers to maintain their life-style of conspicuous consumption and indicate royal support for the aristocracy and an effort to reverse their fortunes. The Statute of Apparel in 1533 specified the types of clothing that were forbidden to people below each of twelve social ranks. For example, wearing sable was forbidden to anyone not a baron or above, and it was forbidden to anyone below the rank of men with over £ 5 per year (which included yeomen, freeholders, husbandmen, etc.) to wear most kinds of foreign cloth, any kind of silk, and any cloth costing more than 6s. 8d. per yard.

On the other hand, the monarchy saw a strong and independent aristocracy as a potential threat to its own centralizing project; the Tudors, Stone writes (1974: 71), "deliberately built up the authority of the gentry as a means of destroying the local power bases of their over-mighty subjects." By the early seventeenth century, "the process of subordinating the English nobility to the crown had been effectively completed," and though the nobles still might have exerted authority in the localities, their recovery never restored them to the political position of a *ruling* class, though they remained at the top of a status pyramid (Hirst, 1986: 55; see also Hill, 1986: 26).[1]

The celebrated "rise of the gentry" is the mirror image of the decline of the aristocracy, and as such, is more apparent than real, reflecting other phenomena less than manifesting its own. To be sure, the gentry grew sharply, tripling (5,000 to 15,000) between 1540 and 1640; that it constituted 2 to 3 percent of the population and owned close to 40 percent of the land (Hirst, 1986: 14). As the gentry commercialized its holdings to take advantage of trade opportunities, it left the insular and introverted world of the countryside and developed close associations with London merchants, who, in turn, began to purchase estates in the countryside (Durston, 1981). The commercialization of agriculture demanded new forms of productive relationships in the fields, which, even when unaccompanied by enclosures, transformed the customary relationships between rural workers and estate owners, especially concerning social control. "Nothing is more unprofitable than a farm in tillage in the hands of servants where the master's eye is not daily upon them," one Yorkshire steward wrote to his master in the 1620s (cited in Thirsk, 1967: 198).

Below the gentry were the various ranks of peasants, whose rank was determined by their relationship to land tenancy. The freeholders, or yeomen, were, according to Thomas Fuller (cited in Thirsk, 1967: 301) "an estate of people almost peculiar to England, living in the temperate zone between greatness and want." In the sixteenth and early seventeenth centuries, the yeomen were making that transition from want to greatness, "advancing as a class both absolutely and relatively," often at the expense of smaller holders and the laboring poor (Thirsk, 1967: 305; see also Hill, 1986: 46). The "chief force behind peasant enclosures," the yeomen were

raising sheep, consolidating and commercializing their agricultural production, and profiting economically from whatever technical advances they
might (Moore, 1967: 11). These middling property owners were "acquiring
a sense of identity which detached them from the previously relatively
homogenous village community, and led them to devise new mechanisms
for imposing their own conceptions of order on those below them"
(Underdown, 1986: 28). One Suffolk man linked the rise of the yeoman
and the decline of the aristocracy in transforming English class relations
by 1618, when he wrote:

> Continual underliving, saving, and the immunities from the costly charges of
> these unfaithful times, do make them so to grow with wealth of this world that
> whilst many of the better sort, as having passed their uttermost period, do suffer
> an utter declination, these only do arise, and so lay such strong, sure, and deep
> foundations that from thence in time are derived many noble and worthy families
> [cited in Thirsk, 1967: 305].

Beneath the yeomen were copyholders and leaseholders, who held their
land for the duration of a lease, either for the life of the holder or for a
fixed length of time. The renewing of leases was a potential source of
revenue for both local landlords and the crown, and the small holder was
also prey to the vagaries of the market and hit hardest by enclosures. This
led to an "almost revolutionary deterioration of [his] position" as the
small cultivator struggled "to protect his interests against the changes
caused by the growth of the great estate" (Thirsk, 1967: 310, 231).

Below these layers of the peasantry were the laborers, cottagers, and
paupers, who constituted up to 47 percent of the population, and whose
economic status was also in sharp decline (Thirsk, 1967: 399). The poor
were "getting relatively and absolutely poorer, were becoming a permanent part of the population, unable to spare the labour of their children to
give them the education which was the necessary condition without which
upward mobility was virtually impossible" (Hill, 1986: 46).

The decline of the moral economy of the traditional English village was
the consequence of this unprecedented amount of upward and downward
mobility among the rural classes in Tudor and early Stuart England.
Throughout the countryside the divide between rich and poor was growing,
and traversing it was becoming less and less likely, for "new and sharper
class divisions were arising" as a result of these profound changes (Hill,
1986: 46). The dramatic upward and downward mobility generated serious
social dislocation and insecurity:

> In the upper ranks of society, high social mobility generated jealousy, envy, and
> despair among the failures, and status anxiety among the successful. In the

lower ranks extraordinary geographic mobility and periodic catastrophes due to epidemic disease, combined to shatter the traditional ties to family, kin, and neighbors, and to wrench men away from their familiar associations and surroundings. [Stone, 1972: 112]

The enclosures of the sixteenth century can no longer be seen as the preeminent cause of the English Revolution, for recent research has downplayed the enclosures to stress more demographic factors, as well as more local political factors (Goldstone, 1985). Still, the enclosures represent perhaps the most graphic and profound *illustration* of the impact of expanding population, increased commercialization of agriculture, and the growing gap between prices and wages. It is through the enclosures that we witness "the slowly disintegrating village community," the erosion of the customary and traditional bases of the moral economy of the English village (Hill, 1964: 122). The enclosures were symbolically important, representing "the final blow that destroyed the whole structure of English peasant society embodied in the traditional village" as they "greatly strengthened the larger landlords and broke the back of the English peasantry" (Moore, 1967: 21, 28). The enclosures, writes Tawney (1912: 150), were "encroachments made by lords of manors or their farmers upon the land over which the manorial population had common rights or which lay in the open arable fields." The possibilities of the international wool market encouraged the amalgamation of holdings into larger leasehold farms, the transformation of common fields into grazing areas for the lord's sheep, and the increasing commercialization of agricultural production to permit more profitable participation in international trade. In the lowland districts, "where common grazing rights were highly prized because the pasture steadily diminished as the arable was enlarged, enclosure constituted . . . a painful and socially disturbing reorganization of land and ways of living" (Thirsk, 1967: 6).

The dissolution of the oppressive coherence of the preindustrial English village was profound and devastating. Thirsk writes (1967: 225):

In champion country, people had to work together amicably, to agree upon crop rotations, stints of common pasture, the upkeep and improvement of their grazings and meadows, the clearing of ditches, the fencing of fields. They toiled side by side in the fields, they walked together from field to village, from farm to heath, morning, afternoon and evening. They all depended on common resources for their fuel, for bedding, and fodder for their stock, and by pooling so many of the necessities of livelihood, they were disciplined from early youth to submit to the rules and the customs of their community. After enclosure, when every man could fence off his own piece of territory, and warn his neighbors off, the discipne of sharing things fairly with one's neighbors was relaxed, and every household became an island unto itself. This was the great revolution in men's lives, greater than all the economic changes following enclosure.

Underdown agrees (1986: 284):

> Enclosure and the logic of the market often destroyed the villager's access not only to land, but also to the commons on which the sports and festivals ritually expressing the neighborhood's identity had been held. A conception of land as a commodity to be exploited for profit, protected by absolute rights of ownership, had triumphed over an older one under which ancient custom had guaranteed rights of access and use by the community. In that change a process occupying several centuries came close to fruition.

The "Ballad of Nowadays," penned in 1520, expresses the change eloquently (cited in Tawney, 1912: 149):

> Envy waxeth wonders strong,
> The Riche doth the poore wrong,
> God of his mercy suffereth long
> The Devil his workes to worke.
> The Townes go downe, the land decayes;
> Of cornfields, playne layes,
> Gret men makinthe now a dayes
> A shepcote in the Church.
>
> The places that we Right holy call
> Ordeyned ffor Christyan buriall
> Off them to make an ox-stall
> These men be wonders wyse;
> Commons to close and kepe,
> Poor folk or bred to cry and wepe;
> Towns pulled down to pastur shepe,
> This ys the new gyse.

Enclosure symbolized a dramatic transformation in the relationship between people and property, between lord and tenant, and among the tenants themselves; the "traditional bonds of lordship and natural obedience were strained and finally broken" as the rights to property came to dominate over the customary obligations that various classes owed to one another, a "definite decline in the sense of responsibility to dependents and a widening psychological gulf between gentry and peasantry" (Smith, 1970: 259; Thirsk, 1967: 464). At the same time enclosures heralded the "breakdown of practical cooperation and brotherliness among men" (Tawney, 1912: 338). And, as we will see below, the disintegration of the traditional moral economy produced an important set of reactions against both enclosing landlords and the centralizing monarchy.

In the cities as well, profound changes mark the Tudor era. As the population of the nation as a whole expanded, nowhere was this more acutely registered than in London, where the population jumped from 40,000 in 1500 to over 250,000 in 1600, and to more than 400,000 on the eve of the Revolution in 1640 (Hirst, 1986: 2). London was the center of a rapidly expanding commercial society, by 1600 handling seven-eights of all English trade (Hill, 1967: 29). London merchants were divided among three groups whose different economic activities and social positions eventually led to different political positions during the Civil War (Brenner, 1974). The older merchants relied on monopolies for income, and were deeply tied to the monarchy, upon which they relied for economic favors. A new set of merchants had arisen from the ranks of the artisans and small traders or had come to London as the sons of rising gentry and yeomen; they favored decreased royal intervention in the market and advocated freer trade. The Merchant Adventurers constituted an anomalous third group, according to Brenner (1974: 82–83): newer merchants involved in older-style trade monopolies, and their fortunes were mixed. This tripartite division among the merchants helps to understand the divisions among the merchants in the Civil War; the older monopolists, "court merchants," sided with the crown, and the newer free trade merchants sided with Parliament (the Merchant Adventurers were almost evenly divided).

Below the merchants was a wide array of craftsmen, artisans, and journeymen, as well as small traders and shopkeepers, who exercised considerable economic control over their product and, through the guilds, considerable control over the production process as well. Their economic autonomy was coupled with a strong sense of moral economy, of traditions, again traceable to guild organization (and later to the organization of Independent and Dissenting church meetings), that stressed decentralized political decision making within the community. Below them were the nonapprenticed laborers and urban poor.

Here, too, the great economic changes were having deleterious effects on all ranks below the merchants, for merchant capital was removing production from the crafts guilds and taking it into the countryside, where local peasants were working outside the control of the guilds. The decline of guild autonomy spelled the breakdown of artisan control over the production process and the products themselves, and frequently led to outbreaks of discontent. Take, for example, the great London riot known as Evil Mayday in 1517, when mobs of apprentices, shopkeepers, artisans, and women attacked the Italian, French, and other foreign craftsmen and merchants in the city. The economic resentment of mobs was so great, they declared, because "the poor English artificers could scarce get any living" (cited in Zagorin, 1982, vol. 1: 235).

As commerce was expanding dramatically, so too was industrial manufacturing; in fact, the expansion of commerce and industry in England far outpaced that in France or any other European country. Between 1540 and 1640 England was "marked by a remarkable speeding up of production" as the output of older industries multiplied four-, five-, or even sixfold (Nef, 1967: 209). The textile industry and coal production are only two of the many industries that underwent such remarkable growth. Industrial growth was evidenced in more than increased quantity; there were dramatic and decisive shifts in the goal of production, a "shift in the major resources of capital and labor away from production primarily for the sake of beauty, of delight in contemplation, toward production primarily for the sake of usefulness in the purely economic sense of substantial comforts in greater quantities" (Nef, 1967: 211). The transformation of the organization of production was equally significant as the guild system gave way to the putting out of craft production, from city to countryside, and there was a "steady strengthening of private enterprise at the expense of government regulation and participation in mining and manufacturing" (Nef, 1967: 211).

The Tudor State and the "Administrative Revolution"

Tudor political administration counterposed a strong and relatively centralized monarchy to a loose confederation of political and economic interests centered around the wool trade, and the economic and social status of the local administrators in county and shire government. Thus, Tudor political administration rested upon a triangular relationship among the king, a coalition of landed gentry and urban merchants, and the hereditary ruling class and gentry in the county government, all of which were suspended over both "the people" and the rural and urban poor. Thomas More's somewhat sarcastic definition of government as "a certain conspiracy of rich men procuring their own commodities under the name and title of a Common Wealth" was only slightly exaggerated, although the tensions among these elements of the foundation remains unobserved (cited in Tawney, 1912: 372).

The development of the English state is marked by the presence and absence of forces that structured the efforts of Tudor and Stuart kings to construct an absolute monarchy. Although there had been a relatively long tradition of centralized government, the absolutist effort could not rely on a national bureaucracy, expansive fiscal resources, or a permanent army, all of which would be important to tame the autonomous impulses of various social groups and regions. The early centralization of the monarchy under the Norman and Angevin kings, in fact, gave rise to correspondingly strong Parliaments, which were the repository of unified noble aspirations because the landed feudal class had not fragmented into semiautonomous jurisdictions. Parliament provided a strong negative check on royal powers, and also precluded the development of a freestanding royal bureaucracy, for local administration was largely carried out by noble judicial and administrative structures at the local level. The crown "accepted the basic pattern of local authority rather than attempting to penetrate it with its own bureaucracy. Government functions of justice, military organizations, economic regulation, and taxation were exercised by local landowners in the king's name" (Thomas, 1978: 79). Local administration was accomplished by sheriffs and justices of the peace, offices staffed by local nobles.

The crown also lacked a standing army as a result of England's geographic position; the apparent lack of a need for an army had also led to the demilitarization of the nobility, which, as we have seen above, freed it for capitalist agriculture and commercial ventures. As a result of the absence of a standing army and a structure of local political administration, the crown was "dependent upon aid from the magnates when it came to suppressing revolts" (Thomas, 1978: 79).

Further, the English state lacked an adequate tax base. The king was forced to live "on his own," largely from fines and from residual feudal dues from customs and ancient crown lands. Parliament controlled the voting of extraordinary taxation for war, which took the form of the subsidy. Sale of crown lands and sale of monastic lands would provide some income, but rarely enough, as we shall observe. The low level of taxation, in turn, inhibited the growth of the bureaucracy and impeded the possible development of a standing army because there would be no money to pay them. Thus, the English crown was faced with a constant fiscal crisis, "arising from an inability to cope with cumulative inflationary pressures due to inflexibility in the early modern English tax system" (Goldstone, 1986: 285).

The task of the Tudor and Stuart kings, as they saw it, was to circumvent these deficiencies that might impede state centralization, and to attempt to concentrate royal power at the top so as better to pursue the growing possibilities provided by international trade, and to participate more fully in geopolitical competition. For the early Tudors, the tasks were relatively small and their progress was incremental. Henry VII inherited the tradition of state centralization matched by an equally long tradition of opposition by customarily privileged groups, especially the hereditary peerage. The decimation of the aristocracy during the Wars of the Roses, 1455–85, permitted Henry VII, the first Tudor, who reigned from 1485 to 1509, to establish the strongest claims to a centralized monarchy that England had ever witnessed. Henry was a capable ruler who realized that "in order to be strong he had to be rich," so he attempted to raise his income through the more expeditious use of household revenues and increased taxation (Elton, 1974: 47). This latter method of revenue raising provoked violent opposition, as in Yorkshire in 1489, when war taxation prompted popular rebellion, and in the Cornish rebellion of 1497, during which the common people argued that grants to the king should be dependent upon the crown's undertaking of specific military expeditions (Fletcher, 1963: 13–14). (Each of these uprisings was brief and easily suppressed.) Henry also managed to balance his budget, if only by a small amount. In 1497 royal income totaled £ 142,000; expenditures, £ 138,000 (Elton, 1974: 53). By the end of his reign he had even accumulated a small surplus, which he bequeathed to his son.

The surplus was hardly sufficient for the ambitious Henry VIII, who reigned from 1509 to 1546. It was soon exhausted as the demands of war and poor financial administration depleted the treasury. Cardinal Wolsey, his chief administrator, determined to raise £ 800,000 in taxes in 1523, a startling jump from the £ 62,000 collected in 1513. Unable to make do with existing revenues or effectively to increase them, Wolsey devised a method of collection to be spread out over four years, but only £ 136,578 was collected by 1525 (Elton, 1974: 77; Fletcher, 1968: 13).

To resolve what they perceived as a deepening fiscal crisis, Henry and Wolsey in 1525 announced the Amicable Grant, hoping to parlay their military victory over the French at Pavia into a windfall profit for the royal treasury because it was, as Wolsey implored the king, a "pity it were they should, for lack or default of money, be impeached" (in Bernard, 1986: 53). The grant, "perhaps the most violent financial exaction in English history," called for voluntary contributions equivalent to one-sixth of the value of all goods owned by laypeople and one-third of the value of all goods owned by the clergy (Pollard, 1965: 142). Hardly designed in an amicable spirit, the grant provoked widespread refusal to pay. Reports to the king indicated that compliance was not forthcoming. "The burden was so grevous, that it was denied," wrote one reporter; another commented that "in the same season through all the realm, this demand was utterly denied, so that the Commissioners could bring nothing to pass" (in Bernard, 1986: 115).

Resistance to the grant centered in the clothing towns of southwest Suffolk and around Laverham, Sudbury, and Hadleigh, and the Stour valley; here Bernard observes a "spontaneous and understandable reaction to the unemployment, or fear of unemployment, arising from the impact, or feared impact, on their local economy of the Amicable Grant" (Bernard, 1986: 148; see also ibid.: 136). Such firm resistance prompted

Wolsey to withdraw the demand for the grant, persuading the government to reduce its demands, and reminding Henry that "the monarchy was still founded upon an implicit partnership between King and people, and that the King's will could be enforced only so far as it did not actively and seriously harm the interests of the dominant classes of the nation, the taxpaying classes" (Wernham, 1966: 109). The failure of the grant suggests the weakness of the Tudor government in achieving a resolution to its fiscal crisis, but it also suggests Henry's flexibility; the king was able to withdraw his demand and not press the drive for absolutist centralization too far. In this sense the grant reveals Tudor government at its "least effective but also at its most ambitious" (Bernard, 1986: 157).

Following Cardinal Wolsey's death, Henry VIII engaged Thomas Cromwell to carry out a series of administrative reforms, which, taken together, amounted to an "administrative revolution" in the words of G. R. Elton, the reign's most careful historian (Elton, 1966, 1973, 1974; Starkey, 1986). The administrative revolution, he argues, centered on the increase in royal bureaucratic control over financial administration, which would "forge a financial system out of the chaos of separate treasuries" and thus free the king to pursue his ambitious foreign policy objectives (Starkey, 1986: 205). The essential ingredient of the Tudor administrative revolution was the concept of national sovereignty, the primacy of the political nation over the interests of any of its constituent parts. National sovereignty implied the supremacy of the state over social classes, the primacy of law over feudal custom and privilege, and the primacy of the monarchy over religious doctrine. In this sense the administrative revolution resembles Cardinal Richelieu's revolution without reform in early-seventeenth-century France. A century before France did so, the English royal advisers had developed an ideology of national sovereignty, which, like the doctrine of reason of state, promoted the autonomy of the state. And like Richelieu's administrative revolution, the Tudor revolution in government attempted to separate political relationships (relations between classes and the state) from social and economic relationships; its architects believed that administration could be transformed without a concomitant transformation of structural relations of production. In each case "external forces exerting pressure upon fiscal administration were of sufficient magnitude to call for extensive, deliberate restructuring" and yet each was marked by a revolution without reform, and was, therefore, guaranteed to provoke profound opposition (Alsop, 1986: 152).

The rise of Thomas Cromwell in Tudor political administration also parallels the rise of Cardinal Richelieu in Bourbon political administration. Cromwell was motivated more by political Protestantism than by any doctrinal disputes with Rome, and his meteoric rise in the administration, including the amassing of powerful titles and positions and a substantial personal fortune, also finds close associations with Richelieu. During his administration, a series of reforms both increased royal control over the realm and institutionalized political administration, "providing a more centralized, less personal and potentially more efficient machinery" (Elton, 1973: 98). Cromwell placed a check on the spread of enclosures, administered the dissolution of the monasteries, restored traditional tillage rights to holders of copy and lease, promoted the textile industry and trade, and helped to rebuild decaying towns. His Poor Laws were designed "to provide relief to the victims of society rather than merely punish those whom destitution made a social danger" (Elton, 1973: 122). Landlords, the king wrote in 1538, should so govern that "the poor people be not oppressed, but that they may live after their sorts and qualities" (cited in James, 1974: 38).

Cromwell was hardly a flamboyant Renaissance royal councillor who surrounded himself with the accoutrements of political power. He was a sober bureaucrat whose sole mission was the nationalization of the governmental apparatus, to turn England into "a unified, independent sovereign state, ruled by a constitutional monarch through national and bureaucratic institutions" (Coleman, 1986: 2). Toward that end he built up the power of the Privy Council as a bureaucratic mechanism of state centralization equipped to deal with foreign affairs, domestic issues, the king's household, and the redress of petitions (Elton, 1966: 342). Cromwell sought to transform Parliament "from a body of local representatives charged with communicating the locality's grievances to the king's government into an aspiring partner in the political government of the nation" (Elton, 1966: 249). He rationalized political administration into a bureaucratic organization, and reorganized the treasury under the Exchequer. He abandoned the pension as the foundation of royal finance, and shifted administration from personal servants to bureaucratic departments of state (Alsop, 1986: 156). By 1532 Cromwell had begun to act "as a special treasurer for national revenues," and by 1534 he promoted a subsidy that for the first time in English history justified the levying of a tax on the grounds of the king's service to the commonweal, rather than pleading necessity because of war or the threat of war (Elton, 1973: 159).

The pivotal moment in the administrative revolution in both France and England appears, on the surface at least, to be a change in traditional religious arrangements. In France this occurred in 1636 when Richelieu entered the Thirty Years War on the side of the Protestant princes and against the Catholic Habsburgs, a move seen by many as a declaration of political independence from Rome. In England this came exactly a century earlier with declaration of the Act of Supremacy in 1636. By declaring the king to be supreme in England, Henry not only resolved his marital problems but freed his hands to move against the Catholic clergy, to incorporate a politically and economicly independent social group, and to bring the bishops, "but half our subjects," under control (cited in Harriss, 1963: 13). One immediate consequence was economic: the crown's dissolution of the monasteries and the sale of church lands (mostly to local gentry) brought windfall profits to the royal treasury (Wernham, 1966: 144; Dietz, 1964: 46). By exploiting Henry's prerogatives over the church, Henry and Cromwell had a more reliable short-term source of revenue, and had also drastically altered the pattern of rural landownership. In the West Riding district of Yorkshire, for example, the church owned 43.8 percent of all land in 1535; by 1546 it owned only 17.2 percent. The crown's share had meanwhile increased from 8.8 percent to 26.8 percent (Smith, 1970: 214).

The Tudor revolution in government was a comprehensive effort at political unification and the rationalization of the nation's finances. It involved enlargement of the monarch's powers and a correlative extension of the sacred foundations of his power. Henry VIII was cast as an "agent of the godhead" so that "the state, embodied in its monarch, took on an air of almost divine, at first in the eyes of its own propagandists, and later in the eyes of most of its subjects" (Williams, 1963: 44–45). Justified by the conception of the divine right of kings, coupled with the notion of reason of state, Cromwell pressed for the curtailment of individual privileges and the suppression of various pockets of religious, regional, and political autonomy that might weaken or threaten the process of bureaucratization.

Administrative decentralization was combated by efforts to develop a central judicial apparatus as well, a process that Hirst (1986: 34) calls the "single major centralizing force in English history." The Court of Augmentations was established in 1536 to administer the lands of the dissolved monasteries as well as all lands purchased by the kings, to insure that they would not be administered by local landlords. Two more courts, the Court of First Fruits and Tenths and the Court of Wards and Liveries, were established in 1540, and assize judges were used to tighten up local judicial administration and oversee the increasingly independent justices of the peace.

Cromwell and Henry were also motivated by persistent fiscal crisis, which became progressively worse during the last years of the reign as new wars on the Continent stretched the treasury beyond its capacity to respond without serious increases in royal income. In the 1540s the wars with France and Scotland cost £ 2.2 million (Thirsk, 1967: 263), and although Parliament granted over £ 656,000 in subsidies between 1541 and

1547, more than £ 130,000 over what had been granted for the entire thirty years previous, it was still not enough. The war against France in 1544 prompted Henry to implement a series of fiscal expedients, such as the increased sale of crown lands and timber, devaluation of the currency, domestic loans backed by the London money market, foreign loans raised in Antwerp, enforced collection of delinquent revenues already owed to the crown, and even a set of short-term loans and a levy on the clergy of £ 60,000. One report noted that "the exchequer hath nothing, the chamber ministereth nothing, so that all resteth upon the mint and the augmentation" (Richardson, 1954: 36, 46ff.).

The administrative revolution and the increasingly desperate search for revenues were not uneventfully foisted upon a passive population. Two reforms—the abolition of the Welsh language and the abolition of diversity of religion—were never implemented because of the fear of popular opposition (as various reforms under Richelieu were also abandoned because of the threat of resistance). Throughout the century England was the scene of popular uprisings that fused antimonarchical sentiments with religious passions and strong elements of class antagonisms. Even after Cromwell himself was stripped of office, tried for treason, and executed by order of his king (1540), these sporadic rebellions continued to plague the Tudor monarchy.

Opposition to Tudor Centralization

> *For, upon these taxations*
> *The clothiers all, not able to maintain*
> *The many to them longing, have put off*
> *The spinsters, carders, fullers, weavers, who*
> *Unfit for other life, compelled by hunger*
> *And lack for other means, in desperate manner*
> *Daring the event to the teeth, are all in uproar,*
> *And danger serves among them.*
> —William Shakespeare
> *Henry VIII*, act I, scene 2

The Tudor administrative revolution was an effort to generate sufficient revenues for the implementation of a foreign policy independent of any domestic social constraints while freezing traditional social relationships that would prevent further erosion of the traditional social foundations of the monarchy. In addition, the sixteenth century witnessed a constant religious tension in England, as in France, as the ideational foundations of political power were an object of contention. Each Tudor monarch faced significant political opposition, and though the social groups and ideological motivations of the alliances that comprised the oppositional groups shifted in each case, the major rebellions often carried similar themes. Many of the popular rebellions were local risings, parochial and conservative in their outlook, triggered by perceived excesses of the English Reformation and the radical religious policies adopted by Cromwell and Henry VIII.

The chief cause of popular rebellion under the Tudors was the abridgment of traditional relationships, either between landlord and cultivator or between rural classes and the central government. In some cases popular disturbances resembled peasant rebellions in medieval England; they were often caused by actions of "landowners or governments, or both, together, which altered the customary relationship or disappointed normal expectations," that is, the rebellions were often defenses of the traditional moral economy against outside interference (Hilton, 1973: 118). Enclosure of arable lands often was accomplished without incident, taking place, as one resident of Somerset noted in 1578, "at their will and pleasure, without denial of anyone" (cited in Thirsk, 1967: 74). Still, enclosure of common lands disrupted the moral economy, and protestors seeking to "restore common to common again" were inspired "by the values of a vaguely sensed 'moral economy,' in contrast to the values of the market economy now being adopted by increasing numbers of the middling sort" (Tawney, 1912: 334; Underdown, 1986: 118).

Enclosures remained the "main target" of agrarian protest during the entire Tudor period, exacerbating class conflict on the land (Zagorin, 1982, vol. 1: 209). "Rich men, to make room for themselves, would jostle the poor people out of their commons," noted Thomas Fuller (cited in Underdown, 1986: 19). Tawney concludes his pathbreaking if rather exaggerated tome on the enclosures with imaginary reflections of a peasant, musing about life without enclosures (1912: 409):

> True our system is wasteful, and fruitful of many small disputes. True, a large estate can be managed more economically than a small one. True, pasture-farming yields higher profits than tillage. Nevertheless . . . our wasteful husbandry feeds many households where your economical methods would feed few. In our ill-arranged fields and scrubby commons most families hold a share, though it be but a few roods. In our unenclosed village there are a few rich, but there are few destitute, save when God sends a bad harvest, and we all starve together. We do not like your improvements which ruin half the honest men affected by them. We do not choose that the ancient customs of our village should be changed!

The threat to the traditional moral economy of the English countryside came from both landlords and royal agents, and was exacerbated by the dramatic inflationary price spiral, and the difficulties of English agriculture in surmounting bad harvests and crop failures to expand sufficiently to accommodate England's expanding population.

Enclosure was of serious concern to the crown as well as to the enclosing landlords because it led to depopulation of the countryside and increased problems of vagrancy and rural poverty. The sixteenth century lived "in terror of the tramp," as Robert Cecil warned in 1597 (cited in Tawney, 1912: 273): "the decaying and plucking down of houses, . . . and not only the plucking down of some few houses, but the depopulating of whole towns . . . and keeping of a shepherd only, whereby many subjects are turned out without habitation, and fill the country with rogues and idle persons." The crown was concerned because, as one statute against depopulation noted, "the defense of this land against our enemies outward is enfeebled and impaired" (cited in Tawney, 1912: 343).

Some of the major rebellions of the period pitted the centrifugal forces of the locality against the centripetal forces of the state. Henry VIII's unification of the nation had substituted royal power for the traditional power of the local gentry and magnates, who saw themselves as defenders of local rights against the centralizing state. Rebels opposed innovation; often, as in the Pilgrimage of Grace or the Prayerbook Rebellion, these defenses of local political tradition fused with religious issues as rebels confronted state centralization through its innovative policies of religious centralization. "Even when the old religion was the cause that took the gentry into the field," Tawney reminds us (1912: 318), "the humbler rebels were brought out as much by hatred of agrarian as of religious innovations." Thus, "though all classes were united against the regime . . . all classes were not moved by the same degree by the same grievances."

The Pilgrimage of Grace, for example, was set off by the Act of Supremacy, which was seen in the local communities as a "harbinger of further interference from without" and stirred large numbers of rebels to call for Cromwell's removal, the return of local privileges to the north counties, and the reversal of Reformation policies (James, 1974: 46; see also Fletcher, 1968: 27). It was a genuine "mass movement" that brought a "wide spectrum of the governing class" into an alliance with popular forces protesting against "the unprecedented intrusion by the Crown into their local communities and traditional ways" (Fletcher, 1968: 50; Williams, 1979: 321). The king, they insisted, "should demand no more money of his subjects except for the defense of the realm" (Fletcher, 1968: 37), and one popular ballad declared, "This cursed Cromwell by his great policy/ In this realm has caused great exaction" (cited in Williams, 1979: 322). The principal grievances "arose from changes in lordship and land-ownership following the dissolution of the monasteries" (Thirsk, 1967: 219); one can discern a correlation between the geography of revolt and the patterns of landownership (Smith, 1970: 197). The Pilgrimage of Grace was "an important turning point in the complex relationship between the Crown, the nobility, and the gentry, and one whose results were to the advantage of the Crown" (Smith, 1970: 205). The revolt failed, ultimately, because of the crown's success at undermining the political power of the magnates at the local level, so that their authority "was no longer an adequate basis for successful rebellion; and because devotion to a principle was not in itself sufficient basis for a movement powerful enough to defeat the Crown" (Smith, 1970: 262).

Similarly, the Western Rebellion in 1547 was, on the surface, against Edward's religious policies, and even demanded the return to Latin of the celebration of the Mass. "We will have our old service of Matins, Mass, Evensong, and Procession in the Latin and not in English, as it was before," they proclaimed (cited in Rose-Troup, 1913: Appendix K). "And so we the Cornish men utterly refuse this new English." But underneath the religious rebellion was a resistance to the erosion of local power and prestige of the western gentry (Fletcher, 1960: 61).

The revolt of the gentry against Mary Tudor's announcement of her impending Spanish marriage, which became known as Wyatt's Rebellion, was also a political revolt with a religious mask. Mary's mission had been to restore England to obedience to the Vatican and thereby save her country from the mortal sin of heresy, but numbers of the gentry saw this rapprochement with Rome in political terms, fearing "for their country's independence" in a decidedly "nationalist" revolt (Wernham, 1966: 214, 211). Though unable to dissuade the queen from her plans, the gentry did learn that regional, provincial rebellion was less efficacious as a means to effect political change, and that grievances channeled into parliamentary opposition might have more impact.

Other revolts cast the landlords as the innovators, abridging traditional rights and privileges, and it was they who were opposed by the common people in the localities. These revolts "were *not* caused by cultivators protesting the loss of land, but by rural artisans and squatters fighting against the conversion of waste and forest to arable fields and protesting food scarcity and high prices" (Goldstone, 1986: 263). In the Northern Rebellion of 1536, for example, "poor commoners gathered in hundreds to throw down enclosures and defend tenurial privileges" (Thirsk, 1967: 408). In 1549, the culmination of a decade during which prices for agricultural commodities rose to unprecedented levels, there were more riots and rebellions than in any other year of the reign. A revolt in Yorkshire that year consisted of a plan "at first rush to kill and destroy such gentlemen and men of substance about them as were favorers of the king's precedings or which would resist them" (cited in Dickens, 1939: 243). Four members of the gentry were actually murdered, and "after they had stripped them of their clothes and purses, they left them naked behind them in the plain fields for the crows to feed on" (cited in Jordan, 1960: 452–53).

In June 1549 a group in Norfolk threw down the hedges of the enclosing landlords. Ket's Rebellion, "the greatest agrarian uprising of the period," was "less a rising against the State than a practical illustration of the peasants' ideals, a mixture of May-Day demonstration and successful strike embodied in one gigantic festival or rural good fellowship," according to Tawney (1912: 332), and a "sad resistance of common folk caught up in the turmoil of economic change," according to a less sanguine observer (Zagorin, 1982, vol. 1: 208, 213). "Exasperated at the exploitation of the gentry," the rebels made several demands that were distinctly economic, among them the abolition of enclosures, the protection of the commons from noble intrusion ("that no lord of no manor shall come on upon the commons"), the protection of copy and freeholders to the profits from their lands, and the now-traditional demand that "all bond men may be made free" (Tawney, 1912: 335; see also Fletcher, 1960: 77).

Opposition to enclosure was specific to it as innovation, not to enclosure in general: "It is not where a man doth enclose and hedge in his own proper ground, where no man hath commons," as John Hale put the case in 1548, "but it is meant thereby, when any man hath taken away and enclosed any other men's commons, or hath pulled down houses of husbandry, and converted the lands from tillage to pasture" (cited in Zagorin, 1982, vol. 1: 209). The goal of the rebellion was the defense of the traditional moral economy, to

> restore the old usages, and the end of all is to be a sort of idealised manorial customary enforced by a strong central Government throughout the length of the land, free use of the common lands, reduced rents of meadow and marsh, reasonable fines for copyholds, free fisheries, and the abolition of the lingering disability of personal villeinage. [Tawney, 1912: 337]

Elizabeth Confronts the Fiscal Crisis

Elizabeth inherited a monarchy that was faced with deep cleavages and smoldering hostilities, in which innovations in the countryside brought persistent revolt and increasingly strong fiscal pressures to mobilize the country for war. Mary had reduced household expenses and raised tonnage and poundage, and had also made some successful strides toward more efficient tax administration, although she left a legacy of opposition and anger. Edward's reign had been marked by the crown's attempt to "surmount financial difficulties by diverting tax income to meet ordinary expenses," so that taxation became incorporated as a mechanism of government finance (Alsop, 1982: 28, 23). Although the "costs of successive wars, political turmoil, and inflation helped create a climate of retrenchment" during the 1550s, Elizabeth attempted to turn this to her advantage. Her policy of compromise, the famous *via media*, was in effect a new strategy of state centralization by which the crown would suspend itself as a disinterested party over all opposing positions, and thereby mediate the friction to its own advantage and accumulation of power (Alsop, 1986: 152).

Domestically, Elizabeth's middle course steered her through a resolution of the religious crisis left by Mary Tudor, so that neither the returning Marian exiles' fanatical Protestantism nor the recently reestablished Catholic Church was apparently favored. Both fanaticisms were subordinated to "national unity, national independence, even national comfort" (Dickens, 1950: 50) as the Act of Supremacy and the Act of Uniformity reestablished the Henrician reforms and the Edwardian prayer book. Again, this return to the religious status quo ante suggested also a political face to Elizabethan religious doctrines, which were most evidenced in the Northern Rebellion, which hoped to place the Catholic Mary, Queen of Scots on the throne. Elizabeth treated the revolt as a political rebellion, not a Catholic resurgence, and because "ecclesiastical unity was essential to political unity," Catholics were persecuted for treason, not for heresy (Klein, 1968: 183; see also Trevelyan, 1953: 131; Hill, 1967: 24; Neale, 1958: 117).

Radical Protestants also threatened the centralizing ambitions of the queen, for they opposed both religious uniformity and political harmony (Rose, 1975: 220). Elizabeth attempted to appease the Puritans, whom she detested as an "abomination" but who had "captured" Parliament, where they were seeking to push the queen into increased persecution of the Catholics and military confrontations with both Spain and France (Neale, 1958: 121, 436). The Puritans also had urged that each parish be directly sustained by the local congregation, which Elizabeth resisted because it would have weakened central government's influence at the local level (Heal, 1977: 118).

Elizabeth's increasingly ambitious foreign policy program encouraged further efforts to centralize political administration, which further provoked increased popular resistance. After 1550 the major domestic objective of the government was "preventing large scale riots and disturbances among the poor," a possibility so terrifying that many local nobles joined in the queen's efforts, and refrained from revolting themselves (Williams, 1979: 215; see also ibid.: 238). As a result, the rebellion in 1569, which fused religious opposition to Elizabeth's religious settlement with the disgruntled nobles' unhappiness at being replaced by new men in local power positions, soon fell apart because "northern feudalism and particularism could no longer rival Tudor centralization," and because "internal Catholic discontent could not serve as the primary force for the overthrow of existing conditions" (Fletcher, 1960: 106; Klein, 1968: 36). Class antagonism, which smoldered throughout the period, surfaced occasionally, as one observer noted (cited in James, 1974: 79):

> Lads with money are counted men,
> Men without money are counted none;
> But hold your tongue why say you so?
> Men will be men when money is gone.

The suppression of the rebellion provided the Vatican with the opportunity to move against Elizabeth, but her excommunication for heresy in 1570, provided her with the legitimation for new fiscal maneuvers against the Catholics, such as fines, and the confiscation of both lay and church property.

Elizabeth's relationship with her Parliaments also expresses the tension between locality and central government. Her persistent needs for taxation and legislation compelled the calling of Parliament, which she attempted to pacify by the manipulation of court patronage. Rather than the elaborate layering of venal officeholders as in France, Elizabeth controlled the position of patronage broker. Here, she was at her most highly personal in administration, apparently reversing Thomas Cromwell's systematization of political administration, and generating significant political corruption at court. Contrary to these appearances, however, Elizabeth's policy contained a systematic and rational quality; she aimed "not at the adherence of a party or faction, but at the goodwill of a whole class" and so she deliberately built up local nobles' traditional clientage ties and patronage at the local level—even allowing some regionally based power brokers like Lord Burghley and the Earl of Leicester, and later Essex and Cecil to compete for her closest confidence—while she simultaneously attempted to subordinate all patronage to her direct command.

Elizabeth's chief concern was the successful implementation of her foreign policy, and it was toward this end that her apparent domestic compromises were aimed; foreign policy was "of transcendent importance, and determined the issues of national life and death" (Tanner, 1966: 5). Even here, however, she pursued a middle-of-the-road course, a *via media,* much to the chagrin of her adviser, Sir Walter Raleigh, who complained that if the late Queen would have believed her men of war as she did her scribes, we had in her time beaten the great empire in pieces, and made their kings kings of figs and oranges as in old times. But her Majesty did all by halves and by petty invasions taught the Spaniard how to defend himself and to see his own weakness which, till our attempts taught him, was hardly known to himself.

But, it was never Elizabeth's intention to destroy Spain and "break the great empire in pieces" as Raleigh might have preferred. Instead, severely limited financially, she was also politically committed to maintaining the balance of power between her two Continental rivals, Spain and France, so that English trade could flourish and political opportunities multiply. Elizabeth's foreign policy was conservative, negative, and defensive, designed to check the expansion of Spain and France rather than to expand England itself.

Foreign policy, especially war, was expensive, and perhaps too expensive for Elizabeth to mount a major offensive against a Continental power (Lockyer, 1964: 212; see also Williams, 1979: 444). The strains of an aggressive foreign policy demanded political unity at home, which would make religious uniformity and control even more imperative for a monarchy wishing to mobilize for war. To prevent Spain's reconquest or French conquest of the Netherlands, and to prevent an outright victory for the Catholic League in France was enough for Elizabeth, and even that was quite expensive (Anderson, 1974: 130).[2] As the crown began to gear up for war in the late 1580s, expenses steadily rose (based on issues of the Exchequer) from £ 150,000 in 1582–83, to £ 367,000 by 1586–87, and to £ 420,000 the next year (Wernham, 1966: 404). Chested treasure (the reserve treasury) was depleted from £ 300,000 in 1584 to only slightly more than £ 50,000 four years later. Expenditures outran subsidies voted by Parliament, and in 1588 Lord Burghley worried that "treasure grows less" (cited in Dietz, 1964: 57). In January 1588 Elizabeth was forced to borrow £ 75,000 from wealthy taxpayers and £ 30,000 from the City of London.

The war with Spain, which Elizabeth had attempted to avoid for twenty-seven years, had finally been declared, the outcome of increased military and economic competition with Spain at a moment when France's weakness offset any potential gain the French would achieve from the English-Spanish conflict. England was, for Spain, "the one obstacle to Spanish hegemony of western Europe," and preventing such hegemony became a colossal headache for the queen because of the enormous money required (Wernham, 1966: 372). Expenditures spiraled, especially because during the war England upgraded its military technology, replacing the crossbow with the more expensive gunpowder and musket. "The normal revenue of the Crown was perfectly capable of meeting the ordinary requirements of the administration," writes Stone (1947: 114). "But the passionate desire to acquire a war chest in time of peace and the desperate search for ways and means to meet the cost of military enterprises in time of war exercised a persistent and ever-increasing influence upon economic policy."

Because ordinary income was insufficient to meet the increased fiscal demands of a war economy, Elizabeth was forced to abandon her intention "not to increase her income, but to exercise a rigorous control over expenditure" as the strategy to resolve the fiscal crisis (Russell, 1973: 96). Sale of crown lands brought a windfall of £ 645,000 in the 1590s, and brought in over £ 813,000 during the reign (Thirsk, 1967: 268). In 1610 Sir Julius Caesar called crown lands "the surest and best livlihood of the Crown" (cited in Dietz, 1964: 138). Revenues were also generated by sale of trading monopolies, rent and recusancy fines, forced loans, benevolences, and, of course, taxation (Elton, 1977: 363; Unwin, 1927: 47). During each war Parliament voted war subsidies (1585, 1587, 1589, 1593, 1601). And, Elizabeth borrowed at usurious rates of interest, and tried to "skimp the war" by conducting it "by the curious expedient of joint-stock companies financed partly by herself and partly by private persons" (Elton, 1977: 363). Finally, Elizabeth encouraged privateering by London merchants, whose booty provided additional revenues, and brought merchants into an important position in Tudor administration. "It was war finance, not depression economics," writes Stone (1947: 114), "that gave the merchant capitalists their chance."

Elizabeth always came up short. Even after she scored the decisive victory over the Spanish Armada in 1588, England was unable to pursue the victory because of the shortage of money. To defeat the Armada had cost over £ 13,000 per month to maintain the navy, and by 1603 the war had cost over £ 2,858,000. Subsidies had yielded more than £ 1.5 million, but that left the crown almost £ 1.3 million in debt (Cal. State Papers, Domestic, 1603; see also Russell, 1982: 15; Russell, 1971: 245).

After the defeat of the Armada, pursuit of the war remained extremely expensive, and also generated renewed opposition. One observer noted that the Parliament called in 1593 was "only for money to maintain the troops in Brittany" (cited in Dietz, 1964: 70). At the 1601 session, one M.P. complained that "the granting of the subsidy seemed to be the alpha and omega of this Parliament," and the next speaker opined that "seeing the subsidy was granted and they had yet done nothing, it would please Her Majesty not to dissolve this Parliament until some acts were passed" (cited in Neale, 1949: 403). New advisers urged withdrawal and nonintervention in Continental warfare because neither France nor Spain was capable of achieving Continental hegemony after the defeat of the Armada. With the exception of Ireland, where the suppression of Tyrone's Rebellion in 1598 cost nearly £ 2 million, Elizabeth withdrew from costly war making, and concentrated her energies on naval power and encouraging and attempting to control overseas trade.

The Tudor Legacy

Elizabeth's death in 1603 ended one of the nation's longest reigns as well as the Tudor dynasty, and ever since historians have been debating her legacy. Some historians, like Pollard and Elton, have stressed the administrative revolution under Thomas Cromwell and Henry VIII as a decisive break with the past that enabled Elizabeth to leave her Stuart successors a modern and bureaucratic state apparatus, "the establishment of national sovereignty, which freed men from the restrictions of the Middle Ages by establishing the order that was essential to liberty" (Pollard, 1920: 426). Other historians, such as Hurstfield and Stone, emphasize the structural problems and inherent weaknesses of the Elizabethan polity that, after her death, split the nation into two irreconcilable camps and eventually resulted in the outbreak of the Civil War. "The paradox of Tudor administration and perhaps the ultimate cause of the collapse of the whole system is to be found in the extent to which its program of the paternalist state, of social justice and conservatism, was sacrificed to the implementation of the more pressing need of planned autarchy and opportunist war finance" (Stone, 1947: 115). As one Fifth Monarchist commented in the 1650s (cited in Stone, 1972: 116), "some compare Queen Elizabeth to a sluttish housewife, who swept the house but left the dust behind the door."

The Tudor legacy was mixed, and important successes were balanced by the persistence of serious structural weaknesses. Religious uniformity had been imposed, an adequate food supply seemed secured, vagrancy had been controlled in large part, law and order seemed ensured, and overseas trade had expanded significantly. Bankruptcy, religiously motivated civil wars, and reckless and expensive foreign intervention had all been avoided. Elizabeth had "helped the French monarchy to its feet, saved half the Netherlands from Spanish 'tyranny' . . . kept the other half out of French possessions, and England itself out of bankruptcy" (Wernham, 1961: 368). The Tudor monarch's policies toward the nobility had propped up a declining class while insuring that its continued stability was dependent upon the largesse of the crown, thus suppressing private violence and potential sources of autonomous political opposition. The continuing struggle between the crown and the magnates also pressed the crown to make political concessions to the gentry, which parlayed its rise into political maneuverability and prevented the crown from developing the administrative bureaucracy that an absolute monarchy might have required.

Persistent problems and structural weaknesses remained, especially in fiscal matters; all government initiatives, as Tawney wrote, were "smeared with the trail of finance." Inflation had eroded revenues from land and commerce; the tax base of the subsidy had been narrowed substantially; domestic sources of credit were less than adequate. In short, "the solid financial foundations required by a modern state had not been laid by 1603" (Williams, 1979: 80). The debt of close to £ 400,000 that Elizabeth bequeathed to the first Stuart kings left a "shaky financial position," which the Stuarts "were to find the biggest obstacle to autocratic government" (Elton, 1974: 364).

Fiscal instability was the legacy of the administrative revolution without reform that characterized Tudor administration, from Cromwell to Elizabeth. Particularly, the reliance on monopolies, the inability to sell offices on a large scale, which minimized revenues and precluded the development of an adequate administrative bureaucracy under royal control, and the inability of the crown to generate an adequate tax base all spelled that continued financial troubles would be built into the structure of the Stuart polity (Stone, 1972: 61–62). As a result,

> the propertied classes had become accustomed to avoiding taxation, and efforts by the Stuarts to tighten things up and to tax the rich at a realistic level by means of impositions, fines for wardship, forced loans or ship money ran into serious legal and political obstacles. The early Stuart monarchy was financially boxed in at all points, since it could only achieve fiscal solvency and the equitable distribution of the tax burden at the cost of a political crisis.

Fiscal instability was coupled with increasing political opposition to Tudor policies. England may have been, by 1603, the "most centralized of states" notes Thomas (1978: 75), but "the scope of governmental action was limited by the interests of the economically powerful classes." A large number of groups had been disaffected by Tudor administration, and drew support from political, religious, economic, and social sources. England was "notorious for her political instability." "It is well known how many civil wars the English have had," wrote one observer in 1589 (cited in Thomas, 1978: 45), "how many changes of regime and how many new kings." Threats to what shaky stability had been achieved were everywhere. The hereditary peers were angered at their declining fortunes; religious minorities sought pluralistic religious policies at their most generous, outright religious takeover at their least generous; and class hostilities based on enclosures and other agrarian innovations all threatened the stability of the monarchy. The gentry, too, was irate because the heaviest financial burdens of war financing fell on its shoulders. Growing opposition in the countryside sought national expression through Parliament. In the 1590s the government's financial troubles "made it possible for the members of the Commons to make their voices heard in no uncertain terms" (Smith, 1967: 41). By the early years of the seventeenth century political opposition had not yet congealed into a coalition that had national form, but the "instrument was tempered with which the Crown was to be resisted and conquered" (Neale, 1949: 307). It remained for the first two Stuart kings to alienate and drive into opposition, through their increasingly desperate search for funds, the other elements that would come to compose that coalition of political opposition.

Notes

1. This position differs, therefore, from that of writers like Coward, who argues (1982: 77) that for the Stanleys, Earls of Derby from 1504 to 1642, "their authority underwent no 'crisis' in the early 17th century" largely because they retained key positions in the relations between the crown and local community and within the local community itself. I maintain, to the contrary, that although many aristocrats retained these formal positions, the content of the positions had changed as the balance of class forces in the countryside and the relationship of each with the crown had shifted.
2. The only notable exception to this negative foreign policy, of course, is the military conquest of Ireland, which integrated the "perimeter of English authority" at the Celtic fringe but did not try to expand it (Anderson, 1974: 131; see also Hechter, 1975).

6

Absolutism and Its Discontents in England, 1603–1628

James I, the first Stuart, who succeeded to the throne upon the death of Queen Elizabeth, has not enjoyed the kindest of historical treatments. Renowned for his extravagance, his sexual preferences, his lavish court life, he was openly denounced in sermons, newsletters, and correspondence throughout his reign as "a bungling, alcoholic homosexual," and has been remembered as "an irritating and inept sovereign" whose "ungainly presence, mumbling speech and dirty ways" made him "a pedantic and undignified person with gross and unseemly personal habits" (Stone, 1980: 25; Mitchell, 1957: 25; Stone, 1972: 89; Hill, 1966: 67). But such personalizing only obscures the structural contradictions of the English monarchy of the sixteenth and seventeenth centuries.

James was not as inept as his nation was increasingly ungovernable by a centralizing monarchy whose social, financial, political, and religious institutions rested on increasingly shaky foundations. Although his efforts to resolve its fiscal crisis and to pursue an aggressive foreign policy made things worse, they did not cause its problems. Elizabeth had left James a sizable debt—the result of her own generosity toward the end of her reign which was the fruit of her efforts to buy off potential opposition and her inability to resist the growth of faction and corruption at court (Prestwich, 1966: 17). James inherited a crown "weakened by inflation and by the costs of war with Spain, a government undermined by faction and administration polluted by corruption" (Prestwich, 1973: 140).

James's intentions often seemed quite honorable. He desired peace when his countrymen thirsted for war; he proposed religious toleration when Puritans, among others, burned for revenge against Catholic conspirators; he urged moderation in trade and industry while the landowning classes pressed for extreme protectionist measures. He had no interest in structural reforms; his object was only "to maintain the stable hierarchical society of degree" (Hill, 1966: 68). But, he had come into possession of a shaky and untenable financial situation. Without the pretense of war, which legitimated fiscal exactions, and concealed by extraordinary wartime expenditures that permitted extraordinary measures to generate revenues, the unstable Tudor fiscal system lay exposed. The most pressing issue throughout James's reign was money, and his efforts to resolve his fiscal crisis, the difficult fact that "his expenditure always exceeded his income," pushed him to abridge traditional relationships between state and society, and brought him into constant conflict with the various social groups that composed the political nation (Prothero, 1954: lxxx; see also Russell, 1971; Appleby, 1978: 32). It was this constant scramble for money that pressed James to attempt to impose, piecemeal and against his own wishes, the English form of absolutism.

As Russell (1979) argues, James and his son, Charles I, had no intention of introducing absolutism to England. Like all early modern kings, he tried to stretch existing social limits on royal powers, especially fiscal powers, searching always for new possibilities to secure revenues within the structure of the old regime. But James also was forced to search for new structural sources of revenues, altering political and social relationships to his advantage in a haphazard policy of state centralization that lacked the overarching ideology of *raison d'état* that was guiding Richelieu and Louis XIII, the immediate presence of wartime exactions, and the systematic efforts that marked Richelieu's efforts to freeze social relations and transform political and economic relations. James relied on the divine right of kings as a rationale for his absolutist policies, voicing the belief that "all property was held of the king as ultimate Lord and that all laws and rights originated in royal grace" (Hirst, 1986: 111). Early Stuart absolutism never amounted to a program but was instituted incrementally. Its chief motivation was fiscal, the recognition that it was impossible "to administer a modern state with medieval methods of finance" (Ashton, 1960: 15). James thought defensively, recognizing the limitations on his pursuit of any aggressive policies; he sought to raise money to ensure the protection of the realm and the preservation of law and order, defense, and administration (Smith, 1967: 53). Thus, though he did not intend to introduce absolutism, James I presented a program that must have felt like absolutism to the English people at the time. Sir Simon D'Ewes remarked that "all his actions did tend to an absolute monarchy" and the Apology of 1604 noted that "the prerogatives of princes may easily and do daily grow" (cited in Hill, 1986: 53, 29). James's own defense of monarchical rights, at the opening session of the Parliament of 1621, rehearsed the traditional supremacy of king over Parliament but also, given the contentious nature of that Parliament, must have been perceived as a strong argument for absolutism: "Parliaments are instituted by monarchs, and that there were no Parliaments but in monarchies, that consequently Kings and Kingdoms were long before Parliaments, contrary to the fond opinion of some that thought otherwise" (cited in Russell, 1979: 140). Sir John Eliot offered an intriguing defense of absolutism to his peers (cited in Hirst, 1986: 144): "Cut off the king's revenues, you cut off the principal means of your own safeties, and not only disable him to defend you, but enforce that which you conceive an offence, the extraordinary resort to his subjects for supplies, and the more than ordinary ways of raising them."

Living "On His Own"

Both king and people had subscribed to the idea that in peacetime the king "live on his own," that is, from the ordinary revenues that accrued to the king by virtue of his ownership of land and possession of various titles. The king appreciated the independence of social constraints that dependence on Parliamentary approval indicated, and the political nation remained free of unwanted taxation. The sources of revenue that were available to the king included the sale of crown lands, feudal rights such as fines for recusancy, first fruits and tenths, and the sale of wardships, and a series of indirect taxes that had become part of the ordinary revenues. These duties on imports and exports, tonnage and poundage, and customs were especially important because they kept pace with inflation, increasing as trade increased. Finally, the crown also had access to a series of extraordinary taxes, such as military subsidies and fifteenths and tenths, an irregular income from the sale of monopolies and patents, and small profits from judicial administrations (fees for writs), the right of purveyance (the compulsory purchase of food from royal officials), loans from corporate bodies, loans from private individuals, and "benevolences," another euphemistically named loan.

These were the fiscal resources that James had at his disposal, but they were inadequate to meet his ordinary needs in peacetime, let alone finance an aggressive foreign policy against the Habsburgs. Besides, James's court costs were astonishing and rather disproportionate to his revenues. For example, after Parliament had voted £ 453,000 in supply in 1601, James celebrated by giving three Scottish friends £ 44,000 to pay off their debts, and spent £ 800 on "spangles" for the guard (see Hirst, 1986: 109). James's first course of action was to attempt to generate funds by selling off what he could. Sale of crown lands, which had been relied upon earlier for revenues, was limited because that "had to be used as part of the stock of political patronage, which made it difficult to raise a fully commercial revenue from them" (Russell, 1971: 32). Elizabeth had used sale of crown lands to buttress a parliamentary war subsidy that covered only half her expenses, and had generated almost £ 650,000 through their sale. Sale of crown lands under James was "extensive," both to defray debts and meet current charges, but hardly sufficient (Ashton, 1960: 90).

Royal borrowing also became big business during James's administration. At first James borrowed from corporate groups, such as the Corporation of the City of London, which granted loans of £ 70,000 in 1608 and £ 100,000 in 1610. By 1614, however, royal credit had already deteriorated so much that the Corporation of the City of London voted to grant the king £ 10,000 outright rather than meet his request for another £ 100,000 loan. In 1617 he raised another £ 100,000 through the corporation, but only after he put up remaining crown lands as collateral and promised a 10 percent return on the loan (Ashton, 1960: 113–29; see also Prestwich, 1966: 201).[1]

Royal borrowing was necessary to James's financial solvency, "no longer confined to situations of national emergency, though from the financial point of view, the very presence of James on the throne was emergency enough in itself" (Ashton, 1960: 160). Still, resistance on the part of corporate groups to royal borrowing efforts increased, indicating serious erosion of political legitimacy and forcing James to seek loans from other sources.

James also attempted to use tax farming through the customs. Beginning in 1604, the crown urged customs farmers to overpay what was due to the king, to be applied against anticipated future revenues. This undisguised "cheap way of borrowing" became increasingly "an essential part of the king's finances" (Ashton, 1960: 90; Russell, 1971: 273). Later in 1604 James also demanded a forced loan of over £ 111,890 from Parliament, and again in 1611 demanded a loan of £ 116,381 (by July 1618 only £ 4,000 had been repaid by the crown to the Parliament) (Ashton, 1960: 35–36; see also Bernstein, 1963: 31).

James also borrowed short term on security from earmarked revenues from the City of London customs farmers individually, the "worms of aldermen," as Bacon contemptuously sneered (cited in Prestwich, 1966: 115). He developed from these urban financiers a group of men "who acted as intermediaries between the crown and the money market" (Ashton, 1960: 24). Like the financiers in France, they were private capitalists who were involved in the credit sector, lending to the crown or guaranteeing crown debts by their own credit. This thwarted capitalist development, as in France, siphoning off potentially productive capital into the state sector, and making some state financiers, like Burlamachi, extremely wealthy. "The King payeth usury to his own subjects, and sometimes for his own money," one contemporary quipped (cited in Tawney, 1958: 151).

Budget tightening was also tried, without much success. In 1618 Lionel Cranfield instituted dramatic belt-tightening in the royal household, hoping to generate revenues by saving. His rigorous accounting procedures—he calculated exactly how many cuts of meat could be had from an ox, for example, as part of mechanisms to ensure competitive pricing of supplying the king's household—resulted in savings of roughly £ 120,000 per year.

All these means to raise revenues without direct interference in either the relations of agricultural production or the relations of urban circulation were efforts to bypass parliamentary control, to provide the king with access to funds without subjecting him to the demands of Parliament for redress of grievances. As such, they assured him not of the desired funds— ordinary revenues rose from about £ 315,000 in 1606 to only about £ 460,000 in 1610 (Hirst, 1986: 110)—but of growing opposition, both in and out of Parliament. Without serious political and financial reforms, a nettlesome task that James was reluctant to undertake, these efforts to streamline crown expenditures and augment income through ordinary channels were bound to fail. James was thus forced to "choose between revenues and popularity" (Russell, 1971: 37). He chose the less popular route, and accompanied his program of state centralization with efforts at developing a standing army, and a "Parkinsonian proliferation of subordi- nate officials at the lower levels of the existing structure," as well as fiscal expedients designed to curtail the autonomous economic positions of various social groups, while bringing more money to the royal treasury. The net result of Jacobean absolutism was both greater central authority and markedly increased opposition to central authority, a steadily "wors- ening crisis of authority" during the first four decades of the century (Zaller, 1971: 4).

James Moves against Rural Autonomy

James first turned to the hereditary nobility as a mechanism to generate funds, but the earlier crisis of the aristocracy made its potential contribu- tion far less than desired. The crown attempted to reap some financial benefits from reviving feudal privileges. Inflation of honors and the sale of offices never reached a level approaching that of France, but James resorted to both fiscal expedients occasionally until 1620, and from 1621 on "in almost every session of Parliament the desirability of a better law against the selling and buying of offices was argued" (Swart, 1954: 53; see also Bernstein, 1963: 31). A 56 percent increase in the peerage between 1615 and 1628 was accomplished "almost all by sale," and the number of peers doubled between 1600 and 1641 (Hill, 1967: 84; Brustein and Levi, 1987: 11). The creation and sale of baronets in 1611, at £ 1,095 each, by 1614 had brought in over £ 90,000; two earldoms in 1619 added £ 18,000 to the royal treasury, and the "wholesale creation of baronets" brought in another £ 12,480 (Hirst, 1986: 113; Dietz, 1964: 179). In 1620 Sir Henry Montague paid £ 20,000 to become lord treasurer (Hill, 1966: 47). In all, Hill estimates that between 1615 and 1628, thirty English titles and forty Irish and Scottish titles were sold for about £ 350,000, of which the crown actually saw less than half (Hill, 1966: 47). The resort to sale of noble titles reveals "the Crown's desperate financial straits" (Aylmer, 1961: 232). The aristocracy was "diluted" by sale of the titles, but even so, the market was soon saturated; the asking price for a baronetcy, for example, in 1622 had fallen to £ 220 (Hill, 1966: 47; Hirst, 1986: 114). Many merchants and gentry came to oppose the practice as well (Swart, 1954: 66). One contemporary observed that he "did and do think the honour of baronets a great injury to the crown, it taking off the dependence of so many considerable families in every county which, having as much honour as their estates are capable of, are not at all solicitous to serve and apply to the crown" (cited in Hill and Dell, 1949: 126).

James also drafted a bill for Parliament in 1621 that would have imprisoned anyone who issued a challenge for a duel who was below the rank of baron, and would have members of the Privy Council imprison anyone at the rank of baron or above who had issued a challenge for a duel or had fought one (Russell, 1978: 47). (The bill never received a first reading in Commons, and was apparently tabled by the Privy Council.) In addition, the crown attempted to substitute the authority of royally appointed lieutenant governors and justices of the peace for the traditionally private and autonomous jurisdictional powers of the aristocracy. These new arrivals in the localities were selected from the non-noble squierarchy, and directly undercut the local political power of the aristocracy (Brustein and Levi, 1987: 11). Similarly, the monopoly patents and efforts to license alehouses from the central administration deleteriously affected local political power structures by threatening to create "a rival system of government" that would not require the patronage and support of aristocratic oligarchs in the countryside (Hill, 1986: 39).

The crown was unable to press its desperate moves against the aristocracy too far. Nobles were the foundation of the monarchy, and had to be relied upon should moves against others, further down the social scale, provoke revolt. Hill (1967: 32) notes a "loss of some powers, but survival of privilege and great influence" as the House of Lords became a bulwark against the demands of the gentry and the merchants, attempting to preserve both religious purity and traditional social structure. As in

France, the social foundation of absolutism was the landed aristocracy; the "underlying nature of the absolute monarchical state was government through and in the interests of a ruling class of landowners" (Manning, 1967: 264). The unity of king and aristocracy was shaken but remained relatively intact.

The gentry, on the other hand, was consistently the target of royal initiatives to generate revenues. In the countryside members of the landed class had "forged a crucial link" between market incentives and farming practices, a link providing handsome profits for commercialized agriculture (Appleby, 1978: 55; see also Moore, 1966). The economy had moved beyond the overriding concern for provision of an adequate food supply and had developed new techniques for a new market (Appleby, 1978: 98). New methods of estate administration (such as raising rents and copyhold fines, shortening leases, converting copyhold into leasehold) combined with new agricultural techniques (such as enclosures and the development of common lands, redistribution and consolidation of holdings, and new techniques of soil fertility) and productive activities (demesne farming, coal mining, lead mining, and the manufacture of iron) gave the gentry the potential of transforming the rural base of the English economy. Reoriented toward trade in wool, the process of agricultural production was itself transformed.

Often such changes increased the class-based hostility between tenants and landlords. As John Selden wrote in *Table Talk,* "When men did let their lands under foot (at nominal rents) the tenants would fight for their landlords, so that way they had their retribution. But now they will do nothing for them, nay, be the first, if but a constable bid them, that shall lay the landlord by the heels" (cited in Stone, 1965: 130). Riots and protests against enclosure (which will be dealt with in more detail in the following chapter) broke out often in the late sixteenth century and early seventeenth century, often lasting several weeks and involving thousands of people.[2] Simultaneously, the government intervened directly in agricultural production. For example, the crown imposed a static rent roll on local landlords that froze rents, angering the landlords and pressing them to search for other means to raise their incomes. The crown sought, too, to limit enclosures by gentry. This intervention did not eliminate the hostility between landlord and tenant but served only to deflect part of the ire of each onto the state, for the crown did not limit enclosure out of compassionate concern for the rural poor but, rather, in the interests of increasing revenues and furthering the interests of the state.

Enclosure of the common lands resulted in rural depopulation, and destroyed many families' margin of independence. The Tudors had earlier moved to limit depopulation directly by edicts (1536) or through edicts restricting sheep farming (1534), but agricultural labor relations changed dramatically as larger and larger numbers of people were working for wages, and there was a large number of landless and dependent wage earners in both town and countryside (Everitt, 1967: 435ff.; Williams, 1966: 214). The crown's concern was maintenance of public order. Bowden writes (1962: 111):

> Depopulation enfeebled the military strength of the system and was financially disadvantageous to the crown, and turned loose in the country large numbers of vagrants whose idleness was a menace to the social order; in addition, it was felt that the accompanying increase in pasture was politically dangerous, tending as it did to make a country dependent upon foreign powers for supplies of corn.

The crown also opposed enclosure because it meant a loss of taxable income; the church often opposed it because it would yield smaller tithe payments.

Governmental policy on enclosures attempted to contain them, but it was consistently inadequate. Coke declared in 1620 that depopulation was against the laws of the realm, and asserted that the encloser who kept a shepherd and his dog in the place of a flourishing village was hateful to both God and man (Bowden, 1962: 126). The enclosure fine, the most common method to limit enclosure and generate revenues for the crown, brought little relief to the poor and small returns for the royal treasury (Hill, 1967: 51; Lublinskaya, 1967: 96). One contemporary verse had it that

> The law locks up the man or woman
> That steals the goose from off the common
> But leaves the greater villain loose
> That steals the common from the goose

Because enclosure fines brought little revenue to the crown to compensate for the loss of taxes, James attempted to enlarge his share from the gentry in other ways. He increased all manner of taxes, especially the fines for wardship; increased purveyance, which swelled his court; defended church property against encroachments from the gentry; and made peace with Spain, thus ending opportunities for privateering (Trevor-Roper, 1966: 185). A rising gentry was finding serious constraints placed on its ascent; a declining segment of the gentry was pressed even further downward. The reign of James I only exacerbated the complaints of the gentry and assured his son of their continued opposition.

James also endeavored to unify England under one central administration, a policy that would increase fiscal solvency and also insure greater control over potential opposition. After the Act of Supremacy, the Tudors had continued to use the parish as a unit of secular administration, and they also integrated English towns into a "single national unit" (Hill, 1967: 13). Administration relied on the local gentry, whose "county identity" militated against acting consistently in the royal interest (Everitt, 1969: 5).

> Without a professional bureaucracy in the shires, the crown was heavily dependent on the county gentry in the field of local administration. It was the gentry who were largely responsible for the maintenance of law and order, the collection of taxes, the implementation of the crown's social legislation and the organization and training of the county's militia. [Cliffe, 1964: 231]

Elizabeth had built up the lords lieutenant as agents of royal centralization in the countryside, and they had formed "a vital link betweeen the central government and the localities," but James preferred to concentrate instead on using justices of the peace, and later patentees deliberately to offset the local autonomous powers of the great magnates, whose dependents were excluded from service (Smith, 1967: 90).

The justices of the peace were never as effective agents of state centralization as were the intendants in early modern France. J.P.'s were natives of both the county and usually of the division for which they sat, and although they were "loyal and hardworking servants of the Crown," their service "normally took third place behind their concern for the welfare of their counties and for their own pockets" (Russell, 1979: 8; see also Kenyon, 1966: 492). If not directly supervised, they were "liable to be more responsive to local interests and needs than to the tasks imposed from London" (James, 1974: 157). "The centrifugal tendency of the Commission of the Peace," writes Kenyon (1966: 492), "the dangers that its members would come to regard themselves as representatives of the localities against the government, was always present, and the ministers of James I and Charles I made recurrent efforts to limit their duties and place them under stricter supervision." Like the élus and the trésoriers in France, these local men who were appointed to serve the king's efforts at state centralization and more efficient fiscal administration themselves became part of the growing local opposition to Stuart absolutism.

As in France, local administration consisted of layers of administrative bureaucrats, and if the J.P.'s could not be relied upon to serve the administration faithfully, then other agents needed to be found. The patentee, who paid for the position of local administrator, and who was charged with searching for financial and administrative abuses in the countryside, is as close an English parallel to the intendant in France as we are likely to find. A "device for coping with deficiencies of local government by unpaid amateurs," the patentee also collected the penalties for rural abuses, and undermined the autonomous powers of the justices of the peace, who themselves had become deeply embedded in traditional rural social structure (Hirst, 1986: 44). Of course, the J.P.'s reacted angrily to this decline in their administrative authority, and Parliament was so alarmed by the number of patentees James appointed that it suspected a systematic policy and partially eliminated the system by statute in 1624 (Hirst, 1986: 45).

James also turned to the local Anglican bishops as potential allies and royal administrators in the countryside. The bishops had the advantage of religious legitimacy, and were "outside the local web of kinship and common interest which involved both the gentry families from which the J.P.'s were recruited, and the great landlords of peerage status who became lords lieutenant" (James, 1974: 157). By recruiting the lords lieutenant, who were hereditary peers, the justices of the peace, who were members of the gentry, and the bishops, who were local heads of the state church, the crown attempted to mobilize all the members of the traditional rural ruling classes to its service in the localities. Unfortunately for James and Charles, the structurally ambivalent and contradictory relationship between the crown and these groups prevented their full mobilization for royal purposes, and in fact, pushed one of them to the forefront of the opposition. The other two, enfeebled by their dependence on the monarchy, were the crown's last defenders in the local community.

James Moves to Control Commerce

Just as James moved to resolve his persistent fiscal crisis by intervention in agricultural production, so too he sought to raise his revenues by intervening directly in the urban world of trade and commerce. Though the crown had been involved directly in the economy for some time—as landlord, minister of currency, debtor—and indirectly as recipient of taxes, the early seventeenth century presented new opportunities and increased the necessity of state intervention (Williams, 1979: 142). "Whosoever commands trade of the world commands the riches of the world, and consequently the world itself," Sir Walter Raleigh had noted in a brilliant if primitive espousal of mercantilism, and reminiscent of Montchrestien a couple of decades later (cited in Shennan, 1971: 89). Never had the state so many opportunities for intervention, and never had the need been so great; the result was a "lush bouillabaisse" of government regulations and strategies to intervene directly into economic life (Williams, 1979: 144).

The most successful expedient developed by James in his search for revenues was the sale of a monopoly: the sale to a specific individual of the exclusive rights to produce and/or to distribute a particular commodity. Such monopolies were seen as a relatively painless way to raise revenues, and a mechanism to bring industry and trade more fully under royal control (Hill, 1940: 25). The fiscal benefits brought to the crown were "considerable" and monopolies also brought some political benefits, linking some of the larger trading companies closely to the crown's political agenda (Hill, 1940: 34; see also Pearl, 1961: 92). There were about 700 monopolies by 1621, and their extent is well illustrated by Hill (1966: 32), who describes how the typical Englishman

> lived in a house built with monopoly bricks, with windows (if any) of monopoly glass; heated by monopoly coal . . . burning in a grate made of monopoly iron. His walls were lined with monopoly tapestries. He slept on monopoly feathers, did his hair with monopoly brushes and monopoly combs. He washed himself with monopoly soap, his clothes in monopoly starch. He dressed in monopoly lace, monopoly linen, monopoly gold thread. His hat was of monopoly beaver, with a monopoly band. His clothes were held up by monopoly belts, monopoly buttons, monopoly pins. They were dyed with monopoly dyes. He ate monopoly butter, monopoly currants, monopoly red herring, monopoly salmon, monopoly lobsters. His food was seasoned with monopoly salt, monopoly pepper, monopoly vinegar. Out of monopoly glasses he drank monopoly wines and monopoly spirits; out of pewter mugs made from monopoly tin he drank monopoly beer made from monopoly hops, kept in monopoly barrels or monopoly bottles, sold in monopoly-licensed ale-houses. He smoked monopoly tobacco in monopoly pipes, played with monopoly dice or monopoly cards, or on monopoly lute-strings. He wrote with monopoly pens, on monopoly writing paper; read (through monopoly spectacles, by the light of monopoly candles) monopoly printed books, including monopoly Bibles and monopoly Latin grammars, printed on paper made from monopoly-collected rags, bound in sheepskin dressed in monopoly alum. He shot with monopoly gunpowder made from monopoly saltpetre. He traveled in monopoly sedan chairs or monopoly hackney coaches, drawn by horses fed on monopoly hay. He tipped with monopoly farthings. At sea he was lighted by monopoly lighthouses. When he made his will, he went to a monopolist.

The levying of customs duties was also a useful and profitable expedient for James. In 1608 new customs were levied on 1,400 articles, a 30–40 percent increase in the number of imported articles subject to custom regulations. These customs were believed to produce £ 70,000 a year, "with no pretense that this was a tariff reform in the interests of trade" (Prestwich, 1973: 149). By 1609 customs farms generated one-fourth of all ordinary revenues, and this increased to almost one-third by 1620 (Tawney, 1958: 98).

The success of James's fiscal expedients depended only in part on the willingness of the merchants to tolerate his interventions in trade relations;

it also required a healthy overseas market, and a strong domestic market to consume the items on which the crown had imposed its duties. The collapse of the overseas market in the 1610s and 1620s placed all of James's hopes in jeopardy and increased the political opposition he was facing. By 1615 trade began to decline precipitously from its peak the year before, and before the year was out, John Chamberlain complained that there was "plenty of all things but money" (cited in Russell, 1979: 85). Falling prices, dwindling rents, and a general lack of capital and lowering of the price of land threatened the crown's ambitions (Prestwich, 1966: 280). The cloth industry was paralyzed: markets shrinking, credit tight, wool prices falling, stocks of unsold cloth mounting, bankruptcies widespread, and unemployment rising. England appeared to be "enveloped in the gloom of depression" (Supple, 1959: 53). "When," it was asked (cited in Dietz, 1973: 112), "was it seen a land so distressed without a war?"

The state alliance with the capitalist classes in the cities was shaken by the fiscal crisis that began in the 1620s and lasted well into the 1630s, prompting increased royal incursions into the freedom of trade. As Goldstone notes (1986: 266), "It was the intractable financial difficulties of the Crown . . . that shook the whole mutually supportive arrangement." Opposition to Jacobean meddling in trade and commerce was also met with increased opposition. In the sixteenth century merchants had advocated a strong state presence in the commercial economy to stabilize markets and protect their cargoes from foreign aggression. By the seventeenth century, however, internal order had been secured and foreign threats eliminated, so to the merchants "the burdens of government seemed more obvious than its advantages" (Hill, 1967: 38). Merchants protested against taxation and the restrictions on finished products, although they continued to urge restrictions on raw materials (Fisher, 1969: 70). They believed, as the Venetian ambassador reported in 1624 (cited in Tawney, 1958: 237), that "the king has always detested business, and now he hates it more than ever."

Merchant opposition to royal initiatives grew throughout James's reign. When a merchant refused to pay his allocated customs duties, for example, in the famous Bate's case, the king's response was to reiterate that the principle of the divine right of kings reserves to the crown the power to regulate trade and to impose any customs duties he desires. The king's success permitted Lord Salisbury to impose new tariffs on every import except basic foodstuffs, munitions, and ships' stores; to Sir Julius Caesar, the Exchequer, it was "the most gainfull to the king and his posterity as any one day's work" (cited in Hirst, 1986: 110; see also Davies, 1959: 12). In 1606 clothiers complained because they believed they had been charged too much and got paid too little, but the king countered with his own needs, based again on the theory of divine right, and did not even deign to listen to their complaint (Bowden, 1962: 153–54).

Later in the reign James's rhetorical arguments did not hold up any longer. The Welsh drapers had argued that because freedom of trade gave people employment and made them grow rich and therefore able to pay taxes, they "wished to be able to sell their cloth to anyone" (cited in Russell, 1979: 62). In 1620 some unemployed Wiltshire cloth workers petitioned the Privy Council with a covert threat of violence, declaring that "to starve is woeful, to steal ungodly, and to beg unlawful," but "to endure our present estate anywhere is almost impossible" (cited in Underdown, 1986: 117). Merchants were successful later in forcing a general loosening of trade restrictions; it is a mark of the failure of Jacobean absolutism that it "never had sufficient power to hold the capitalist sector of the economy in check, to reduce it to central regulation and control" (Hill, 1966: 103).

Monopolies met with sustained opposition. They "distorted the whole pattern of trade" and did not facilitate capitalist development; rather, monopolies thwarted capitalist development (Appleby, 1978: 33). In its granting of the privileges of monopolies, the crown provoked a split among the merchants, and paid the price of opposition from one group to gain the loyalty of the other. The great merchants of the City of London benefited greatly from monopolies, "establishing their dominant position over trade, industry and municipal government" at the expense of the smaller merchants in the outport cities (Manning, 1976: 163). These smaller merchants did not share in the profits of monopolies but nevertheless picked up a good deal of the cost. Monopolies limited output, did not achieve the social objectives of protecting the interests of consumers and employees, and brought inadequate revenues to the Exchequer, even less than free trade would have done (Hill, 1966: 35). Merchants in outport cities thus allied with the provincial gentry in the Parliament and opposed these grievous controls on industry and trade, and fueled the antipathy of the "country" faction against the alliance of court, crown, and the City of London. The 1624 Statute on Monopolies declared them contrary to the "fundamental laws of this realm" (in Hill, 1966: 35). In this way the "bitter struggle of the outports under James I against the monopoly privileges of the chartered companies of the city became intimately bound up with Parliament's attack on the prerogative power of the crown" (Pearl, 1966: 132).

The most famous of the king's disastrous attempts to control trade was the Cockayne Project of 1616, an attempt to bring the clothing industry under royal control and subsequently to expand exports. Dutch clothing manufacturers usually had received unfinished cloth from the English, which they then dressed, dyed, and sold. In 1614 James gave the monopoly for the manufacture and sale of dyed cloth to Sir William Cockayne and his associates, and withdrew the charter of the Merchant Adventurers, who earlier had had the right to export the unfinished cloth. Although this may appear to have been sound mercantilist policy, it was an economic and political disaster for James. The Dutch refused to import the finished cloth, and Cockayne's firm was so "guilty of bad workmanship" that James was forced to withdraw the privileges he had granted to Cockayne and to restore the charter of the Merchant Adventurers. Still, "the damage was done. Good trade was lost, the English textile industry went into depression, and there was unreasonable, if understandable, resentment against the Dutch" (Howat, 1974: 59). The Cockayne Project was an utter failure for everyone, including the racketeers, who sought to gain by conspiracy a share in the profitable monopolistic trade (Supple, 1959: 51). The project yielded almost universal condemnation (Dietz, 1973: 111).

Political Opposition, 1603–1624

James's efforts at resolving his fiscal crisis through intervention in trade relations and in rural agricultural production met with resistance at points of both production and circulation, and opposition was heard in political institutions like Parliament and also in nonparliamentary circles. During the first few years of James's reign, religious issues played a large role as the king's policy of "alternately permitting and relaxing persecution" of the Catholics "created distrust among the Protestants and failed to win the confidence of the Catholics" (Davies, 1959: 8). The Gunpowder Plot of November 1605 found Catholic extremists, led by Guy Fawkes, planning to destroy Parliament, which would serve as a call to all Catholic gentry to revolt against the king (Hurstfield, 1970: 97). The failure of the plot, and Fawkes's execution destroyed Catholic efforts to dislodge an Anglican king, and pushed the Catholics into an alliance with the crown, which alone could protect the religious minority from random violence of religious Protestant zealots. Catholics remained "far more loyal to the crown than to the pope" (Hirst, 1986: 81). Like the Huguenots in France, the institutionalized religious minority in England, the Catholics, remained loyal to the crown throughout the seventeenth century, believing their continued survival was contingent upon royal protection, and as fearful as the king of Puritan drives for religious uniformity.

Discovery and suppression of the Gunpowder Plot did not solve James's financial problems. In 1606 the royal debt was calculated at £ 550,331, and had been increasing by over £ 50,000 per year (Dietz, 1964: 121). By 1608, when James named Robert Cecil as lord treasurer, the debt had climbed to almost £ 1 million (Russell, 1971: 274). A loan of £ 69,000 from the Corporation of the City of London helped James stagger through to his Parliament of 1610, where he requested both supply (a grant to pay off his debts) and support (a substantial sum to meet the current deficit and to prevent debt). "What can be our hopes," asked Cecil of Parliament in the opening session (cited in Dietz, 1964: 133), "if we keep a King poor and low that is great and glorious?"

Resistance to James's efforts preceded the calling of Parliament, and Commons seemed reluctant to grant either supply or support. To the assembled Commons, "inefficient administration, high fees, corruption in high places, burdensome taxation, the over-exploitation of 'fiscal feudal' sources of income" had led to mounting distrust of the king's intentions (Munden, in Sharpe, 1978: 48–49). Thomas Wentworth, an M.P., suggested that James's extravagance indicated that "God is angry with the King's treasury" (cited in Gardiner, 1861: 144). Lord Salisbury's offer of the Great Contract was a defensive initiative by the king, a compromise that would insure adequate revenues to the king in return for fiscal concessions to Parliament; its acceptance generated an additional £ 200,000 a year for the king. But, the king relinquished his claims on rights of wardship and purveyance, each of which had been a steady source of income, as well as renounced the use of informers to raise money on penal statutes. Trading these sources of income that had been linked to the inflationary spiral for a fixed annual sum prompted Sir Julius Caesar to comment that the king might be facilitating "a ready passage to a democracy, which is the deadliest enemy to a monarchy" (cited in Hill, 1966: 52).

Before the opening session of the Parliament of 1614, Francis Bacon advised James to open the session with a strong claim of the rationale for absolutist government, urging him to declare that he would not, "for all the treasure in the world, quit any point of his just power of sovereignty and monarchy, but leaves them (as they are) sacred and inviolate to his posterity" (cited in Prestwich, 1966: 149). James's demand for a subsidy— without which he would be forced to live "like a Shell-Fish upon his own Moisture," as one contemporary put it (cited in Prestwich, 1966: 161)— was transformed into a benevolence by Parliament, as it used his fiscal needs to refrain from outright grants in peacetime.

James's consistent need for money during the decade of the 1610s led him to the traditional French expedient of venality of offices. When he created and offered earldoms for £ 10,000 each, however, he found the market for offices "flooded" (Russell, 1971: 281). James was thus thrown onto the less stable and more politically volatile credit market, and I have documented above his increasing reliance on all manner of loans.

The 1620s changed the magnitude of the fiscal needs of the crown, and also the structure of political opposition. Until 1621, when he again called Parliament, James had been able to avoid participation in the Thirty Years War, and had profited by the continuation of war, and the rivalry between Spain and France (Lee, 1970: 139–40). Though James did not share the prevailing anti-Spanish attitude in Parliament and did not want war, he was unable to dissuade Philip III from assisting the invasion of the Palatinate, and thus was drawn into the war because he could not "sit idly by while his son-in-law was despoiled of his hereditary lands" (Davies, 1959: 23). Of course, war only "accentuated social tensions that were already there," and other matters pressed on the minds of the "discontented gentlemen and angry merchants" who assembled in Parliament in 1621 (Hill, 1986: 42; Prestwich, 1966: 131). A "serious depression" in industry had dramatically affected merchants' trade, so that, as one M.P. put it (cited in Supple, 1959: 54), "Trade is like the moon on the wane . . . the counties that suffer are several, the sufferings several . . . trade runs high in importation . . . low in exploration . . . the kingdom is hindered even within the kingdom by a decay of the trade of cloth."

The whole country suffered greatly in the serious economic downturn of the 1620s, and the tightening of royal fiscal screws to generate sufficient funds for the king's projects only made things unbearably worse. One Staffordshire gentleman reported in 1620 that "the country is much oppressed, so much that . . . it is a grief to hear the cry of the poor" ring true throughout the realm. And, his conclusion indicated the ways in which royal fiscal exactions were exacerbating the crisis: "Not a week is there, that some payments are not made, and what becomes of the money the Lord knows" (cited in Hirst, 1986: 125).

By looking at the structure of oppositional discourse and the various proposals made by the Parliament of 1621, we can get a good sense of the growing opposition of the local gentry and merchants, and also of the explanatory power of the fiscal crisis model I am employing in this work. Wallerstein, for example, argues that the origins of the English Revolution can be found in the trade crisis of the 1620s because it turned capitalists, interested in exploiting world markets, against the king (Wallerstein, 1974). For the world-systems model to be valid, then, we would expect those capitalist merchants who were most involved in overseas trade to voice their opposition to James I, and to begin to do so from the 1570s, when the decline of overseas trade began. However, these merchants were largely supportive of the king because he had granted to them profitable monopolies, and had granted numerous trade concessions to garner some additional revenues for the monarchy. (That the opposition from these groups grew most rapidly not from the 1570s, as Wallerstein's model might have suggested, but from the 1610s and especially after 1620, when the crown attempted to resolve its fiscal crisis by selling offices and confiscating lands, gives increased credence to the fiscal-crisis model I am proposing here as a superior explanation to one relying upon patterns of overseas trade.) The Parliament of 1621's first bill was to limit monopolies and patents, an important "statutory invasion of the royal prerogative" (McIlwain, 1940: 138). Patents and monopolies were opposed not by the largest capitalists, of course, but by the local gentry and the justices of the peace, the latter because they thwarted competitive trade and the former because they represented "rival agencies of local government" (Russell, 1979: 101). In fact, the chief opposition came from middle-level traders who were the victims of royal monopolies and also from landowners who objected to the erosion of their local privileges. Parliament represented middle-level outport merchants against the larger London monopolists, and denounced the "sinister conspiracy by the London cartels" when Alford argued (cited in Russell, 1979: 313):

> London will beggar the whole Kingdom for the Londoners and Merchants have raised the prices of all foreign commodities to a great rate, and yet all our Country Commodities were never so cheap, as now are Wool Cloth, corn, and the like, and they will engross their Merchandise, and have our own native Commodities at their own Prices.

Parliament opposed monopolies and promoted free trade; "faced with a crisis of national scope, it was in no mood to respect the sanctity of chartered organizations" (Supple, 1959: 68).

Parliament's protestation demanded far-reaching fiscal reforms as a condition of continued financial support of the war with Spain. James's efforts to placate Parliament by offering Chancellor Bacon for impeachment rather than promoting reform, and by pleading with it that while it resisted "the business of my state lies ableeding" had little impact on a determined Parliament, whose resistance was so stiff that one observer joked that England was turning into a republic (Prestwich, 1966: 314; Hinds, 1911: 184; Zaller, 1971: 82). Ultimately, James dissolved Parliament, throwing himself into the hands of the Spanish rather than giving in to demands for structural reforms.

Also, throughout the 1620s opposition to James settled on the duke of Buckingham as the architect of the grievous policies. The duke's centrality as patronage broker and policymaker angered large numbers of people. To the Lords, he had debased the peerage through the sale of honors and by "blocking the King from his aristocratic councillors"; to the Commons, he was the evil genius behind monopoly (Sharpe, 1978: 242). In fact, Buckingham's monopolization of power brought the two Houses of Parliament together in common cause (Zaller, 1971: 116, 123).

The dismissal of Parliament did not resolve the fiscal crisis. Lord Cranfield wrote unhappily of "the want of money in the kingdom. The great dearth. The decay of trade," and declared that "His Majesty can neither borrow in City nor Country considering the great debts he owes both" (cited in Prestwich, 1966: 330). Forced loans of £ 76,458 in 1622 and only £ 10,492 in 1623 were hardly enough to overcome a debt of over £ 1 million. James required mechanisms to raise money that would allow him to "approach a critical House of Commons, not as a self-made mendicant imploring relief, but with the assurance of a solvent and respected partner" (Prestwich, 1966: 337). Cranfield warned against increased monopolies, extortion, and bribery as expedients, and wrote in 1623 of the impossibility to "conceive into what straits I am daily driven for supply of money for his Majesty's occasions, which the exchequer is not able to support, they are so infinite and of so many pressing natures" (cited in Dietz, 1964: 200). Cranfield's fall was more a victory for Buckingham, who deflected criticism away from himself, than for the king's ability to resolve his fiscal worries or for Parliament, which again registered its opposition by impeachment of a royal official.[3]

By 1624 war expenditures had increased so rapidly that a new Parliament had to be called (Russell, 1971: 298; Ashton, 1960: 39). If the king wanted war, he must have money; if he was to have money he required a Parliament. But, if the "pursuit of a costly war policy and the failure of another benevolence" forced calling the Parliament of 1624, James would have to confront its unrelenting opposition and demands for administrative reforms. Parliament offered the Statute on Monopolies, declaring that "all monopolies, commissions, grants, licenses, charters and patents for the role of buying, making, working, or using any commodities within the realm were contrary to law," which Buckingham found utterly impossible, declaring his opposition to the making of foreign policy in Parliament or even taking account of parliamentary opinion in the formulation of foreign policy. (Price, 1966: 34; see also Adams, in Sharpe, 1978: 158). Parliament was dismissed once again, without voting the needed funds, its opposition growing but unresolved. The king did not live to see another Parliament but left his son, Charles I, the task of attempting to meet expenses and coping with serious political opposition.

Charles I Comes to the Throne, 1625–1629

The death of James I and the ascension of his son, Charles I, to the throne in 1625 did little to alleviate the problems of the monarchy. In fact, things went from bad to worse. James's "muddled" foreign policy left England involved in war on at least two fronts (Scotland and Spain) without adequate funds to pursue either (Prestwich, 1966: 283). The persecution of the Huguenots in France prompted many English Protestants to call for increased foreign involvement to assist their religious brethren. Civil expenses had risen more than 25 percent over the level during Elizabeth's reign, and this during a period of deflation (Mann, 1978: 41). James left his son both a troubled treasury and a serious erosion in the prestige of the monarchy, alongside increasing opposition from a variety of quarters. Roberts (1966: 41) sums it up:

> The House of Commons was filled with confident, aggressive, and ambitious men, and the House of Lords with peers jealous of their privileges. James's prodigality drove the tight-fisted gentry to oppose importunate courtiers. Government by patentees angered every justice of the peace in the land. The grant of monopolies persuaded the merchants to join in the hunt for monopolists. The collection of impositions aroused the lawyers and merchants. The failure to enforce the laws against recusants exasperated the Puritans. The prevalence of extortion in the administration angered all who had to pay its price. Indecision at court impelled courtiers to seek support in Parliament against their enemies. In sum, . . . an impoverished King, indifferent to good government and the opinions of his subjects, met an ambitious Parliament, determined to use its power to secure good government and the pursuit of national policies.

Charles faced such an array of opposition, so much of it generated by the structural problems of the absolutist drive to resolve an endemic fiscal crisis, that it is hard to attribute his mounting political difficulties to psychological variables. It is no doubt true that his "authoritarian temperament," his "fundamental insecurity," and his almost "fatal stubbornness and indifference to public opinion" made the structural situation worse, but even here there is room for disagreement (Hirst, 1986: 161, 162).[4] But Charles's vision of Stuart England, his political objective, was "a deferential, strictly hierarchical, socially stable, paternalist absolutism based on a close union of Church and Crown" (Stone, 1972: 126).

When Charles took the throne, the fiscal crisis that he had inherited was immediately obvious. One observer wrote in 1625 (cited in Dietz, 1964: 223) that "there is neither money in the exchequer left, not means to maintain the ordinaries for this year, nor any credit at all," and another commented that the government was "in such straits for money as is not to be spoken of." The legacy of war found Charles already committed to large expenditures to his allies: £ 360,000 as a subsidy to the king of Denmark; £ 240,000 to various mercenaries under Mansfield's command; and £ 100,000 to troops in the Low Countries (Russell, 1971: 300). A loan upon his ascension of £ 60,000 from the Corporation of the City of London was granted at 8 percent interest on security of crown lands, but even here the goodwill that accompanied the ascension was soon dissipated when the king defaulted on the interest payments. Another loan of £ 100,000 was turned down by the 300 wealthy London citizens who had been gathered together to consider it (Pearl, 1966: 72). Charles knew that borrowing would not nearly repay his debts, let alone generate increased revenues to provide the fiscal maneuverability he needed to pursue the various fronts of war. He needed Parliament.

Opposition to Charles's policies was voiced as soon as Parliament assembled.[5] Royal demands for supply for the war effort were met with counterdemands for "redress before supply," which the king could hardly afford. The war was costing over £ 50,000 a month for land forces and mercenaries alone, which was close to the king's entire annual income, and the expenses for the navy were in addition to it (Russell, 1979: 73). Charles's assertion that "since they had drawn him into a war, they must find the means to maintain it" was answered with two "pitifully inadequate" subsidies, and tonnage and poundage for the year only, although this customs duty was traditionally voted to the king for life at the first Parliament of his reign (Dietz, 1964: 223; Russell, 1971: 300). Royal efforts to pursue an aggressive and independent foreign policy were constantly thwarted by Parliament, which failed to vote needed funds and registered opposition to various fronts of the war. The plans to support the Huguenots at La Rochelle were scrapped because of parliamentary opposition, hardly, Cogswell writes (1984: 267), an example of "imperious indifference to an insignificant institution."[6] Lack of funds also allowed the Spanish to gain significantly, which in turn reduced even further Parliament's willingness to subsidize the war effort. Thus, Charles found himself, quite early in his reign, facing squarely actualization of the maxim "There is nothing which decreases the popularity of wars so easily as defeat" (in Russell, 1971: 261).

Because finance was "continuously the central problem of royal government and policy," and Parliament was not to be forthcoming with the needed funds, Charles's only recourse short of pursuing peace was "the use of arbitrary measures to raise money." So, the king developed a number of expedients to attempt to raise funds without resorting to Parliament again (Aylmer, 1961: 40; Dietz, 1964: 233). He ignored crown debts entirely, and royal creditors who did not demand repayment often and vigorously were habitually disregarded (Dietz, 1964: 258). Charles tried to collect gifts, loans, and benevolences, but the aversion to paying was so great that their value was very low. He was eventually able to raise a loan on the security of the crown jewels. This source of funds was, naturally, painfully inadequate, and Charles called another Parliament because the Spanish war could not be sustained without one. After he had reminded the members that Parliaments "are altogether in my power for the calling, sitting, and continuance of them, therefore as I find the fruits of them either good or evil, they are to continue to be or not to be," Parliament voted three subsidies and three fifteenths, about a third of what Charles needed, and this contingent upon the removal of Buckingham from ofice, for he was blamed for casting the king into "all kinds of wars." It was a condition that the king refused to consider (cited in Russell, 1979: 292; see also Russell, 1971: 71, 267; Russell, 1979: 291ff.). Charles dismissed Parliament without receiving any funds.

Reliance on the credit market had proven inadequate, "unable to bear the strains of war" (Hirst, 1986: 149). In the winter of 1627 Charles alienated the last large block of crown lands, for which he received about £ 350,000 in return for canceling past debts and the extension of another loan. This "ended the traditional role of land as a major source of royal revenue and with it, it might be said, the medieval monarchy" (Hirst, 1986: 149). Charles came to rely increasingly on the unreliable credit market for funds.

To resolve the fiscal deadlock, Charles proposed a forced loan, a barely disguised euphemism for a parliamentary subsidy, which came more and more during Charles's reign to approximate direct taxation without parliamentary approval (Ashton, 1960: 36). This desperate fiscal expedient, the *"enfant terrible* of a financially embarassed king," was the "greatest in magnitude of demand and the greatest in magnitude of accomplishment" of the reign, and rescued Charles from immediate bankruptcy" (Barnes, 1961: 163; see also Hirst, 1986: 148). The forced loan of 1626 "aroused fierce opposition from unexpected and influential quarters"; one Suffolk clergyman, John Rous, noted in late 1627 that "men be disposed to speak the worst of state businesses" (Ashton, 1960: 164; Rous cited in Hirst, 1986: 149). A young M.P. named John Hampden refused to pay his share of the loan, an action that foreshadowed his later symbolic importance in opposing Ship Money. Other fiscal expedients in 1627 included the Loan of Five Subsidies, another "thinly disguised tax" intended to substitute in loans what the subsidies would have provided but that also provoked serious opposition. England was at war with both Continental powers at the same time, a situation that had not obtained for over a century, and, as Lord Goring wrote to Buckingham in 1627, "All the revenue is anticipated for the next whole year, which being so, the farmers and such like bonds are little worth, for the King may break all those assignments at his own will, and where then shall they be paid?" (Cal. State Papers, Dom., 1627–8: 422). Resistance to the Loan of Five Subsidies was high throughout the realm, and the Corporation of the City of London refused to lend any more money to the king. The king ordered to be arrested those gentlemen who refused to pay the Loan of Five Subsidies, but popular opposition was so strong that seventy-six of them were released in January 1628 (Cliffe, 1961: 293). Buckingham's client Pye wrote to his patron to consider "how far his Majesty's revenue of all kinds is now exhausted. We are upon the third year anticipation beforehand; land, much sold of the principal; credit lost; and at the utmost shift with the Commonwealth" (cited in Prestwich, 1966: 463). "They wish to make war against heaven and earth," wrote the French agent Dumoulin in 1627 (cited in Russell, 1979: 323), "but lack the means to make it against anyone."

Opponents of the king's policies felt themselves to be in a stronger position when they assembled in Parliament in 1628, and they presented the Petition of Right, a far-reaching attack on absolute monarchy, which demanded the abolition of arbitrary imprisonment, the elimination of arbitrary taxation, and the establishment of martial law, as well as the end to the billeting of troops, which they argued caused unnecessary financial burdens on the populace and "brought the war home to the people" (Russell, 1971: 336; see also Hill, 1986: 53). The presentation of the Petition of Right, which used natural liberties and natural law as the rhetorical sources of opposition to absolutism (and claimed to confirm old liberties as rights, not to extend new privileges, hence the use of the petition and avoidance of a formal bill), was the final blow to the pretense of amicability between Charles and his Parliaments; relations now were at "the point of collapse" (Russell, 1979: 64). Though Charles grudgingly accepted it, the petition indicated a "functional breakdown" in English political adminis-tration that was manifest in the strained relations between central and local government; between a king representing the claims of national interest over local power brokers, afraid of both military absolutism and the threat of social revolution from below, and among agencies of administration. Although Russell argues that the crisis of 1628–29 was the "result of a decade of war, and unsuccessful war, rather than of any longer-term factors," it seems clear that the king's fiscal inability to conduct an independent foreign policy, and the desperate search for revenues to offset a persistent and structurally based fiscal crisis brought the king and the Parliament to loggerheads (Russell, 1979: 484).

By 1629 Charles was pressing for peace with the French, and his abandonment of the effort to rescue the Rochellais indicates his fiscal incapacity to pursue that war effort. When Parliament assembled once again in 1629, Charles informed them that he had ordered the officers of the customs to seize the goods of any who did not pay tonnage and poundage (Roberts, 1966: 73). Sir John Eliot attempted to sway public opinion, declaring "collectors and payers of Tonnage and Poundage to be capital enemies of King and Kingdom," which invited the public to institute a taxpayers' strike; it was an appeal to a growing body of public opinion to bring pressure on the king to change his policy (Russell, 1979: 416). As far as Charles was concerned, Parliament was now the chief impediment to successful government; if government could not be conducted with it, he would rule without it. Of course, to do so, Charles needed to be at peace with Spain and present at least the pretense of fiscal solvency. The Treaty of Madrid, negotiated in 1630, ended England's formal participation in the Thirty Years War, with Charles renouncing all claims to the Palatinate, and withdrawing from foreign adventures. In "renouncing Parliament," Russell writes (1971: 312–13), "Charles had, in effect, renounced his right to a foreign policy, and could do nothing." In addition, the crown's reliance on fiscal subterfuge provided only an illusion of solvency; Hill writes (1973: 31):

> The government's alliance with a ring of big London capitalists, who produced loans in return for baronetcies and privileges like farming the customs, alienated London citizens outside the favored circle, and this alliance gave the government a sense of financial security which was wholly illusory. . . . Bankruptcy was concealed, but it was bankruptcy all right.

During the next eleven years of prerogative government Charles's needs for revenues diminished not at all; in fact, they increased prodigiously. What did decrease were the mechanisms by which he could legitimately raise revenues. The absence of Parliament meant that all fiscal expedients were fraught with contention and controversy; they became increasingly desperate and provoked increasingly hostile reaction. Without Parliament as the locus of legitimate opposition, this resistance remained divided among various groups. When wartime necessities again forced the calling of Parliament in 1640, the elements of the coalition of political opposition had found their mouthpiece, and in the ideology of Puritanism (and especially in the politicized religious opposition to Laudian clerical administration) the coalition had found the cohesive glue to maintain its unity for a revolutionary challenge to absolutism.[7]

Notes

1. Another attempt to raise money that year, about £ 200,000 through the farmers of the great customs, failed because the customs farmers would not overdraft, and the developments of the war with Scotland had prodigiously increased the royal need for funds and decreased significantly the likelihood of repayment (Ashton, 1960: 161).
2. An enclosure riot in the midland counties in 1607 lasted about a month, and involved crowds of about 5,000 people. Of special interest is that the rioters called themselves Levellers, a name that became increasingly important politi-

cally during the 1640s as the spearhead of the popular social revolution (Zagorin, 1982, vol. 1: 179).

3. Impeachment was one of Parliament's chief methods of registering its opposition. Between 1610 and 1625 Parliament impeached seven servants of the king, arrested eight others, expelled four from the House, and censured one (Roberts, 1966: 10).

4. For example, Barnes (1961: 143) argues that Charles was a king whose "motives were pure and in whom sincerity was dominant." "Few kings," he continues, "who have sat on England's throne and few ministers who have counselled them appear to have been more genuinely desirous of the subjects' good than were Charles I and his principal counsellors." Barnes probably goes too far, however, when he argues that "the disafforestation and drainage schemes, the Book of Orders, the revitalization of the militia, and even the ship money fleet were all aimed at securing benefits for the nation" (1961: 144). Fiscal expedients designed to augment royal power over and against the autonomous social groups in countryside and cities can be seen as nationally beneficial only in a scheme that posits, as Mousnier does for France, a centralizing, absolutist monarchy as the progressive and enlightened force in political organization. Given that absolute monarchs saw themselves as defending a feudal, patriarchal, and seigneurial system, casting the monarchy as the force of progress against retrogressive capitalist merchants and enclosing gentry, while dimming the once-bright light of Whiggish history, is also itself untenable, and one of the few places where I disagree with Professor Barnes's illuminating study.

5. I recognize that the term *Parliament* might be read as a monolithic entity in the traditional Whig sense that "Parliament opposed the monarchy." I am aware, of course, of the deep divisions within the Parliament, not only between Lords and Commons, but also between middle-level merchants from outports and the larger monopolist merchants in London, among various adherents to different religious sects, and also among the allegiances to which any M.P. might answer. Where possible, I shall be specific about which factions in Parliament I mean, but in no case do I mean *Parliament* to connote a single, monolithic entity of one mind and one unified opposition.

6. The reference here is to Russell, who argued that Parliament was a relatively "insignificant institution," and that in the 1620s "the majority of important events took place outside Parliament" (Russell, 1979: 1). No doubt Russell is right to point our attention to the countryside, to which we shall turn shortly, but Cogswell's important caution that the government constantly shifted its foreign policy initiatives in an effort to placate Parliament suggests that the institution was quite significant, even if not uniquely so.

7. It is important not to overstress the significance of Parliament in any analysis of the English Revolution. Frequently, scholars have cast the Revolution as a strictly parliamentary affair, without much discussion of the layers of social groups composing the coalition of political opposition. But to focus exclusively on Parliament's role in the Revolution is like looking at a barometer and blaming it for bad weather. Parliament reflected the deep divisions of mid-seventeenth-century England; it expressed the powerful conflicts, but it did not create them. One could see in Parliament many of the powerful political currents at the time, and one could have seen storms approaching, as with a barometer.

7

Toward Revolution in England:
Prerogative Reign and Fiscal Crisis,
1629–1640

Dismissing Parliament in 1629 and concluding a peace with both France and Spain the following year only slightly alleviated the fiscal crisis that had beset Charles I since he had come to the throne. Expenditures dropped hardly at all, and the monarchy was still not solvent. Charles could continue without Parliament only so long as he kept out of war, and yet with Parliament, he was limited as to the funds that he could raise. He limped along, augmenting his income wherever it seemed possible, choosing short-term fiscal expedients over longer-term structural reforms, even though these expedients violated the "central dualism between the ordinary and extraordinary expenditures which lay at the heart of financial policy" (Ashton, 1960: 38). During the 1630s Charles sought to resolve his fiscal crisis by reviving old feudal sources of revenues, exerting royal control over economic activity, rehabilitating outmoded sources, and, of course, inventing new possible sources of income. The reliance on short-term expedients was "like the shearing of hogs," wrote one contemporary (cited in Prestwich, 1966: 560), "which makes a great noise but yields little wool."

New elements were being added to the list of groups that were withdrawing their support, both financial and political, of the Stuart monarchy. A fiscal crisis was rapidly becoming a legitimacy crisis, as increasing numbers of urban lower-middle classes and also urban and rural Puritans were disaffected from royal policies, and were beginning to question the capacity of the king to rule as well as to reign. The various elements of the coalition of political opposition were now all set in motion. The religious opposition of the Puritans lent a unifying ideology that supported revolt, while the increasingly loud voices of the urban lower-middle class and poor pushed the other oppositional elements to articulate a program that would appease the popular elements without becoming a social revolution.

Charles's Search for Funds

During the first few years of the 1630s Charles "resorted to every possible feudal and non-feudal device in the quest for tax revenues capable of sustaining an enlarged state machine beyond Parliamentary control" (Anderson, 1974: 141). He exploited purveyance, revived wardships, and sold noble titles (although far fewer than his father had done because there was so little market left). In January 1630 Charles decided to impose fines for knighthood. Originally, the law of knighthood had been instituted to compel all those with incomes over £ 5 per year to be knighted so that the king would be assured of having enough knights for military protection. James I had earlier attempted to raise revenues by putting knighthoods up for sale, but many had refused what had become simply an honor, and one that was somewhat costly without providing any immediate political, social, or economic benefit. Charles replaced the fee for knighthood with another: he issued a fine for all those with incomes over £ 40 per year who refused the expense of becoming a knight. When one country gentleman received the order to be knighted and declared his wish to comply, his request was refused and he was fined for not being knighted. The last thing Charles wanted, after all, was for anyone to become a knight; "he wanted to fine them for not becoming knighted" (Russell, 1971: 318). This thinly concealed nonparliamentary tax of the landowning classes brought in over £ 150,000 in 1630 and 1631 alone; by 1635 £ 173,000 had been paid in fines. But, fines for knighthood were easily seen through, and not the stuff of which long-term solutions to fiscal crises are made. As the Venetian ambassador commented, they were "false mines for obtaining money, because they are good for once only and states are not maintained by such devices" (cited in Hirst, 1986: 174; see also Hill, 1973: 54).[1]

Charles also resorted to the trusted Tudor and Stuart expedient of exploiting crown lands, although outright sale was much less profitable than offering them as collateral on loans.[2] However, because the Corporation of the City of London was increasingly resistant to lending money to Charles, he borrowed from individuals or syndicates whose entire fortunes were tied up in royal credit markets (Ashton, 1960: 173). Even these individuals and syndicates were stretched to their limits by Charles's needs, especially toward the end of the decade when preparations for war again increased the fiscal pressures on the king. What's more, the "incessant and overriding demand of the Crown for revenues" pushed these individuals and syndicates, many of whom were city magistrates, into alliance with others who began to share their political and social outlook. The king's threats, his tactical separation of creditors from their institutional base, his failure to husband his credit, and the prolonged amounts of time he took to repay his loans all combined to encourage these creditors—many of whom were wealthy merchants and monopolists—to abandon royal finance as a source of income and as a method of maintaining the king against his opponents.

The farming of the customs also exchanged short-term relief for longer-term opposition, and was the only source of revenue that increased significantly during the decade. In fact, Hirst argues (1986: 175) that Charles "limped along by courtesy of the customs farmers." That the crown imposed customs duties on an increasing number of imported commodities was contentious enough to some, but that the crown then farmed out the collection to financiers was even more heinous. During the 1630s Charles added alum, currants, French wines, silks, tobacco, sugar, and coal to the list of items on which custom duties were to be collected, and collection was farmed out to financiers.[3] Customs farms brought in £ 210,000 per year between 1631 and 1635, and another £ 245,000 per year between 1636 and 1641. New customs farms added £ 53,091 a year between 1631 and 1635, and another £ 119,583 per year between 1636 and 1641. Coal duties and farms accounted for an additional £ 8,400 a year between 1631 and 1635, and £ 18,400 a year between 1636 and 1641 (Aylmer, 1961: 64).

Charles also attempted to intervene directly in trade, both by the continual sale of monopolies and other fiscal maneuvers. Sale of monopolies was "the line of least resistance for governments in financial difficulties," and Charles continually relied on them (Hill, 1973: 39). The sale of a monopoly on soap production brought in £ 29,000 per year after 1636, and when monopolies were opposed in courts, Charles bypassed the common law courts and administered them through the Star Chamber. In 1635 Charles licensed a second East India Company—to the great damage of the shareholders of the first, who had paid heavily for the monopoly—and generated a small windfall from the monopolists involved in the second company. (Hill, 1973: 100). (This splitting of royal officers, the monopolists, is analogous to the splitting of venal offices of Cardinal Richelieu (either by splitting the semester of their contract or creating a whole parallel set of offices) as a way either to bring new officers into the realm of royal credit or to undermine the privileges of the first group.)

Monopolies generated increasing opposition, and in the character of this opposition we can observe the gradual coalescence of the strands of opposition. For example, the soap monopoly was opposed on economic grounds because it doubled the price of an inferior soap that made the hands of washerwomen blister, and also on economic grounds because the monopolists were Papists (Hills, 1973: 39). As one pamphlet had it (cited in Hill, 1973: 39),

> No freeman of London after he hath served his years and set up his trade, can be sure long to enjoy the labour of his trade, but either he is forbidden longer to use it, or is forced at length with the rest of his trade to purchase it as a monopoly, at a dear rate, which they and all the kingdom pay for.

The opposition to monopolies was only a part of the general opposition of smaller merchants in the cities and most merchants in the countryside to royal intervention in trade. The wool industry was damaged by the fiscal manipulations and chicanery, as well as by the general decline of exports through the 1630s. Epidemic compounded the problems, especially with the outbreak of the plaque in 1636, which brought "financial distress to merchant, clothier, the familes of weavers, spinners, carders, and sorters, as well as the landlords who raised the sheep" (Appleby, 1978: 35).

Everywhere opposition to royal financial expedients was growing. "Government interference in business, in agriculture, trade, industry, building and mining was a widespread grievance under Charles I. But it was a grievance against the policy of the Crown, especially its many fiscal expedients" (Aylmer, 1961: 462). Sir John Oglander wrote in 1632 of the effect of these fiscal policies on the gentry, whose members had expected to benefit (cited in Stone, 1965):

> It is impossible for a mere country gentleman ever to grow rich or to raise his house. He must have some other vocation with his inheritance, as to be a courtier, lawyer, merchant, or some other vocation. If he hath no other voca-tion, let him get a ship and judiciously manage her, or buy some auditor's place, or be vice admiral in his county. By only following the plough, he may keep his word and be upright, but he will never increase his fortune.

Although Charles had raised revenues during the 1630s from about £ 300,000 a year to almost £ 500,000 a year, the "price of fiscal solvency by reliance on prerogative exaction was political disaffection" (Prestwich, 1966: 547; see also Hirst, 1986: 174). "As the government's finances shrank, the thirst for money tended to become the end in itself and to obscure the motives which desired the commonwealth's good" (Barnes, 1961: 144). In 1639 Sir Jacob Astley, who had been requested to assist in collections of royal revenues in Yorkshire, wrote, "Your Honor will not believe what trouble they give me to set them even as they should be for amongst them there be those that talks no good purpose" (cited in Cliffe, 1961: 313). The secret Parliament of 1637 registered opposition to Arminianism, the High Commission, the Star Chamber, the notion of a triennial Parliament, and the inclusion of bishops in the House of Lords, and demanded reversal of the judgment of the Bate's case from the early years of the reign of James I, which had given the king the power to levy the customs duties without parliamentary consent (Russell, 1971: 330). Fiscal opposition began to center on the fiscal expedient known as Ship Money.

Ship Money and the Escalation of Political Opposition

Ship Money was perhaps the most successful and the most contentious of all the fiscal expedients developed by Charles I in his effort to resolve his fiscal crisis and continue to rule without Parliament. As an extraparliamentary measure, Ship Money became a symbolic juncture for the growing political opposition of landed classes, merchants, and lower classes in both city and countryside. It was "taken as conclusive evidence of the king's intention to consolidate absolutism"; its levying "completed the alienation of the Country from the Court" and "outraged the sensibilities of men who respected the sanctity of the law and valued their neighbors' respect" (Zagorin, 1982, vol. 2: 144; Barnes, 1961: 242). Ship Money shifted the terms of political opposition; "by placing the King's authority at the center of a claim for extraparliamentary taxation [Ship Money], played a key role in forcing opposition to royal policy out of conventional, localist forms into more general, ideological modes of expression" (Lake, 1981: 71).

Some writers disagree with this interpretation, suggesting that Ship Money was "no would-be absolutist attempt to bolster [Charles's] general revenues. . . . Neither was its administration the new departure that might have ushered in absolutism"; rather, Ship Money was simply "one more product of the council's fiscal antiquarianism" (Hirst, 1986: 177). These writers stress two important themes to support their argument. First, Ship Money had a long history, and its legitimacy was, in principle, widely accepted. Thus, Clifford writes that however beset by problems the collection may have been, "there is recorded nowhere any complaint about the actual principle of Ship Money, no one seems to have doubted its legality. Most accepted that it should be collected, it was merely the means of doing this which were in question" (Clifford, 1982: 99). Second, Ship Money was such "an enormous fiscal success" that writers suggest that it could not also be seen as a turning point in the generation of political opposition, even if it also provoked "limited passive resistance" (Morrill, 1982: 3).

Ship Money was, despite its initial financial success, pivotal in the development of the coalition of political opposition for several reasons. Although Ship Money maintained a long and venerable history, Charles's efforts to have it assessed at the parish level by the local sheriffs was an administrative innovation and made the imposition of the tax appear new to contemporaries. As an unprecedented intrusion of the centralizing monarchy into the locality, Ship Money was perceived as a ruthless violation of the traditional moral economy of the English villages and towns, a "threat to ancient liberties," and an "affront to popular as well as elite notions of law and good rule" (Underdown, 1986: 131, 124). The Somerset grand jury complained in 1638 of "the great and heavy taxations by new invented ways upon the country" (cited in Underdown, 1986: 124). In addition, the distribution of the assessment brought middle- and lower-rank people into common cause with the gentry and merchants because all felt themselves to be unjustly assessed (Hill, 1986: 37).

Although Ship Money's legality as an emergency measure may have remained unchallenged, and its financial results been quite successful, each succeeding effort to collect it brought in less and less money and generated more and more opposition to an imposition that suddenly appeared to be a permanent fiscal feature of the relations between the locality and the crown. Opposition to Ship Money was a "defence of local rights and interests," which was "only one aspect of a general defence of ancient custom" (Underdown, 1986: 124), and brought together social groups whose earlier class antipathy may have prevented making common cause against Stuart efforts at absolute rule. In 1637, for example, in Somerset "the opposition hardly made any pretence at dutifulness, took few pains to conjure up legitimate grounds for a complaint, and seldom bothered to dissemble its true motive. Resistance was overt. Husbandmen, yeomen, and gentlemen attacked Ship Money in the most effective manner that any financial exactions can be attacked: they refused to pay it" (Barnes, 1961: 222).

Ship Money had originally been imposed on port cities, so as to provide ships for the royal navy. Each border county and the City of London, an inland port, was asked to contribute one or more ships, fully equipped, to the navy, or the money such a ship would cost, based upon the assessment of the county's wealth. Sheriffs were charged with breaking down this aggregate assessment into smaller portions payable by the borough and individual property owners in the shire in proportion to their wealth and landholdings. It was a logical and legal imposition, the crown reasoned, because port cities were protected by the royal navy from plunder and invasion in wartime, and ought therefore to be responsible for supplying the navy.

Ship Money was successful early, though it was never popular. In 1588 Elizabeth had levied about eighty ships from coastal towns, thirty of which had come from the City of London, and Ship Money had brought the treasury the equivalent of four parliamentary subsidies. But, Lord Burghley also noted, in July 1588, "a general murmur of people and discontented people will increase to the comfort of the enemy" (cited in Wernham, 1966: 404). Elizabeth extended Ship Money beyond the coastal towns to coastal shires when she levied the tax again in 1591, 1594, 1595, 1596, 1599, and 1603. Because she reasoned that inland towns benefit from secure boundaries and naval protection, she also extended the imposition to include inland towns; she devised a plan in 1603 "for every county, inland and coastal, to contribute money to standing fleets for the protection of merchants' shipping" (Williams, 1979: 76). (Her plan was never implemented, however, for opposition was gauged to be too great; the extension of Ship Money as a tax on inland ports "aroused resentment and opposition" [Williams, 1979:77].)

Inspired by Elizabeth's early success with Ship Money, Charles I determined to levy the assessment, hoping to collect the money in lieu of raising ships. In 1627 Essex justices refused to join with Colchester in providing a ship; the king's reply insisted that "the defense of a kingdom in times of extraordinary danger [is] not tied to ordinary and continued precedents" (cited in Barnes, 1961: 204). In March twenty-three Somerset judges also declared that they would undergo the charge "with great unwillingness, because we conceive it will beget upon us and our posterities the precedent of a charge which [neither] we, nor our predecessors did ever bear," and reminded the council that they were "from a county that hath not been backward in public service when custom and ancient usage hath been the grounds of those commands" (cited in Barnes, 1961: 204). Again in 1628 the expenses of aiding the Huguenots at La Rochelle and Re inspired the Privy Council to extend Ship Money beyond the ports; the king wrote (cited in Swales, 1977: 165):

> This great business of setting out ships used to be charged upon the Port Towns and neighboring shires . . . [but] we have thought fit with the advice of our Privy Council and agreeable to the precedents of former times to cause the whole charge of this fleet to be cast up and distributed among all the counties.

The project was abandoned when significant opposition again seemed to be forthcoming; Charles requested only £ 173,411 from the seaport cities, and negotiated a loan through the money market "for satisfying arrears of wages, for repairing ships, and supplying stores" (Cal. State Papers, Domestic, 1628, vol. 92: 93; Swales, 1977: 172).

During the prerogative reign, Charles revived Ship Money as a potential source of revenue, and again sought to extend its assessment and collection. It was originally opposed by Lionel Cranfield as a "most lewd project," but Attorney General Noy rehabilitated the imposition after Cranfield's impeachment (cited in Prestwich, 1966: 560; see also Gordon, 1910: 153). The pivotal change came in 1635 when Charles announced his intention to extend the tax to inland towns at his own discretion; as the king's councillors put it, the imposition meant "that for the supply of shipping to defend the nation, the King might impose a tax upon the people: that he was to be the judge of the necessity of such supply, and of the quantity to be imposed for it; and that he might imprison as well as distrain in case of refusal" (cited in Hill and Dell, 1949: 159). Writs in 1634 had asked for £ 104,252 from the maritime towns, and had yielded only £ 89,895, which could not meet the expenses of the navy (Cliffe, 1976: 305; Gordon, 1910: 154; Dietz, 1964: 275). The challenge implicit in the king's insistence on his right to tax without parliamentary consent was not lost on the Venetian ambassador, who wrote in January that the king's intention was to prevent the need for summoning Parliament, and "by these steps to approach more nearly to that advantageous position over his subjects, and to that independent dominion over affairs . . . which it has obviously been his aim to attain by every means" (cited in Hill and Dell, 1949: 160).

Ship Money was not only a violation of traditional privileges but a signal of Charles's absolutist designs. The change in 1635 was crucial. Sir Simon D'Ewes noted "the liberty of the subjects of England received the most deadly and fatal blow it had been sensible of in five hundred years past" (cited in Hill and Dell, 1949: 158). D'Ewes continued to link the innovation of Ship Money as a fiscal expedient to the most serious violation of the contract between state and society:

> The sum now to be levied came to some £ 320,000, and if this could be done lawfully, then by the same right the King upon the like pretense might gather the same sum ten, twelve, or a hundred times redoubled, and so to infinite proportions to any one shire, when and as often as he pleased; and so no man was, in conclusion, worth anything. . . . This taxation was absolutely against the law, and an utter oppression of the subjects' liberty, who had such a property in their goods as could not be taken from them by any taxes or levies, but such only were enacted and set down by Act of Parliament. . . . All our liberties were now at one dash utterly ruined if the King might at his pleasure lay what unlimited taxes he pleased on his subjects, and then imprison them when they refused to pay. . . . What shall freemen differ from the ancient bondsmen and villeins of England if their estates be subject to arbitrary taxes, tallages, and impositions? . . . It is the honor of a king to have his subjects rich.

. . . In all my life I never saw so many sad faces in England as this new taxation, called Ship Money, occasioned.

Ship Money had become a regular tax, no longer subject to parliamentary approval. In a sense Ship Money announced Charles's absolutist project.

Ship Money was also a remarkably successful fiscal expedient, if we judge simply by the amount of money that came into the royal treasury as a result of its imposition. Between 1636 and 1640 Ship Money yielded about £ 200,000 per year, with a significant drop in 1639 because of the widespread refusal to pay during the celebrated trial of John Hampden. In Cheshire, for example, Ship Money was collected smoothly, with only sporadic objection, and in Hampshire resistance never questioned the legality of the levy because "no one wanted to be thought disloyal" (Clifford, 1982: 94; see also Lake, 1981).

Yet, opposition did build across the countryside. Although the levy continued to bring in a steady amount, the amount of money due but not received by the crown grew dramatically. In 1636 £ 201,000 was collected and £ 4,536 remained unpaid; in 1637 £ 196,779 was collected and £ 6,907 went uncollected; in 1638 £ 196,400 was collected and £ 17,738 went uncollected; and in 1639, when writs for Ship Money totaled only £ 88,567, almost £ 14,000 went uncollected. The most dramatic jump came in 1640 when £ 216,622 was collected and £ 166,983 went uncollected (Gordon, 1910: 154; see also Bard, 1977: 179).

Ship Money also put additional strains on the crown's local administration. Local sheriffs were responsible for assessment, and they "felt the weight of ship money on their hearts as well as on their backs. . . . They had to make the choice between the claims of their neighbors and their King" (Barnes, 1961: 242). And the sheriffs, themselves, were held to be responsible for the assessed amount, even if they were unsuccessful at collecting it, although no sheriff appears to have been forced by the king to pay the difference between the assessment and the amount collected.

Throughout the latter half of the decade the opposition to Ship Money was registered in several quarters. The Venetian ambassador wrote in December 1636 that the "unwillingness of the people to contribute becomes more strongly felt. Not only the lower classes but the greatest lords are beginning to make themselves heard seriously," and Richard Baxter noticed that the levy "made a wonderful murmuring all over the land, especially among the county nobility and gentry; for they took it as the overthrow of the fundamental laws or constitution of the kingdom, and of Parliaments, and of all property" (cited in Hill and Dell, 1949: 159–60). To men of property, even the financing of the royal navy ran counter to their mercantile interests because the "ships for which they had paid were being used to further a policy that seemed pro-Spanish and unnecessarily anti-Dutch" (Howat, 1974: 46). The efforts to avoid parliamentary control over taxation was also heinous to these landed classes.

Opposition also developed among the lower and middle classes, directed both at the rural wealthy and at the crown. After all, the burden of the assessment rarely fell evenly across all classes, and the gentry and merchants could pass on the costs to the lower orders; the intention of the levy was to reverse this trend, but the crown "had little or no success in this because . . . the gentry had too much influence in making the assessments and conducting the levies" (Manning, 1976: 172). Wiltshire clothiers complained that they had been "immoderately fleeced" to the benefit of the gentry, and one political pamphlet expressed this hostility when it urged Parliament to consider "the inequality, and unconscionable disproportion of rating of the subsidies" that meant that "the poorer sort cannot pay the King: the greater sort, as having the law in their own hands, will pay but what they please, but the middle sort, they must and shall pay; and in such a disproportion as is insufferable" (cited in Manning, 1976: 172, 173). In Durham the Privy Council was informed that the mayor, instead of assessing the Ship Money on the inhabitants "with an equality, that the service be not disgraced, or the poor oppressed," made the levy "disproportionately in the most, and unworthily upon the poor ones," which has "caused the greatest clamour that I have hitherto heard" (cited in James, 1974: 172).

Resistance to Ship Money took two forms. Some complained about the severity of the fiscal burden but did not challenge the legitimacy of the levy nor of the king's right to generate revenues without parliamentary consent. For example, in Buckinghamshire, local common people declared that they were "much grieved and complain they are overcharged with the rate" (*Ship Money Papers,* 1965: 38; hereafter SMP). One town's petition stated that the inhabitants, "many of us being poor tradesmen, yet we are willing to pay according to our ability, but they have rated us five fold." The petitioners concluded by asking only for a new "indifferent" assessment (SMP: 33).

In 1637 John Hampden, a Buckinghamshire squire and M.P., also refused to pay his assessment, a paltry, and likely underassessed twenty shillings, and the ensuing court case was a long and well-followed event. As Russell writes (1971: 322),

> The Crown defended Ship Money, like impositions, by creating confusion between two lines of legal precedents. Charles claimed that the relevant precedents were not those which said the king could not raise taxes without the consent of Parliament, but equally valid precedents which said he could, in an

emergency, conscript ships and men for purposes of national defense. He might also compel people to contribute financially to the conscription of a ship.

If the king perceived such an emergency, the king's lawyers argued, how could the judges disagree? "Alas, it is not Parliaments that can keep us safe," one lawyer noted (cited in Adair, 1976: 120), and another involved the spectre of democracy, warning that if Hampden's line of reasoning were followed to its conclusions, "What will be the consequences of it but the introducing of a democratical government?" (cited in Adair, 1976: 118). After a lengthy deliberation, the judges returned a 4–2 verdict against Hampden, and he duly paid his £ 1. The Venetian ambassador suggested that this decision "at one stroke . . . roots out for ever the meeting of Parliament and renders the King absolute and sovereign. . . . If the people submit to this present prejudice, they are submitting to an eternal yoke" (in Hill and Dell, 1949: 160–61).

In 1638 Essex, Oxfordshire, and Gloucestershire had also registered refusal to pay, and Somerset achieved the distinction "of troubling the council more concerning rating to Ship Money than any other county" (Barnes, 1961: 213). London merchants refused to pay, and when writs were once again sent to Buckinghamshire, "no one seems to have paid" (Adair, 1976: 124; see also Pearl, 1966: 244). "No person of quality will pay voluntarily," observed the Venetian ambassador, who also wrote that when the king summoned various sheriffs to reprimand them for their negligence in collection, they "told him frankly that it was impossible to induce any person of account to pay amicably by persuasion or threats" (cited in Hill and Dell, 1949: 161). Although Charles promised that Ship Money "shall be proceded in regardless of Parliament" in 1639, nothing was collected that year from Northumberland, Montgomery, and Westmoreland, and by 1640 Bedfordshire, Cambridgeshire, Hertfordshire, Staffordshire, Yorkshire, and Brecknock all joined the opposition (cited in Dietz, 1964: 291; see also Gordon, 1910: 142). Resistance was "stiffening" as people "who had only previously complained of their assessments began a massive campaign of tax refusal" (Russell, 1971: 322).

For a brief term Ship Money had been a successful fiscal expedient, bringing in over £ 750,000 to the royal treasury, in addition to the actual ships supplied by the City of London. The entailed political costs were enormous, and indicated both an escalation and a coalescence of opposition to Charles's efforts as state centralization. Hampden's refusal to pay what was perceived as a new imposition, abridging the traditional relationship between state and society, had inspired many others to resist, and indicated the withdrawal of confidence by a significant segment of the propertied classes. Charles's arrogance appeared significantly muted when he opened Parliament in 1640, and the lord keeper declared that "His Majesty never had it in his royal heart to make an annual revenue of it, nor ever had a thought to make the least benefit or profit of it" (cited in Gordon, 1910: 145).

Though Charles's statement is unduly modest, both in its financial and its political understatement, it is also clear that Ship Money became one of the pretexts for the coalescence of political opposition as well as the reason by itself for serious political opposition. It was a convenient reason for opposition, only because the principles at stake were clear to most of the participants. Opposition came less because of the amount of the levy than because of the form of collection; opponents believed "the money was levied in an unconstitutional and arbitrary manner, and was used for purposes which many taxpayers regarded as immoral" (Stone, 1972: 123). In circumventing Parliament, Charles had also given that body an even greater role to play as the institutional carrier of political opposition (Zagorin, 1982, vol. 1: 126).

As the country edged toward open expression of deep political grievances, which were based, in part, on the withdrawal of fiscal support to the crown by the propertied classes, two other factors came into play, factors that would determine an outcome of the English Revolution different from the outcome of the Fronde in France. The two factors were the mobilization of lower-class opposition and religious opposition. Each had earlier evidenced a separate set of issues and had directed their grievances to the crown independent of Parliament. Gradually, however, as religious dissidents and opponents of absolutism among the popular classes joined the coalition of political opposition, the coalition gathered elements that would push for more dramatic solutions to the crisis of the old regime, and also provide the source of social cohesion for so many disparate social and economic groups.

The Genesis of Lower-Class Opposition

The entry of "the people," as they were called[4]—the rural artisans, copyholders, leaseholders, and laborers, and the urban artisans, small producers, craftsmen, shopkeepers, and wage workers—into the coalition of political opposition against Charles I is an important step in the trajectory of the Revolution. Of all the mid-seventeenth-century revolutions, only the English Revolution is marked by such active participation of the rural and urban popular classes. Their participation was decisive for the eventual success of the Revolution, and their participation throughout also determined, in part, the course that the Revolution would take. More than economic and political interests motivated the popular classes to participate. To be sure, these people had been squeezed economically by commercializing landlords, whose enclosures and disafforestation programs had pushed them off the land and torn apart the traditional moral economy of the English village. And surely, they found no relief from either a king who was too preoccupied with his own fiscal crisis to concern himself with poor relief or from clergy who were too busy posturing themselves to curry royal favor to support local gentry or to minister to the needs of the rural popular classes.

The sources of popular participation must also be sought in collective experience, in the psychological impact of various political and economic events, in the cognitive links between structural events and collective consciousness. In this sense, popular participation was caused by the psychological consequences of the breakdown of the traditional moral economy of the English village. Agricultural innovations had severed the seemingly natural and mutually dependent relationships among the various rural classes; they had transformed the fabric of social life, breaking irrevocably the classes' imaginative links with their historic past, shattering traditional local autonomy and (in some cases) control over their labor, and plunging them into the anomic world of landless, propertyless, communityless, and ultimately selfless people. The many former tenants and laborers were forced off the land and into the cities, and they carried in their collective memory the vision of a social world infused with a moral economy. Further, failure of the crown to mediate the struggle between landed classes and their tenants had left a reminder that royal policies were not conceived in the interests of the preservation of the moral economy, nor would these policies have the effect of forestalling its dissolution. In addition, the ease with which radical religious ideas and especially Puritanism spread among the urban lower-middle classes, the shopkeepers and craftsmen, also linked the popular classes to the political importance of the Puritan challenge for religious toleration, and the end to the Laudian reforms. It was more, then, than their economic and political interests that propelled the popular classes into the coalition.

In such an atmosphere, the traditional tensions between agricultural landowners and their tenants often led, paradoxically, to the eventual alliance of these two groups against the crown. Class hostilities in the countryside certainly did not disappear. "Under the surface impression of calm and stability, the years between the Northern Rising and the Civil War saw recurring quarrels between landlords and tenants" (James, 1974: 82). In some cases older landlords, themselves feeling the economic squeeze of rapid inflation and commercialization, increased feudal pressures on tenants for revenues, converting copyholds into leaseholds, and "rack renting," a deceptive practice in the negotiation of leases.[5] Landlords also resorted to "fiscal feudalism," a process by which they could "enforce payment of every obsolete and obsolescent feudal due for which a legal case could be extracted from the medieval records" (Manning, 1976: 133). The revivification of feudal dues that had fallen into obsolescence was compounded by the king's efforts to resort to the same practice to raise royal taxation; both royal and aristocratic fiscal feudalism fell on the shoulders of the peasantry.

While the aristocratic landlords were resorting to intensifying and resuscitating feudal devices, the gentry was also squeezing the popular classes, as its interest in growing export markets led it to commercialize its agricultural holdings. "By clearing trees, draining marshes, fertilizing barren soils and enclosing the improved grounds and parcelling them out into large farms for lease at competitive rents, the lords of the manors could tap great new wealth" (Manning, 1976: 135). These enclosures were nearly always at the expense of the landless peasants hoping to acquire small holding on the wastes, as well as the small and medium peasants, who stood to lose some of their common pasture land, and the rural laborers, who were deprived of access to common lands that often spelled the difference between self-subsistence and poor relief (Manning, 1976: 135). There developed, Manning argues (1976: 135),

> a head on clash between the lords of manors and the main body of the peasantry in many parts of the country over their respective rights and shares in the unimproved commons and wastes. This conflict was to decide whether the landlords and big farmers or the mass of the peasantry were to control and develop the wastes and the commons.

This conflict remained one of the central agrarian issues of the entire seventeenth century leading up to the Revolution.

Government policy on the enclosure issue attempted to forestall opposition from either landowners or tenants, and was designed, like other policies, to freeze existing social relations while generating some return for the crown. The structural ambivalence of the crown's policies in the countryside led the king to attempt to limit enclosures while he simultaneously supported them. On the one hand, the crown tried to limit enclosures because they led to rural depopulation, which destabilized the countryside, allowed the gentry to build up independent political power, and were part of the larger process of secularization and commercialization that the king sought but was frequently unable to control. On the other hand, the crown did not want to limit enclosures too extensively because the enclosing landlords were counted upon as the backbone of royal absolutism. Caroline government was not designed as a welfare state to provide for the needs of its poor, and was ill equipped to do so. Charles wanted to limit enclosures for his own purposes, to "extort fines from offenders" rather than to protect the poor (Tate, 1967: 126). Often the crown itself was seeking to enclose in the very areas that the gentry sought to enclose. Jurisdictional disputes between gentry and kings about the rights to forest, fen, and common land occurred frequently.

The early seventeenth century witnessed the increased exploitation of the royal forests—the sale of wood, enclosure of forests, and disafforestation—to fuel royal hearths as well as to fill royal coffers. In addition, the king sought to enclose forests as deer parks for royal hunting parties, transforming a region from which people drew their livelihoods into a recreational playground for the court (Manning, 1967: 207). Royal statutes declared themselves against "intrusion" by copyholders and freeholders in 1627, and delegitimated all common rights to areas of the forest that the crown claimed for enclosure in 1628 (Sharp, 1980: 95). The king also took the lead in the enclosing of wastelands, marshes and fens, and heaths and moors, indeed every possible area that could be developed for private gain, which "provoked violent conflicts between lords and tenants, and left the peasants involved with little feeling of respect, deference, or loyalty for the King, peers, and most landlords" (Manning, 1977: 149; see also Stone, 1965: 164, 214–17, 299–332).

The popular classes in the countryside experienced not the protection of the king against commercializing and predatory landlords but an alliance of king and nobility against them. Indeed, the "livelihoods of all those small, pasture-farming peasants who lived in or near royal forests, or who dwelt near fens or coastal saltmarshes, or who had grazing rights or holdings on the wastes of manors, came under attack from landlords, *led and incited by the King and the Court circle*" (Manning, 1977: 149; see also Thirsk, 1970: 167; Tawney, 1912: 394–95). The peasants' resulting "resentment and hostility" was directed "mainly against the authority of the Crown" (Kerridge, 1957: 72).

The contradictory governmental policy in the countryside was most seriously exposed during the 1620s and 1630s when a series of climatological and epidemiological downturns pressed all the classes strongly. Disastrous harvests and widespread famines coincided in the early 1620s with a "deep depression," which, as we have seen, also seriously affected cloth exports (Russell, 1971: 184). In 1625 plague broke out among a London population whose resistance to infection had been seriously reduced because of undernourishment and famine; in August the Tuscan ambassador reported 942 dead of the plague one week, 3,400 the next week, and 5,000 the following week (Clark and Slack, 1976: 89; see also Russell, 1979: 213).

The demographic tensions exacerbated the growing political and economic tensions between any two points in the triangular relationship among the crown, the nobility, and the people. A series of popular uprisings marked the decade of prerogative rule, and although these were neither as serious nor as widespread as the series of contemporaneous popular uprisings in France, they were nonetheless important in galvanizing the popular classes and bringing their discontent into the growing coalition of opposition. Riots against enclosures were widespread during the 1620s when expressions of "class hatred for the wealthy, riots in Dorset, Gloucestershire, Worcestershire, Shropshire, and Wiltshire erupted, indicating "the violent reaction of a rural proletariat to fluctuations in employment, constrictions in the food market, and loss of crucial income supplements" (Sharp, 1980: 264, 7). Rural protest seems to have followed a clear pattern: in areas marked by extensive development of the clothing industry and in the most backward areas we find the highest incidence of rural revolt, though often for very different reasons. In the more backward areas any innovation was a serious threat to the precarious balance in the countryside, and pushed the rural people over the edge. In the more highly industrialized areas workers were extremely vulnerable to the slightest fluctuations in the market, having abandoned their earlier involvement in agricultural labor. The clothing industry in some areas had progressed sufficiently that it had ceased to be "by-employment" for a predominantly agricultural population (Supple, 1959: 141). Rural clothing workers were especially hard hit by economic decline, for they had few alternative resources. It is not surprising that the wage dependence of the artisans led these propertyless cottagers to leadership positions in many of the riots (Sharp, 1980: 259). In 1622 the unemployed in Gloucestershire went in groups to the houses of the rich, demanding money and seizing property (Hill, 1967: 27). In May the sheriff of Somerset described local conditions eloquently (cited in Sharp, 1980: 162):

> There are such a multitude of poor cottages built upon the highways odd corners in every country parish within this county and so stuffed with poor people that in many of those parishes there are three or four hundred poor of men, women, and children that did get most of their living by spinning, carding and such employments about wool and cloth. And the deadness of that trade and want of money is such that they are for the most part without work and know not how to live. This is a great grievance amongst us and tendeth much to mutiny.

The depression of 1629 further immiserated the rural artisans, and prompted another series of rural revolts. The clothiers of Essex petitioned to try to revive the sagging drapery industry, complaining of "not being able to subsist unless they be continually set on work and weekly paid and many of them cannot support themselves and their miserable families unless they receive their wages every night; many hundreds of them having no beds to lie in, nor food, but from hand to mouth to maintain themselves, their wives and children" (cited in Sharp, 1980: 166). The crown's investigation surveyed the main cloth-making centers and consistently found the same conditions: "an unrelieved tale of chronic poverty deepened by idle looms and unsold cloth, with the unemployed and hungry wage-earners on the verge of violence" (Sharp, 1980: 166).

By 1635 conditions had become so deplorable and the crown's poor response so provoking that riots in royal forests and against enclosure became commonplace, most especially in those areas in which the popular classes lived closest to the margin and were therefore most susceptible to the devastating consequences of innovations like enclosure (Williams, 1979: 330). In the west counties, for example, massive enclosure riots were "an expression of the social and economic grievances of virtually landless artisans and cottagers" (Sharp, 1980: 155). What became known as the Western Rising was prompted by increasing economic pressure on the cottagers brought about by enclosure and disafforestation, which exacerbated the problems they faced because of the long-term decline in the cloth industry, the trade decline of 1629–31, and harvest failures that drove the price of food up dramatically (Sharp, 1980: 174). Local people, the Star Chamber decree noted, "in Contempt of all Authority, combined together and resolved to pull down and destroy all the present and ancient enclosures" (in Sharp, 1980: 174). Though the Western Rising, like other enclosure riots, evidenced a "considerable hostility toward the gentry or at least toward particular gentlemen," what motivated the rioters in the 1630s was less class struggle at the level of production and more their opposition to innovative agrarian policies, and opposition was registered against any who attempted to implement such policies (Morrill, 1982: 13). Thus, occasionally, royal policies were supported by local gentry and yeomen "as long as they were the beneficiaries. When these things were done, however, for the profit of outsiders, and when in consequence they had to defend law and order against their aroused inferiors, it was a different matter" (Underdown, 1986: 112). Riots against disafforestation were protests against the violation of traditional rights by outsiders, and the "targets were not local gentlemen and farmers, but the clique of courtiers and Londoners intent on disrupting the forest community in the name of improvement and private profit" (Underdown, 1986: 108).

What is important is understanding that the popular classes were no longer the passive spectators of the political process, nor simply the loyal subjects upon whom policy was implemented. If enclosing landlords wanted far less state intervention, the popular classes often wanted far more; yet, both groups wanted to remain free of the intrusions of royal courtiers and appointees, who also threatened the stability of the traditional moral economy. Popular forces were increasingly alienated from the crown, whose activities to resolve its own fiscal crisis, they believed, prevented it from acting decisively in their interests; the people were "less inclined to see the King as their benevolent protector or the court as anything but an oppressive, alien force" (Underdown, 1986: 112). Local gentlemen and yeomen opposed the king because he blocked their own attempts at enclosure and other innovations, and also because they feared the violence of rural uprisings, and therefore often presented local demands to the central government, giving legitimate voice to grievances of the common folk in the countryside. Charles warned the House of Commons to consider the implications of its alliance with the popular classes, that "at last the common people might set up for themselves, call parity and independence liberty . . . destroy all rights and properties, all distinction of families and merit" (Hill, 1972: 20). Although there was hardly anyone in England who might have supported the proposals that fueled Charles's exaggerated fears, his warnings was prescient and more insightful than maybe even he imagined. But, it was not until the outbreak of the Second Civil War, and most distinctively after his execution, that some members of the popular classes articulated a program for a new foundation for the political nation.

The Mobilization of Religious Opposition

Religion's made a tennis-ball
For every fool to play withal.
—Humphrey Willis, 1659
(Cited in *Underdown*, 1986: 255.)

From the beginning of his reign, Charles was faced with increased opposition from religious groups. Although he and his father were as anti-Catholic as Elizabeth had been, they were not anti-Catholic enough for the radical Puritan faction that was growing throughout the country, nor for the Presbyterians, who were a powerful presence in Parliament. Puritans were also fearful of "Popish" policies of the established Anglican church, and the repression of the Catholics came nowhere near the level desired by them (Russell, 1979: 82). The crown's moves against the Catholics— fines, seizure of property, discriminatory taxation, exclusion and dismissal from office and professions—were consistent with earlier policies, but the English Catholics also realized that the crown protected them from more severe Puritan policies. Like the French Protestants, the English Catholics were willing to undergo this limited amount of state repression in exchange for protection against a more severe repression that was possible. An overwhelming number of English Catholics, like the Huguenots, remained loyal to the king throughout the Revolution (Cliffe, 1971: 170, 345).

As in France, the most serious religious rifts were within the dominant religion, not between a majority and a minority religion. The English Reformation had created a permissive religious atmosphere in which new radical Protestant sects had emerged. Their repression and exile by Mary Tudor only fueled their growth after her death, and Elizabeth's reestablishment of the Church of England allowed for significant religious toleration. The established church still maintained the immanence of God in the world, and consequently opposed challenges to the established order; a growing division between bishops and local clergy stemmed from this inherent doctrinal conservatism of the church hierarchy. Puritans, like the Calvinists, argued for the complete and fundamental separation of God and the world, and conflicted with both the ideas of absolute monarchy and an established church that supported the king.

Puritanism manifested a mixture of "holiness and hardheadedness," and was more concerned with a moral revolution in people's minds than with the establishment of a state church (Everitt, 1969: 14; see also Hill, 1967). Puritanism rested on theological assumptions different from those of Anglicanism, but these assumptions alone did not account for the centrality of religion in the English Revolution. Many writers have subsumed political, social, and economic grievances under the larger heading of religious disagreement. Morrill, for example, suggests that historians have been "confused" by a search for parallels with Continental mid-century revolutions, "which were brought on by war and the centralising imperatives of war," because these perspectives (like the perspective being offered here) miss the central defining feature of the English Civil War; it was "not the first European revolution; it was the last of the Wars of Religion" (Morrill, 1984: 178; see also Fletcher, 1981: 418). Bendix (1978: 309) develops a causal sequence that begins with religious opposition:

> The main issue of the period arose out of collisions between King and these propertyholders over the distribution of their respective rights and privileges. Religion was also concerned with property, as for example in the titles to former monastic lands, the collection of tithes or the several livings to which individual church dignitaries were appointed. However, issues of property were secondary to the religious ideas of the Puritan movement which gave the conflicts between King and Parliament a broader meaning. For the main challenge to governance by an exclusive hierarchy of dignitaries originated in the religious sphere.

This seems to reverse the causal sequence. Puritans "tried to spiritualize economic processes" that were already set in motion against royal authority; opposition came not as much from doctrinal dispute as from political and economic differences, which were often expressed in religious terms (Hill, 1974: 97). "It is not ideas," wrote Weber (1964: 264), "but ideal and material interests that directly govern men's conduct," and nowhere is this clearer than in the events leading up to the English Revolution.

Puritanism provided a symbolic language, grounded in nonmaterial and nontemporal absolutes, that allowed political opponents to express their oppositional interests, and bound groups together in opposition despite the differences that they might evidence among them, "unit[ing] the opposition by concealing divergences" (Hill, 1986: 75). Religion can be "an important component in the motives of ideologies of revolutions, and [give] legitimacy and moral strength to rebels" (Zagorin, 1982, vol. 1: 149). What was dangerous to the crown "was not Puritanism, but Puritanism in opposition," because although Puritanism "did not drive men eagerly to preach resistance, it did contribute enormously to the climate of mistrust" that was developing to specific Caroline policies (Russell, 1971: 204; Hirst, 1986: 79). In fact, Russell claims, there was "nothing very revolutionary about the essence of Puritanism" (Russell, 1979: 364). Underdown writes (1986: 275):

> Long before the civil war, especially in towns and pasture regions where clothworking and other industrial pursuits were available, the growing gulf between the people "of credit and reputation" and their less prosperous neighbors was reflected in the emergence of parish elites who saw it as their duty to discipline the poor into godliness and industriousness, and who found in Puritan teaching (broadly defined) their guide and inspiration.

Contemporaries certainly seemed to believe that religious ideas were less central than the idea of religious opposition as a source of political unity and ideological opposition. "It makes me smile sometimes to hear how soberly men will talk of the religion of this or that function," noted one Royalist at the end of the revolution (cited in Hill and Dell, 1949: 310). "He that would rightly understand them must read for Presbytery, *aristocracy;* and *democracy* for Independency." The Leveller newspaper *The Moderate* claimed in 1649 (cited in Hill and Dell, 1949: 337) that

> wars have ever been clothed with the most specious of all pretenses, viz. reformation of religion, the laws of the land, liberty of the subject, etc., though the effects thereof have proved most destructive to them; . . . taking away each man's birthright, and settling upon a few a cursed property the ground of all civil offences and the greatest cause of most sings against the heavenly Deity.

Oliver Cromwell reminded his contemporaries that "religion was not the thing at first contested for," even though he believed that "God brought it to that issue at last" (cited in Hill, 1970: 213). The cynical John Selden summed it up most elegantly when he wrote (cited in Hill, 1966: 99):

> The very *Arcanum* of pretending religion in all wars is that something may be found out in which all men have interest. In this the groom has as much interest as the lord. Were it for land, one has one thousand acres, and the other but one; he would not venture so far as he that has a thousand. But religion is equal to both. Had all men land alike . . . then all men would say they fought for land.

Religious ideology itself was less the cause of the revolution than two forms of structural relationships involving religion, and the ideology of opposition that religious dissenters provided. First, traditional church organizations promoted a parallel hierarchy to the state, and the local parish priests were chafing under the enormous weight of the hierarchy that supported bishops, whose luxurious life-styles were well known. (This was also true, as we have seen, in France, and the religious divisions within the Fronde often paralleled the division between the parish and the centralized church.) Second, the relations between the state and the church were strained and weakened. Although Charles I had said that "the dependency of the Church upon the Crown is the chiefest support of regal authority," by the 1630s the alliance at the local level between church and state had been eroded by the split between parish and central church, and the split between locality and court (cited in Hill, 1966: 77; see also Hirst, 1986: 169). Puritan divines flourished in the countryside, where they encouraged religious toleration and a political openness that threatened the early local triangulation of power among church, nobility, and crown. "There should be more praying and less preaching" wrote the Duke of Newcastle (cited in Hill, 1966: 79), underscoring one of the chief formal differences between the Puritans and the established English church, "for much preaching breeds faction, but much praying causes devotion." Internal church organization and church-state relations, coupled with the utility of religious doctrine as an ideology of opposition, appear to be the key determinants of the trajectory of religious opposition and religious support for political opposition in both England and France in the seventeenth century.

In the 1630s religious opposition joined with political and economic opposition to Charles's efforts to centralize state power, and Archbishop Laud's efforts to centralize religious power. Charles was accused of "Romanizing" the Church of England, leniency toward the Catholics, and inadequate subordination of the needs of the monarchy to the Puritan-defined needs of God. Laudian reforms aroused significant opposition, which took a theological cast but was equally concerned with the distribution of political power within the church, and the relationship of church and state. Laudian reforms were seen as the intellectual justification for royal absolutism, largely because they included the "recovery of the political power and the prestige of the bishops after decades of neglect and contempt" (Stone, 1972: 118). Opposition to those reforms was seen as opposition to state centralization. The Laudians "were not so much *for* the poor as *against* the parish elites, against the growing control of local affairs by the middling sort in alliance with town oligarchies and the gentry" (Hill, 1986: 262). For example, Laudians supported the Book of Sports in 1633, which encouraged men and women to engage in traditional village pastimes on Sundays. Although this seemed to support the traditional moral economy, Puritans believed that the villagers should be improving their minds instead, or at least resting after six days work, and parish elites agreed with the Puritans that the pagan fertility rites that underlay traditional sports were disruptive of the work discipline they were trying to impose. In this way did splits within the church mirror the divisions between Anglican and Puritan, which themselves paralleled the growing rifts between crown and country (Hill, 1986: 262).

In the 1630s, then, Puritans joined the growing coalition of political opposition, a coalition set in motion by earlier opposition to fiscal, economic, political, and social policies, as well as religious ones. The Puritans gave the opposition strength and a sense of moral mission, especially in opposing the Laudian reforms. They lent an inspired passion to the opposition, and concealed differences among the various other social groups, allowing an oppositional unity that was unique among all the political revolts of the midcentury.

The Trigger, 1640

On New Year's Day, 1640, Sir John Suckling offered the following words to his king:

> May all the discords in your state
> (Like those in the music we create)
> Be governed at so wise a rate,
> That what would of itself sound harsh or fright
> May be so tempered with delight.

Such wishes were as well timed and hopeful as they were remarkably naive. As the new decade dawned, the opposition to Charles's fiscal, religious, and social policies had built to such a degree that the very legitimacy of his rule, and of monarchy in general, came into question. Important factions within every social group in England were coming to oppose the king, searching for a platform from which to express their grievances. The opposition included rich and poor, Puritan, Independent, local parish priests, artisan and peasant, gentry and merchants. Several different sources of conflict had become superimposed, creating a potentially revolutionary situation:

> Diverse groups were united against the government. Commoners, yeomen, and some gentlemen opposed enclosing landlords and court patentees. Congregations, led by their richer members, looked to London merchants to help them to get the preaching of which the hierarchy had deprived them. Townsmen opposed royal attempts to remodel their government. Most men of property opposed arbitrary taxation; men and women of all classes opposed monopolies. [Hill, 1958:12]

Christopher Hill argues (1973: 104–5) that in each sphere of opposition three separate strands can be discerned. Immediately below the decisive split in the ruling class was a body of discontented popular elements that threatened to turn each strand of political revolt into social revolution. In the first sphere "court favored monopolists were attacked by freetraders who looked to Parliament and common law," and lurking below was "the mass of consumers and draftsmen, who also opposed monopolies but had little in common with London merchants and gentlemen clothiers." There was also a "rivalry between those who profited those who suffered from the Courts of Wards, between enclosing landlords and the government which fined enclosures," and below that was a "mass of tenants who wanted stability of tenure for their holdings and the throwing open of all enclosures." There was also a "rivalry between prerogative and Church courts on the one hand, common law courts looking to Parliament on the other," and below, groups began to challenge the idea of the rule of law itself. In religion a rivalry between Laudians and moderate Puritans "who wished to subordinate the Church to Parliament and elders" was paired with the "sectaries who rejected the idea of a state church altogether." Finally, there was the rivalry between "those who wanted to preserve a static hierarchical society and those who were busy shaping a more fluid society in which men of ability and means would be able to make their way to the top"; below them were those "whose poverty prevented them [from] . . . even conceiving the possibility of altering the world in which they lived."

Even as these fissures widened and a "remarkable" unity of opposition to Charles's religious, fiscal, and social policies coalesced, the need for funds continued unabated (Fulbrook, 1982: 259). Refused loans in Rome and Genoa, Charles seized £ 130,000 in bullion that merchants had stored in the Tower of London for safekeeping, setting off a spate of bankruptcies. He contemplated debasing the coinage, threatening to replace it with less valuable brass coin. He bought pepper on credit for £ 63,000, and sold it immediately for £ 50,000 cash, and seized some of the pepper and cloves of the East India Company and sold them for less than half their market value (Hill, 1973: 107; Dietz, 1964: 285). These expedients, the activity of a monarch desperate and tottering on the brink of bankruptcy were, of course, not enough. And, London had become a "hotbed of discontent" in which vociferous opposition became more and more visible and a daily occurrence as Charles turned to the City as a possible source of revenues again (Pearl, 1966: 107). Fiscal crisis in 1640 was "not a mere short-term problem brought on by a few decades of depressed trade or bad harvests. Nor was it brought on by the opposition of the gentry to the policies of a backward feudal Crown," writes Goldstone (1986: 280), and the crisis of 1640, he continues, "was of revolutionary import because its roots lay in the failure of the entire structure of Crown revenues to keep pace with a century and a half of inflation during which the Crown assets and credit had already been pressed to the limit." Although, potentially, if rarely solvent in peacetime, English monarchs "had failed to discover and institute an effective means of raising revenues necessary for conducting an independent foreign policy without first obtaining the consent of Parliament" (Fulbrook, 1982: 255). It was in this atmosphere that Charles determined to go to war with Scotland.

Charles's ability to hobble through the last years of the 1630s "depended on the continuance of the peace," and the collapse of his regime was begun "by a government putting unacceptable pressure on its subjects to try and equip itself for war" (Ashton, 1960: 191; Russell, 1979: 83). The resolution to go to war with Scotland was a "folly [that] completely destroyed Charles's solvency" (Dietz, 1928: 133). The king was driven to war, in part, because he simply did not have enough money, and war provided the single pretext under which he could raise money. Unfortunately, "the increased cost of warfare, by reducing the king to the point where he could neither pay his bills nor fight, was *one* of the important forces which drove him to declare war on his subjects" (Russell, 1982: 24). The preparations for war brought the last element of the coalition of political opposition into place. Until the Scottish war, "the municipal government of London had, on the whole, been prepared to accept royal policy . . . and to negotiate with the Crown on matters in dispute, such as the city's title to the Irish estates and of its ancient chartered privileges" (Pearl, 1966: 91). As in the final few years leading to the Fronde in France, the withdrawal of fiscal support from the capital center, and also from key financiers in the capital, provided the final withdrawal of fiscal support for royal policies, the last refuge of an insolvent king.

Charles's fiscal needs overrode his longer-range concerns for maintaining political legitimacy; in March 1640 he attempted to exploit the most desperate fiscal expedient of all: he called Parliament (Ashton, 1960: 184). Although Charles made it clear that Parliament had been summoned only to vote supply for the Scottish war, the Commons claimed the privilege of "redress before supply" and presented a list of specific grievances to the king. These included the Laudian innovations in public worship, the repression of Puritan ministers, Ship Money, monopolies, and free trade. By early May, realizing from his perspective that he had made a serious error of judgment, he dismissed Parliament, hoping to rule again by prerogative reign.

In August it was the Scots themselves who seized the initiative, crossing the Clyde and occupying Northumberland, Newcastle, and Durham. The Treaty of Ripon, concluded in November, granted the invading Scots army £ 850 per day; over £ 12,000 was paid in September and October alone, and by the year's end, over £ 25,000 had been paid to the Scots (James, 1974: 176). The Scottish presence tied Charles's hands fiscally, and also afforded his opponents the opportunity to stage massive demonstrations against him in the capital (Hill, 1978: 90). To pay the Scots, then, Charles had not only to summon Parliament but to allow it to sit until it had voted the necessary funds.

When Parliament assembled later in November, the old regime collapsed. At Parliament's opening, the lord keeper attempted to hold the state together, declaring (cited in Manning, 1967: 268–69):

> From the throne turn your eyes upon the two supporters of it, on the one side, the stem of honor, the nobility and the clergy, on the other side, the gentry and the Commons. Where was there, or is there in any part of the world, a nobility so numerous, so magnanimous, and yet with such a temper that they neither eclipse the throne nor overtop the people but keep a distance fit for the greatness of the throne. Where was there a Commonwealth so free, and the balance so equally held, as here?

An eloquent defense of absolutism, perhaps, but in late 1640 also an exercise in wishful thinking. The center did not hold. Strafford and Laud were impeached by Parliament, the former executed and the latter imprisoned. The entire structure of the monarchy was challenged. The system had cracked "because of the government's inability to cope with war and invasion," its inability "to conduct an independent foreign unpopular

foreign policy, to wage war without the consent of the political nation"
(Hill, 1986: 51; Fulbrook, 1982: 258).

Of course, the failure of the war against the Scots was simply the trigger
that set off the Revolution, the revolutionary moment. That moment was
the expression of a profound conflict between a centralizing state, attempting to resolve its fiscal crisis and develop a financial and political base
independent from traditional domestic constraints, and several layers of
opposition to this absolutist effort, from deeply conservative country
gentlemen "who sincerely believed that they were defending ancient and
traditional rights" to urban artisans and Puritan divines who sought to
reconstitute the nature of English society (Ashton, 1980: 214). The Revolution was caused by far more than a "series of disastrous mistakes and
miscalculations" by an incompetent king; it was caused by the multi-
layered resistance of English society to the creation of an absolute monarchy (Morrill, 1982: 2; see also Zagorin, 1982, vol.2: 138). "The English
Revolution," writes Hill (1980: 111–14), "like all revolutions, was caused
by the breakdown of the old society. . . . By 1640, the social forces let
loose by or accompanying the rise of capitalism, especially in agriculture
could no longer be contained within the old political framework except by
means of a violent repression of which Charles's government proved
incapable."

Long-run changes in the structure of English society—the decline of the
traditional moral economy of the English village and the commercialization
of agriculture; the rise of sectarian religious ideologies; the changing
political relationship between court and country; and the social transformation of the English class structure—provided the backdrop for the
events of the late sixteenth and early seventeenth centuries. The endemic
fiscal crisis of the Tudor and Stuart state was an expression of these
changes, and the crown's search for revenues precipitated the outbreak of
revolution by galvanizing the opposition into a political coalition. The
corner into which Charles was forced by the invasion of the Scots then
triggered the eruption that had been seething below the surface for a very
long time, and that had earlier been given to sporadic outbursts. "The
government was brought down by a revolt of the taxpayers," who had
joined together in an uneasy coalition that heard the calling of Parliament
as a call to restructure the government of England. It was a call to political
revolution.

Notes

1. In 1631 Oliver Cromwell, then a young country squire in Cambridgeshire, was
   fined £ 10 for refusing knighthood (Hill, 1970: 45).

2. Sale of crown lands had become "the most brilliant example of the disparity between actual revenue yields and the amount received by the King," writes Dietz (1928: 126). For example, the sale of lands in 1635 had brought over £ 90,000 to the crown, but after various deductions, only slightly more than £ 25,000 actually found its way to the royal treasury (Dietz, 1928: 127).

3. The story of the tobacco customs provides a curious footnote to the entire period, and explains the historical source of the English preference for Virginia tobacco over the Spanish and Turkish varieties. Though the English actually preferred Spanish tobacco, the war with Spain pressed James to exploit the competition between merchants of Turkish and the Virginia tobaccos. In 1620 he offered the farming of the customs and the rights to monopoly sale of tobacco to the highest bidder. It was thus unclear which type of tobacco English smokers would be using, but when in 1624 the Virginia growers, the Jamestown Company, offered £ 130,000 over five years for exclusive monopoly rights, as well as the right to administer the customs, English smokers had their answer. Charles attempted to extract more money to extend the customs farm and the monopoly of the Jamestown Company.

4. I use the term *people* here in the ways that some English historians have done, notably Manning and Hill, to distinguish between the lower-middle-class and working-class elements that were actively politicized and "the poor," the landless, unemployed urban and rural people who remained without political aspirations and did not participate in, nor articulate claims during, the Revolution. Even the Diggers, the model "poor people's army," was composed mainly of rural laborers and tenants.

5. All leases were negotiated so that tenants paid an entry fee, a sum for the execution and takeover of the lease. Under copyhold arrangements landlords attempted to keep pace with inflation by demanding extremely high entry fines, but then the tenant held the land at a fixed rent for life. Rack renting consisted of negotiating shorter leases (which would allow the lord to raise rents at each negotiation of a lease) and reducing entry fines to the tenant, thus making the transformation appear easier and more in the tenant's interests.

8

Conclusion: Common Causes and Divergent Outcomes

This book has presented a comparative sociological analysis of the historical and structural antecedents to revolution in early modern France and England. In so doing, it has argued that both the English Revolution and the Fronde were movements of resistance against a perceived absolutist centralization of political power in the hands of the monarchy. The various constituent elements of the revolutionary coalition that constituted the Fronde and the English Revolution were set in motion by the separate oppositions to the fiscal, social, and political strategies devised by their respective monarchies to resolve their endemic fiscal crises. Empirically, we have observed how each corporate group—in France, the high nobility, venal officeholders, Catholics, Protestants, merchants, state creditors, and popular forces in the countryside and the cities; in England, the aristocracy, gentry, yeoman and other peasants, merchants, Episcopalians, Puritans and other religious minorities, and urban artisans—came to oppose royal state-building efforts. Theoretically, this analysis has implied that revolutions are not the result of organized class movements competing with one another for political power; they are not like boxing matches in which two mobilized classes "slug it out," with the winner taking the crown. The state, in this sense, is not the object of political contention, but a contender itself, and, in part, the source of the contention (Tilly, 1978). The formation of the revolutionary coalition depends upon state action. Governments develop policies to manage specific crises and meet certain needs; often these conflict with the aims and ideals of specific social groups. Drawn together into coalition, these groups often challenge for legitimate state power.

The antecedents of these revolutions are strikingly similar, but there is a fundamental difference between the Fronde and the English Revolution: the English Revolution was a successful political revolution and the Fronde failed utterly. How can these two events, which manifest such similar middle-range causal sequences, have such different outcomes? I shall argue that internal divisions within the revolutionary coalitions yielded a weaker revolutionary claim in France than in England, where the coalition was cemented by common religious ideology, as well as by a common desire to prevent the success of the social revolution that was set in motion by the political revolution. I shall also argue that the French crown was administratively stronger and more resilient than the English crown, and therefore capable of holding off political challenges.

Each of these arguments returns to the two sides of the relationship between the state and society that has been the major interest of this analysis. Max Weber's deep understanding of this complex relationship may help frame the kinds of questions to be raised. Weber suggests that what differentiates political development in the West (Europe and the United States) from China and India is the presence in the former of "strong independent forces" (Weber, 1964: 62). "Princely power could ally itself [with these forces] in order to shatter traditional fetters" (revolution from above) or, "under very special conditions, these forces could use their own military power to throw off the bonds of patrimonial power" (revolution from below). The latter conflict "was the case in the five great revolutions which decided the destiny of the Occident: the Italian revolution of the 12th and 13th centuries, the Netherlands revolution of the 16th century, the English revolution of the 17th century, and the American and French revolutions of the 18th century." Although Weber then asks, "Were there no comparable forces in China?" he also sets the analytic agenda for a comparative sociology of revolutions, posing questions that have framed the discussion of the genesis of a revolutionary coalition in both Bourbon France and Stuart England. What forces were independent of royal power? What were the structural sources of their independence? How did these forces articulate with other social forces? What were the relations between the state and social classes, and how had they changed over time? What were their motivations in opposing the king? What other forces could be counted upon as allies? What interests and ideologies could hold these forces together?

The Fronde as Failed Political Revolution

There are many reasons that the Fronde failed, why the Fronde was the French Revolution that wasn't, a *revolution manquée* (Madelin, 1931). The

French monarchy was strong enough to withstand a revolutionary challenge, especially because venality of office had incorporated into the structure of absolutism precisely those class elements that might have sustained a revolutionary challenge. Here, the contrast with England is instructive: if, as Aylmer claims (1974), England was a much-governed country with very little government, then venality had made France a very little-governed country with a great deal of government.

Not only was the administrative capacity of the French state resilient enough to absorb potential contendors for state power but the coalition of opposition was extremely weak, and each of the constituent groups was also internally fragmented. The coalition of the Fronde reproduced the divisions within early modern French society; thus, Zagorin (1982: vol. 2: 220) argues, the failure of the Revolution was "due less to the monarchy's strength in the immediate circumstances than to the revolution's weakness." "Town was divided against countryside, one town against the next, one body of officers against another, lesser bourgeois against oligarchs, nobles against grandees, and so on, with each and every group anxious to outmaneuver its rivals in the quest for the protection and patronage of the Monarchy" (Parker, 1980: 188). Other authors agree that the internal divisions within the revolutionary coalition precluded success. Beik (1985: 219) focuses on the consequences of provincial disunity:

> Pushed to their limits during the Fronde, all revealed their true colors in mutual denunciations: The Parliament was a company of posturing dignitaries unable to realize its irresponsible political ambitions; the Estates were a collection of bishops and barons with vested interests in royal taxes and with no local power base of support beyond their own clients; the Comptes was a group of financiers, jealous of their fees.

As a result, "there was no real possibility of a 'provincial front against the crown' because of the very structure of provincial government and because the social interests of the rulers lay with the national monarchy, not the provincial population."

Similarly, Elias comments about how "strong are the rivalries and conflicts of interest between these groups, which impede a common pursuit of the objective. Each of them would like to limit the monarchy in its own favor, and each is just strong enough to prevent others from doing so"; the coalition was "incapable of uniting, incapable of fighting with all their strength and winning" (Elias, 1982: 180). Thus, the Fronde

> exposes once again the structure of tensions which gives the central authority its strength, but which remains concealed from view as long as this authority is firmly established. No sooner does one of the competing allies seem to gain the

slightest advantage than all the others feel threatened, desert the alliance, make common cause with Mazarin against their erstwhile ally, and then partly switch back to his side. Each of these people and groups wants to curtail royal power; but each wants to do it to his own advantage. Each fears that another's power might grow at the same time [Elias, 1982: 191–92].

"Anger and discontent bring them together," wrote Paul Viollet in 1898, "but their interests admit no unity" (cited in Elias, 1982: 206).

To argue that a key factor in the Fronde's failure is the weakness and disunity of the revolutionary coalition, though, is only to beg the sociological questions of what mechanisms might hold such a coalition together and what might generate them, and why they were not operative during the Fronde. One social source of revolutionary unity is an overarching ideology or vision that is capable of a transcendent solidarity to hold the coalition together despite disparate interests. Revolutions do not require an overarching political ideology shared by all the participants, but they do require at least several alternative political ideologies that might serve different groups as visions of the future. Religious dissenters frequently, but not always, provide such alternative visions. Without these ideologies a revolutionary challenge may lose its sense of historical mission, its sense of purpose, its *raison d'être*. Certainly, the Fronde lost that sense of mission, collapsing into a chaotic assemblage of particularistic pretensions.

The collapse of the Fronde stemmed from both the ambivalent royalism of the Huguenots and the divisions within the Catholic church, and especially the anti-Mazarinist sentiments of the parish curés—all of which prevented the emergence of a religiously based alternative political ideology. French Protestantism might have advanced a constitutional form of government and popular consent as an alternative political ideology to absolutism, for Huguenots saw the origin of political order in the covenants among God, king, and people, and advocated a thesis of "government that affirmed popular sovereignty as the foundation of authority, the origin of political power in covenants, agreements, and consent, and the consequent right of the people to resist and remove kings who become tyrants" (Zagorin, 1982, vol. 2: 70). But, French Protestantism had become so defensive and guarded after the siege of La Rochelle, that it saw its survival as contingent on royal protection from Catholic zealots. Hence, Huguenots "solidly" supported the crown during the Fronde. At the same time the growing opposition of other social groups "made it necessary for the Cardinal to tolerate the excesses of the Protestants, and even at times, to court the heretics" (Ranum, 1980: 193; Beik, 1985: 298). Thus, what might have been a relationship of ideological antagonism became, instead, a relationship of mutual political support, for crown and religious minority needed each other as allies.

Catholicism, on the other hand, generated a significant amount of political opposition but was unable to generate an alternative ideology from the official political ideology of absolutism. When the Fronde erupted in Paris in the spring of 1648, many parish clergy saw the opportunity to replace a hated cardinal with another who was more to their liking, Cardinal de Retz. As the curé of Saint-Barthelemy informed Mazarin, the curés "have always acted and still act on behalf of the Cardinal de Retz against the state, the king, and Your Eminence" (cited in Golden, 1981: 63). The Religious Fronde, which erupted within the church itself after the suppression of the Parliamentary and Noble Frondes in 1652, combined several strands of dissident Catholic ideologies, such as Richerism, Jansenism, and Gallicanism, with an internal critique of the church hierarchy by the parish curés. Mazarin had, as one contemporary observed (cited in Golden, 1981: 117), "made a wound so deep in the liberty of the French clergy that it will be difficult to heal it without leaving a shameful scar." The curés, therefore, sought to achieve supremacy over their parishes and independence from other ecclesiastical groups that sought to interfere in parochial affairs (Golden, 1981). The Religious Fronde provided the curés with a "corporate identity," "the formation of a corps and the claim that they exercised sole and complete authority within the territory of their parishes," but it did not mean a politicized ideology capable of sustaining a political challenge to absolutist monarchy (Golden, 1982: 485; Golden, 1981: 68).

Only the Parisian Illuminés, a small group of radical Catholic theorists, extended their theological critiques of church hierarchy and doctrine to the political sphere. For example, Simon Morin articulated a vision that was more consistent with Reformation Protestantism than the Vatican, calling for an end to Mass, sacraments, priests, external ritual, and even the mediation of Jesus in the relationship of the individual to God. He also advocated, as a corollary, the redistribution of wealth, writing that "the king should confiscate the property of the church and give it to the poor" (cited in Golden, 1979: 199). Similarly, François Davant, "the most radical pamphleteer during the Fronde," was one of the few writers who did not condemn the English regicide. In *Avis à la Reyne d'Angleterre et à la France* he argued that because Charles had been a tyrant, regicide was really tyrannicide and thus justified: "Not to rebel against a tyrannical monarchy would be a sin against God," he wrote (Golden, 1979: 203). Davant also advocated complete religious toleration, and developed a contractual theory of kingship, arguing that "kings have been chosen to

administer justice; if they oppress the population, they may be removed''
(cited in Golden, 1979: 203).

The Illuminés were a far too small and radical sect to generate much of
a following, especially in the first years of Louis XIV's reign after the
suppression of the Fronde. In addition, the Catholic hierarchy was too
intertwined with the structure of French absolutism to cast its future with
the Frondeurs. The support of the Catholics, with the exception of a
minority of Paris curés, was often halfhearted, and was certainly neither
republican nor democratic. The clergy shared with the Parliamentaires a
loathing of Mazarin, but they did not share a political vision. In fact, when
Parliament adopted an edict prohibiting cardinals from serving in the
Conseil de Roi, the Assembly of the Clergy protested (A.N. AB XIX 3624,
Coppett ms. 177). Nor did the other sects within the church fill the
ideological vacuum. St. Vincent de Paul preferred to minister to the
casualties of the Fronde in the provinces rather than urge his followers to
seize the political initiative and declare for the revolt. The Jansenists,
though they posited an alternative political community, a republic of the
saints not unlike the English Puritans, confined their opposition to the
realm of religious ideas, preached noninvolvement with the world, and
"professed complete loyalty to the King, and none of them declared
openly for the Fronde" (Keohane, 1980: 217). Without such an ideology
of political opposition generated from the religious sphere, the Fronde
disintegrated into a series of disconnected factions, none of which was
capable of providing the necessary unity.

Another possible bearer of an alternative political vision in the old
regime—the bourgeoisie—was also largely silent during the Fronde, and
commercial regions went "relatively untouched" (Brustein, 1985: 458).
Many wealthier merchants supported the crown, though most were ambivalent about which of the constantly shifting sides might provide the most
economic security (Moote, 1973: 352). Omer Talon recalled how the
"wealthy burghers in Paris actually welcomed parliamentary resistance to
royal taxation during 1648" (cited in Moote, 1973: 352). The parliamentaires attempted to accomplish what the regency had resisted: to guarantee
free trade within the realm and protect French merchants from interference. A key article in the Arrêt d'Union of July 1648 proposed to reestablish free trade, and Article 12 of the Treaty of Reuil that seemed to end
the Fronde of the Judges in 1649 read, in part:

> in order to provide means to all our subjects who deal with merchandise, to
> increase their trade within our realm, we have revoked and revoke as of now all
> the privileges granted individuals to make money on any merchandise whatso-
> ever, leaving all merchants the freedom to act in the future according to the

experience which each has been able to gain, with prohibition to trouble those who wish to become involved in the commerce of the said merchandise.

Yet, the merchants were often more interested in gaining noble status through the purchase of an office than in advancing a class-based ideology that would depart from the feudal basis of absolutist rule.

The venal officers, those newly arrived nobles, had accomplished precisely that upward mobility within the old regime, abandoning their bourgeois class of origin for the pretensions of the hereditary nobility (which explains the importance of the paulette). The scramble for noble privilege in the old regime indicates how this potential source of political opposition framed its interest. This is not to argue that the venal officers did not oppose the centralizing policies of Richelieu and Mazarin; they not only opposed them but provided the necessary leadership to inaugurate the Revolution itself. This does not mean that the venal officers did not generate a competing political ideology; they did, suggesting that "public authority in France is divided between the King, the courts, and the Princes, and during a Regency, the courts and the Princes possess a larger share of authority than normally" (Doolin, 1936: 76). The judges in the sovereign courts demanded consent to taxation, abolition of the intendants, the reduction of the taille, the reinstatement of the paulette, increased parlementary powers of verification and registration of edicts, and the abolition of arbitrary imprisonment, insisting that a person be charged with an offense within twenty-four hours of arrest. They articulated a primitive version of constitutional monarchy, prohibiting the use of *lettres de cachet,* and urged equality before the law.

The venal officers articulated their vision from within the structure of absolutism, not in opposition to it. "Parlement's defense of the ancient constitution during the Fronde was a camouflage for defending the value of patrimonial offices and maintaining the solvency of the Crown's perpetual annuities (rentes) in which they had invested heavily" (Giesy, 1983: 206). Theirs was a vision of increased robe nobility participation, of shared power, of state reform; it was a vision of those who saw themselves as noble, as the social foundation of the monarchy. In fact, these venal officeholders insured the triumph of absolutism, even if they believed themselves to be tempering it. As one of Louis XIV's advisers noted (cited in Tilly, 1986: 161) while observing England in 1688,

If England had as many officials supported by the king as France does, the revolution would never have occurred. For it is certain that so many officials means so many committed people attached to the maintenance of royal authority. Without that authority they would be naught. If it were destroyed they would instantly lose the large sums of money with which they had bought their positions.

By abandoning their class of origin for the political pretenses of their class of aspiration, the venal officers were limited in the extent of their alternative political vision, and powerless to resist the high nobility—their new class allies in the coalition of political opposition—as these sword nobles asserted their vainglorious dynastic aspirations. The noble pretenses of the robe nobility meant that the revolution moved upward into a dispute among nobles rather than galvanizing urban and rural popular classes into a significantly "republican" revolutionary direction.

The Fronde also represents the last attempt to subordinate the monarchy to the high nobility. The autonomy of the state to pursue a distinctly state-centered set of interests is thus a historical phenomenon that develops when various classes are too weak to infuse the state with their own character. One pamphlet, *La Royaliste au Mazarin,* published as the Assembly of the Notables met in 1651 (cited in Saint-Aulaire, 1827, vol. 2: 339), claimed that Mazarin

> does not see at all that in ancient times, a King followed the advice of a bunch of I don't know how many diverse councillors, and undertook his affairs of consequence always securing the advice of the princes of the blood and the *grands* of the state. The French state does not condemn the aristocracy, it placed them within the monarchy; but if the King wanted never to defer to the aristocracy, that is to say to the closest place to the Crown, where the wise have established by their participation a just state, he will become despotic or tyrannical, and, by consequence, he will have to undo all that has been done.

The high nobility generated no alternative political vision, simply reversing the program of absolutist centralization and proposing the reinstitution of a more medieval monarchy in which the high nobility would play a pivotal role. (At their worst, the Princes of the Blood did not even articulate this much of a political vision but acted from within it, seeking to replace the queen mother with one of their own.) They relied on their traditional bases of power in the countryside against the central government in Paris, and on the personal flair and charisma of key nobles in generating popular support in the cities. Yet, these personal politics were outdated in the mid-seventeenth century, and popular support waned in the absence of a truly alternative vision.

The failure of any one group, or any set of groups, to generate a radical alternative political ideology, and the structure of opposition among the various layers of nobility, insured that when the Fronde spread to the provinces, it did not result in class struggle between the producers and landowners (as sociological theories of successful revolution might have it; see Skocpol, 1979). Provincial Frondes were recorded mostly in those provinces that had experienced major provincial rebellions in the 1630s and 1640s, such as Guyenne, Provence, and Normandy, and in which internal factions within the provincial parlements opposed Mazarin's policies, resenting "the steady encroachment upon their authority by the crown's new judicial and financial commissioners, the intendants," and expressing their dissatisfaction with fiscal policies (Kettering, 1982: 276). These factions often combined with a "military emergency precipitated by a hostile governor" to produce a revolutionary situation and an important connection between urban fiscal revolts and the rebellions of regional nobles (Kettering, 1982: 275; see also Tilly, 1986: 142). Despite this potentially explosive situation, the Frondes are marked by the "failure of co-ordinated rebellion" (Bonney, 1981: 829). Each province, indeed each locality and municipality, experienced and expressed the revolts differently. The Fronde in the provinces was in reality many local Frondes, particularistic rebellions against specific targets, never united into common cause throughout the countryside. Although many were provoked by the crown's fiscal exactions and the demands made on local liberties by the twin pressures of wartime finance and state building, each local Fronde took on a different hue, colored by the specific locality. The revolt of the judges did not necessarily bring about the revolt of the governor, nor of urban and rural popular classes, and the "rebellion of a provincial governor did not necessarily bring about the revolt of his province" (Bonney, 1981: 829).

In Provence, for example, the Fronde was modest and reformist, as the magistrates in the Parliament of Aix sought to return the luster to their tarnished social and political images in local politics, to supersede those agents who had usurped their local powers. They were quick to return to the royalist fold to insure their gains, while the revolt spread to the countryside among the popular classes and high nobility, who then found no support among the parliamentaires (Kettering, 1978; Kossman, 1954). In Anjou local citizens rose in revolt against increased fiscal exactions and the "incessant tyranny" of the provincial governor, the Duc d'Epernon (Couyba, 1903, vol. 3: 19). The Angevin Fronde

> was complex and tumultuous and changeable. Yet it returned again and again to the same themes: preservation of local and regional privileges against an omnivorous monarchy, hostility to everyone who profited personally from the royal extension, opposition to the billeting of unruly, demanding troops on the citizenry, resistance to arbitrary taxation, especially when farmed out to financiers, and particularly when applied to the necessities of life. [Tilly, 1986: 98]

In the absence of a local parliament, rebels looked to the city council, whose personal ambitions and ambivalences paralyzed them. The failure of these local merchants and officers to aid the popular forces so severely weakened the revolt that it was easily crushed.

In Normandy a conflict between the provincial governor and Parliament never generated significant popular support, although Parliament did join the Parisian sovereign courts in agitating against Mazarin. In Caen local administrators joined with the Parliament of Rouen in opposition to tax farmers, intendants, and new taxes. In Brittany the Fronde provided the occasion for local conflicts to assume national character, as inter-noble rivalry eventually involved the Parliament at Rennes, and the provincial estates in Nantes. Yet, the rivalry between these two institutions, either of which might have represented popular sovereignty, precluded a unified front against the regency. Toulouse was the "only parliamentary town which failed to resist monarchical centralization, but instead became entangled in a bitter conflict with other provincial authorities" (Lansky, 1977: 21). As a result, the Fronde in Toulouse was rendered impotent by the same rivalry as in Brittany, as provincial estates and urban parliaments struggled for the right to represent a decreasingly enthusiastic popular position.

Only in Bordeaux did a local revolt generate an oppositional ideology that might have challenged Bourbon absolutism. The Bordelais Parliament's refusal to support the local revolt, known as the Ormée, further radicalized the revolt, leading the rebels to seek the destruction of the Parliament, and with it royal government in the province. The artisans, small shopkeepers, and craftspeople who predominated in the ranks of the Ormée generated a republican ideology that sought explicitly "to raise the issue of equal rights and representative government" (Le Roy Ladurie, 1974: 153). Without the fetters of parliamentary vacillation, without a bourgeoisie that had abandoned its class for noble status, the Ormée was transformed from a revolt against royal expedients to a revolt against wealth. In the *Apologie pour l'Ormée* (1651), the pamphleteer writes:

> Wisdom depends neither on wealth nor palaces, and can thrive even when men are wholly destitute. It is equality that makes for perfection among individuals . . . [for] it unifies all parts of the republic, fosters peace, and produces concord among the citizenry. . . . The actual cause of sedition and political strife is the excessive wealth of a few.[1] [Westrich, 1974: 49]

Among all the provincial and regional rebellions of the Fronde, the Ormée had the most far-reaching political implications. It demonstrated how much Parliament and crown needed each other, especially in the face of concerted opposition from below, and also suggests just how limited was the alternative proposed by the venal officers. In addition, it indicates where new groups might fit into the coalition of political opposition. The Ormée was a popular uprising, a revolutionary movement that expressed republican antimonarchical sentiments. The participants rebelled against the old regime and its institutions, Parlement and king, and also against the wealthy merchants, who, they believed (rightly, as it were), "used their control of municipal government to shift the burden of royal taxation onto the lower classes" (Westrich, 1974: 140). If the Fronde in any way prefigures the Revolution, the Ormééists were its sans-culottes.

The fall of the Ormée in 1653 signaled the end of the Fronde, the end of an unsuccessful attempt at political revolution. State activity had generated a coalition of political opposition, but that coalition was unable to sustain its revolt either by persistent lower-class agitation or through the development of an alternative political vision. The Fronde's failure heralded a new era of state building in old regime France, the absolutist state of Louis XIV.

After the Fronde

After the Fronde hopes were high that peace would come at last, both in the debilitating wars against Spain and in the tumultuous social conflict of the king's minority. But the crown had bought short-term peace at the price of longer-term fiscal stability. When Louis declared his personal rule in 1661,

> the government was much in debt. Its income was largely devoted to servicing that debt, partly by paying wages to venal officers, partly by meeting in a halting way obligations to purchasers of *rentes sur l'Hôtel de Ville*, partly by paying interest on outstanding loans; but also, and perhaps largely, by paying out exorbitant sums to men who as state officials often enough wrote out the documents by which, in their private capacity as financiers, they received their illegal profits. [Dent, 1975: 232]

The level of taxation was over double that of 1610, and thousands of debtors languished or died in prison. By the mid-1660s, however, Louis and his finance minister Colbert had balanced the budget and reduced the taille. Colbert, that "grim agent of deflation," reorganized royal finances, shifting away from the "brutal, abrupt impositions of new levies, toward a more subtle blend of indirect taxation, currency manipulation, sale of privileges, and borrowing" (Le Roy Ladurie, 1980b: 9; Tilly, 1978: 44). Colbert bypassed the parliaments entirely and relied on increased utilization of financiers and intendants.

As finance was being modestly reformed in the interests of state centralization, Louis moved to consolidate his absolute power. He ordered all records of the Parliament of Paris relating to the Fronde destroyed, "as if to blot out history" (Knachel, 1967: 262). The Hôtel de Ville was also "ordered to find and suppress all the pieces and documents concerning all public affairs from 1648–1652, that anyone may find" (*Registres de l'Hôtel de Ville*, 1846, vol. 1: iii).[2] The failure of the Fronde had revealed the impotence of the estates, and demonstrated the narrow corporate selfishness of the judges, the equally narrow personal feuding of the high nobility, and the ineffectiveness of the lower classes without a sustained bourgeois challenge; these were not the sources of successful revolt in old regime France. Louis concentrated his power, removing social obstacles to state building from various groups who had defended a threatened autonomy (Zagorin, 1982, vol. 2: 221). As he did so, he also centralized the structural sources of weakness as well as strength, centralizing fiscal problems while he concentrated political power. Finances became decidedly state finances; one royal pamphlet in 1700 (cited in Klaits, 1979: 215) noticed that "almost all private wealth depends upon royal authority. Wages, pensions, huge loans and arrears on rentes are attached to the king. Should the monarchy totter, all this wealth would be endangered."

For the high nobility, the end of the Fronde spelled the end of its political supremacy in French political affairs, and "confirmed the effective collapse of the independent military capacity of the magnates" (Parker, 1983: 119). One contemporary complained, "See how the civil wars have reduced the Princes of the Blood, and how miserable they are to be compelled to act deferentially toward men who are infinitely beneath their rank" (letter from Marigny to Lenet, August 4, 1652; *Histoire des Princes de Condé*, vol. 4: 544). Louis XIV domesticated the high nobility, preserving its social privileges by inviting its members to court at the recently refurbished Versailles but excluding them from political decisionmaking. At Versailles the nobles also became absentee landlords, cut off from their traditional base of popular provincial support, and thus split from the common people and "never again available for alliance with a popular rebellion" (Tilly, 1979: 24; see also Tilly, 1986: 115; Tilly, 1981: 51). Etienne Pavillon, the seventeenth-century poet, offered a fitting epitaph for the political fate of the high nobility in his "Le Gentilhomme de l'arrièrre-ban" (1689; cited in Goubert, 1972: 200; translated by Steve Cox):

> My pride in noble status lay
> In being exempt from what commoners pay
> Today I mourn my birth's nobility:

This glorious rank will be the death of me
By forcing me, in this ill-omened year,
Among the arrière-ban to appear.
O great grandsire, of tranquil memory,
(Pen and ink were your only armory,
Bourgeois in caution and timidity),
Behold in me your true posterity.
Yours was the cash your son and grandson spent
To bring me to this dire predicament,
This noble duty, which I must fulfill,
To be a warrior against my will.

Cut off from the provinces, undermined politically, reshaped as a economic class in the strictest sense, the nobility became a "creation of the state" rather than the "spontaneous social creation" the nobles had earlier believed themselves to be (Mousnier, 1971: 122).

The Fronde's end ushered in no fundamental changes in the relationship between the venal officers and the crown, for venal offices remained a chief mechanism of upward mobility for the bourgeoisie under the old regime, and a central feature in royal policy. Louis further subordinated the robe nobility, removing its right to remonstrate and, in 1669, ordering the sovereign courts to address all judicial grievances to the Conseil de Roi instead of personally to the king. Certainly, the reduction of parliamentary power was not complete, but the court "no longer promoted a broad program of state reform or attempted to forge lasting alliances with other discontented groups" (Hamscher, 1977: 199). "The parliaments resemble ruins," wrote Montesquieu in *The Persian Nights*. Now, "they perform practically no function . . . they have bowed before time . . . and before supreme authority, which has swept all before it." Parliament's resistance to royal initiatives after the Fronde was meager and less than decisive (Hamscher, 1977; Moote, 1972).

The institutional capacity to resist state building had been lost. To Joseph Nedham, an English observer in 1650, what had been lost were the social bearers of individual freedom; in words that are remindful of Tocqueville's two centuries later, Nedham (1650: 24) described the transformation:

For, according to the ancient constitution, that kingdom retained a mixture of aristocratical power; so that the then supreme court of Parlement at Paris had a principal share in the government and nothing was imposed on the people but by consent of their deputies. But now, having been mined out of their authority by the powerful encroachments of their kings and being overawed by armed powers held continually in pay for the purpose, their authority is defunct and their common interest in the affairs of the public translated into a private *Conseil d'Etat*, which depends upon the mere will of the king. And so the Parlement of

Paris, which was once the supreme council, having surrendered its title to the sword of the king, serves now only for a petty court of judicature and a mere mock show of majesty.

As a result, said Nedham (1650: 23), "France is a most sad example at this day, where the tyranny of their kings is founded and preserved by force, not only upon the shoulders of the peasant but on the destruction of the ancient princes and the majesty of Parliament; which retains not so much as a shadow of their old liberty."

Throughout the old regime the relationship between the crown and the robe nobility had been structurally contradictory. What had appeared to strengthen absolutism in the short run and had enabled Bourbon monarchs to accomplish the governmental revolution had also seriously weakened the nation economically, politically, and socially. The consequences were not felt for over a century, but Jacques Necker saw them in 1784; in his *Administration des Finances* he wrote:

> The multitude of official posts which confer nobility and which can be bought (in France) sustains a spirit of vanity (among our merchants and industrialists) and tempts them to renounce their business and manufacturing activities at the very time when their increased wealth could be used to give greater scope to their enterprises . . . and to increase the prosperity of the nation. . . . I will not hesitate to say that this attractiveness of noble status to me prevents the French from realizing their full (economic) potential. This is also one of the principal examples of the superiority in several branches of business of those nations in which social distinctions are less marked, and people are not perpetually preoccupied by all the vain and pretentious concerns which result from the existence of sharp social distinctions. [Necker, 1784, vol. 3: 116–17]

Shortly after Necker penned those words, the venal officeholders in the sovereign courts again refused the absolutist program. This time, however, their revolt was carried forward by another political coalition, and they were among its casualties.

Bourbon absolutism entailed the political incorporation and economic subordination of the outlying provinces. The high nobility had been removed from its traditional power bases, and local officers were increasingly wedded to royal policies. Intendants returned to the provinces, and remained important agents of royal policy. And the provincial estates became a mere registry for the king's wishes. The failure of both the Estates-General and the provincial estates "left French elites without the nationally institutionalized forms of participation that might have been established" (Bier and Grew, 1978: 264), a sad fact well noted by contemporaries. In 1676 on a tour through Languedoc, English liberal philosopher John Locke commented on the provincial estates (1953: 30), writing that "they never do, and some say dare not, refuse whatever the King demands." Madame de Sévigné, when asked to serve as a delegate to the provincial estates at Normandy for her husband who had died during the previous session, wrote in 1671 (1953: 350–52) that she did not much care to go because "the session will not hold long; there is nothing to do but ask what are the King's commands; no reply is made and the affair is over."

The Fronde had far-reaching social implications for the course of French history, manifesting, for the first time, the possibility of a broad alliance between city and countryside, of various social groups and corporations throughout the kingdom. Both geographically and socially, the Fronde was the most widespread of all the revolutions of the mid-seventeenth century. Its failure was the ground upon which the old regime determined it unnecessary to reform itself, unnecessary to change its financial administration. The failure was an indication that absolute monarchy was capable of fending off potential political revolt in a way the more representative English counterparts were not. The circumvention of reforms meant that when the state did reform its administrative machinery, it would be far more tumultuous an event than it might have been in the mid-seventeenth century. The Fronde made the Revolution necessary.

Louis XIV built an enormous political edifice that remained weakened by persistent fiscal crisis. He ruthlessly crushed his political opposition, whether real or imagined, yet allowed the complex structure of privileges, exemptions, and bureaucratic confusion to survive. His efforts to bypass groups that obstructed the effective extension of royal power, so successful in the short run, left in their wake numerous isolated pockets of discontent whose combined strength was considerable. His pursuit of military conquest and the mobilization of resources toward that end left social questions begging and badly needed administrative reforms unaccomplished. His glorious reign had been built upon the backs of many French people and the resentment they felt toward the Sun King was equal only to the awe with which they regarded him.[3] The revolts of the Fronde had left an ambiguous legacy to the old regime:

> There would be sullen resistance to arbitrary taxation, executive justice, and the new intendants in the years to come. And, despite the widespread disenchantment with the anarchic results of the original parlementary Fronde, the financial courts in Paris, provincial parlements, and various social groups could still take advantage of any new disagreements between the chief Parlement and the administration. This was the strange and ambiguous legacy of the series of revolts which had ended in a royalist revival, without giving the royal administration the sweeping victory so often described by historians. [Moote, 1972: 354]

The ambiguous legacy institutionalized a structural tension in the government of the old regime, and insured that significant pockets of discontent survived. It was not until the convocation of the Estates-General in 1789 that these diverse forces of opposition would again unite against the royal administration. At that time, strengthened by popular discontent once again, the forces of opposition decisively destroyed the old regime that Louis XIII and Louis XIV and cardinals Richelieu and Mazarin had struggled so hard to build.

The Failed Social Revolution in England

The coalition of political opposition in England differed from that in France in several crucial respects, and these differences determined the different outcomes of the two revolutions, despite their similar structural causes. First, as we have seen, the coalition met with a different administrative capacity to absorb or rebuff collective efforts to transform the monarchy; the administrative machinery of the Bourbons was far better suited to meet the political challenges of the revolutionary contenders than was the English monarchy, largely because venality of office had brought so many of these potential contenders into the absolutist administration, depriving them of an independent foundation for political challenge. That venal officers were part of the absolutist state insured that their rebellion would not, on its own, proceed very far.

The absence of the ideological mechanisms to maintain solidarity among the various constituent elements of the revolutionary coalition is a second major reason that the Fronde failed and the English Revolution succeeded. Puritanism acted as a moral and ideological glue, which allowed coalition members to work together despite their differing political and economic positions.

The ideological coherence was the way in which the revolutionary coalition was held together by a shared terror of the possibilities contained in the revolt of the popular classes in England. The Fronde largely galvanized upward, mobilizing the sword nobility to press for dynastic changes; the English Revolution set in motion a wide assortment of lower-class groups, especially in the urban centers, and most dramatically in London. These groups posed a threat to the consolidation of the political revolution, for they represented a completely different vision of the reconstitution of civil society in the postrevolutionary period. When the Civil War erupted in 1642, they joined in the opposition coalition in a united front against the royalists. It was their appearance that pushed the Revolution toward both political and social transformation, toward social revolution.

For the Parliamentarians, the revolt against Caroline absolutism was not a question of social revolution but of the relationship between the state and the ruling class. The question was "how to ensure the main burden of supporting the state fell on the lower rather than the upper classes" (Manning, 1968: 270). The monarchy had collapsed because a substantial section of the ruling class withdrew its support. For the ruling class, the Revolution was over as soon as it had begun; it was a successful challenge to royal absolutism. For the popular classes, who pinned their hopes of social transformation on the revolt of Parliament, political changes in the composition of the relationship between ruling class and state were hardly enough. Nor were simple economic changes:

> The popular movement was not merely the reflex of economic distress, it was carried forward by the cries of Liberty and Reformation, and it had its own aims distinct from any conflicting with those of the landlords or middle class. . . . It was no longer a question of the relation of the nobility and gentry to the Church but of whether the State was still to be based on the nobility and gentry. [Manning, 1967: 280–81]

It was the intervention of the popular movement that pushed the rebellion beyond the expectations and ambitions of the moderate reformers among the dissatisfied upper classes.

The outbreak of revolution prompted the articulation of political claims by the popular classes, and their joining the revolutionary coalition had a decisive impact on the trajectory of the Revolution. The Revolution "had arisen essentially from the claims of the gentry and merchant classes to play a larger part in the making of government policy. But the Civil War led to the mobilization of lower social groups who had not previously manifested much political self-consciousness" (Thomas, 1978: 66). If the Parliamentarians and Royalists formed the two principal parties of the Revolution, then this popular movement must be counted as the third part, envisioning a future based neither on the absolutism of the king nor on the laissez-faire capitalism of the Commons. The disintegration of the village community had pushed scores of peasants off the land and into the cities, where, joined with numerous artisans who were struggling to retain their economic autonomy, they developed a distinctive vision of political transformation that was neither feudal and absolutist nor liberal and capitalist (Hill, 1964: 122).

The popular movement exerted a distinctive presence throughout the Civil War, resisting impositions from Parliament to finance its military activities in the same way it had earlier resisted increases in royal taxation and feudal dues. In 1645 in the west and south, a group of rural laborers took up arms against both Parliament and king. The Clubmen, the "most massive popular movement of the entire civil war period," identified with neither party in the Civil War (Underdown, 1986: 155). The Clubmen asked "whether the able and rich who will not join with us be not only counted ill-affected but liable to pay for the poor who do their county service?" (cited in Hill, 1975: 199). The Clubmen signaled a revolt of "whole communities, not merely 'the rabble,' " and they sought to "protect their communities from plunder and to reduce the burden of contributions" to the Parliamentary cause as well (Underdown, 1986: 156, 158). In one couplet they staked their position clearly (cited in Kamen, 1970: 358):

> If you offer the plunder or take our cattle
> Rest assured we will give you battle.

The Clubmen were only one organized example of the enormous popular upsurge during the years of the Revolution, when the popular classes were agitating, presenting demands to the Parliamentarians and articulating their position. The "inferior sort of people," William Lilly, a noted astrologer told Oliver Cromwell (cited in Hill, 1975: 51), "are ascending." Indeed, they were. Dozens of religious sects emerged from the atmosphere of religious opening during the years of Revolution (which was less the product of genuine religious toleration on the part of the Presbyterians or Episcopacy and more the effect of the vacuum caused by the disruption of the hegemonic position of the established state church) and the profound economic and social dislocation experienced in preceding years (Hill, 1975). The Ranters, for example, believed in ecstasy as the road to salvation, and took to drunken carousing, swearing, free love and sexual freedom, the liberal use of tobacco and music, and mixed dancing as expressions of their experience of the divine (Underdown, 1986: 249). The Fifth Monarchists, another radical sect, went as far as envisioning a franchise open to women as well as all men, regardless of property ownership.[4]

For others, the disruption of a prolonged civil war, a series of bad harvests, the devastation of gentry enclosures that sent food prices soaring and increased the cost of living, were all compounded by the impositions of parliamentary taxation—especially the excise—which was levied on tobacco and beer among other consumer goods that were enjoyed by the popular classes (Hill, 1972: 86; Hill, 1975: 199). Some, like the Levellers, sought to sway the mainstream Parliamentary factions of the revolution; others, like the Diggers, took agrarian matters into their own hands and sought to tear down the fences of enclosed common fields and institute an inchoate and visionary cooperative commonwealth.

The popular classes that rebelled during the Revolution were "defenders of local rights against the centralizing state: ancient laws and liberties, an account for the money 'cheated or wrested from us by loans, contributions, taxes, fines, excise or plunder'; government by men 'of visible estates and of unquestioned repute' instead of committee-men of 'broken condition' " (Underdown, 1986: 230–31). To contemporary supporters of the Parliamentarian cause, though, they were a fearsome rabble, "an ignorant, rude, and revelling people," according to William Baxter, who contrasted them with the "small company of converts, who were humble, godly, and of good conversations" (cited in Underdown, 1986: 143). Religious radicals were cast as a "giddy multitude" by philosopher Robert Boyle; in 1652 he wrote (cited in Underdown, 1986: 330) that "this multiplicity of religions will end in none at all." After being driven from political power himself, the Presbyterian Parliamentarian D. Holles wrote in 1649 (cited in Hill and Dell, 1949: 369):

> The wisest of men saw it to be a great evil that servants should ride on horses and princes walk as servants on the earth: an evil not both seen and felt in our unhappy kingdom. The meanest of men, the basest and vilest of the nation, have got the power into their hands; trampled upon the crown; baffled and misused the Parliament; violated the laws; destroyed or suppressed the nobility and gentry in the kingdom.

The war, Baxter wrote (cited in Underdown, 1986: 143), "was begun in our streets before king or parliament had any armies."

The effect of the popular movement was to fracture the political coalition of revolutionary opposition, fragmenting the various constituent elements. The "unity of the forces facing the Crown dissolved when popular uprisings in London, in Ireland, and in the fen and forest regions occurred in 1641–9" (Goldstone, 1986: 267). For example, when fen dwellers opposed crown-initiated fenland drainage projects, Commons initially supported the fen dwellers and Lords staunchly supported the project. Fenmen therefore supported Parliament in the First Civil War. But when popular uprisings among the fen dwellers erupted, however, the upper classes were so afraid of social revolution that Commons was, itself, supporting fenland drainage projects by 1646 (Lindley, 1982). As Hill noted (1980: 129), "What mattered in the English Revolution was that the ruling class was deeply divided at a time when there was so much combustible material among the lower classes." The fear of social revolution fragmented the Parliamentary opposition, and reunified the upper classes in the face of revolution from below.

The Levellers and Social Revolution

Just as the countryside was in open rebellion against the king and often against Parliament as well, the towns and cities of England exhibited a strong movement articulating a radically different political and social vision than either of the two major parties. Drawn from diverse social, religious, and economic elements, these popular forces were a decisive element in the transformation of the Revolution, and one of the key reasons that the political revolution succeeded must be the unity among the ruling classes forged through the threat of revolt from below. By examining in a bit more depth the most significant of these popular movements, the Levellers, we can gain a better sense of who these popular forces were, where they came from, and the vision of social reconstruction that they professed. The Levellers are significant also because if the popular movement in general pushed the Revolution decisively, it was through the emergence of the Levellers that "the popular movement finally became wholly revolutionary, because it then achieved full political consciousness, coherent political objectives of its own, and the means to express itself in secular terms" (Manning, 1976: 283).

The Levellers were fairly short-lived as an organized political movement. Born in 1645 amidst the revolutionary upheaval—their first political pamphlet was *A Remonstrance of Many Thousand Citizens* in 1646—the organization had been effectively silenced in 1649 as Cromwell consolidated the Protectorate. Their influence reached its zenith during the reorganization of the New Model Army in the spring of 1648, but by that fall their ability to promote radical social change had been sharply diminished, first in the Putney debates and later at Ware and Burford. Despite their brief duration, they made a dramatic impact on the course of the Revolution, especially in the late 1640s, and represented a decisive departure from both Royalist and Parliamentary positions.

The Levellers were an urban movement, expressing the position and aspirations of the lower-middle class of artisans, small shopkeepers, master craftsmen and journeymen, "the pewterers, weavers, cobblers, saddlers, clockmakers, and other small tradesmen" (Shaw, 1968: 15). Leveller leader John Lilburne claimed they were "the hobnails, clouted shoes, the private soldiers, the leather and woolen aprons, and the laborious and industrious people of England" (cited in Shaw, 1968: 90). They were frequently religious sectarians, expressing that elective affinity between Protestant ascetic values and a specific economic location. These were men who experienced economic autonomy—control over the product of their labor and control over the labor process through guild regulation of crafts or through independent shop ownership—and at the same time experienced the coherence and solidarity of political and religious community, not as abstractions but as the experience of everyday life. This combination of political community and economic autonomy was fused in a particular lower-middle-class moral economy; the Leveller vision of postrevolutionary social reconstruction sought to preserve both elements in a synthesis that was not envisioned by the moderates in Parliament.

The daily experience of economic autonomy led the Levellers to resist fiercely the "encroaching might of the big capitalists, who were forcing them down to proletarian status" (Hill, 1975: 135). They spoke with the "anger of artisans suffering while the contractors and monopoly companies made fat profits," and they spoke of economic independence that they sought to preserve against both a centralizing absolutist-inspired state and larger merchants whose industrializing visions threatened their independence as well (Hirst, 1986: 273; see also Brailsford, 1961; Manning, 1977).

The ideas of the Levellers derived from their daily experience of political community as well. They believed passionately in common law, which was central to their vision of community. Their political community was a moral entity in which individuals would experience their freedom only insofar as they were members of the larger whole. This notion lies at the heart of the Leveller alternative, for it challenged both the traditional community of the old regime and the concept of individual freedom that England was soon to proclaim. The Levellers rejected the negative freedom of capitalist industrialization—the freedom from constraints on individual activity—believing that "liberty is a right demanded by the very nature of human beings: not merely a freedom from the restraint of others but a conscious and deliberate share in such arrangements as the community finds it necessary to make" (Gooch, 1954: 179). To the Levellers, society was not composed of autonomous disconnected individuals who, in the pursuit of their own rationally derived interests, banded together into contractual collectivities. It was the community, the moral economy, that was transcendent, not the individual, and individuals were free so long as they partook of common life. Individual liberty was indissolubly linked to political equality, and hence to political community. As Richard Overton wrote in 1646 (cited in Stone, 1980: 35),

> To every individual in nature is given an individual property by nature, not to be invaded or usurped by any: for everyone as he is himself, so he hath a self propriety, else he could not be himself. . . . For by natural birth all men are equally and alike born to like propriety, liberty, and freedom.

Such a vision derived from the religious origins of the Levellers; their radical Protestantism informed their vision of political community "on the analogy of one of the 'gathered' churches, whether Independent or Anabaptist, in which they enjoyed their deepest experiences of social life" (Brailsford, 1961: 259). Membership in the religious community or radical Protestant sects "meant their voluntary entry into a closely knit community and the signing of a covenant with each other for mutual aid and discipline, in which they collectively subscribed to certain beliefs" (Brailsford, 1961: 259). Anabaptism, with its refusal to take oaths, celebration of communion only as a symbolic act of fraternal commemoration, and the eschewing of baptism at birth, was particularly important in framing the Leveller vision; in the Anabaptist tradition, the individual chose baptism consciously as an adult and thus joined a moral community in which all things were held in common.

What concerned the Levellers was not so much the great disparity of wealth and status in mid-seventeenth century England but that since the Norman Conquest, formerly free Englishmen found themselves in a dependent status. The myth of the Norman Yoke—that dependency of feudal statuses were not indigenous to England but imported in 1066—sustained the Levellers' belief that their vision would emancipate the nation from foreign influences, and return it to all freeborn Englishmen. Their vision of political community would replace the dependence of one individual upon another with the universal dependence of each and every person upon the community. Community was overarching, all-embracing, and inevitably moral. It is in this sense that the Levellers were a democratic movement, envisioning a dramatic enlargement of the political nation and eliminating bonds of feudal dependence without replacing them by the bonds of dependence that characterize capitalist wage relations. In this sense the Levellers prefigured, in both ideology and daily experience, the political philosophy of Jean-Jacques Rousseau, the sociology of Emile Durkheim, and the revolutionary community of the sans-culottes in the French Revolution, none of which could have been envisioned during the Fronde, except perhaps by isolated popular uprisings before the Fronde.[5]

From these notions of community and dependence, the Levellers developed compelling political programs for the establishment of the republic of virtue. They advanced a notion of full religious toleration, for they believed that freedom of conscience implied a full separation of church and state. Lilburne wrote (1646: 11):

> Unnatural, irrational, sinful, wicked, unjust, devilish and tyrannical it is for any man whatsoever, spiritual or temporal, clergyman or layman, to appropriate and assume unto himself a power, authority, and jurisdiction to rule, govern or reign

over any sort of men in the world without their free consent, and whosoever doth it, whether clergyman or any other whatsoever, do thereby as much as in them lies, endeavor to appropriate and assume unto themselves the office and sovereignty of God (who alone doth and is to rule by his will and pleasure). . . .

Because religious beliefs could not be imposed from outside, it followed that the Levellers advocated the abolition of tithes, and argued for local parish autonomy from central clerical control. As Leveller leader Richard Overton wrote in 1647 (cited in Wolfe, 1944: 193–94),

That the grievous oppressions by tithes and forced maintenance for the ministry be removed, and that the more easy and evangelical practice of contribution be granted and confirmed for the benefit of the subject and his freedom therein, for prevention of the lordliness in, and the commotions, oppressions and tyrannies that might happen by, the clergy.

Instead, the Levellers argued that there should be "no power to impose ministers upon any respective parishes" but rather that "the parishioners of every particular parish" shall have "free liberty . . . to choose such as themselves shall approve" (cited in Wolfe, 1944: 408).

The Levellers were hostile to the encroachments made by all types of larger-scale capitalist enterprises, and demanded governmental control of economic activity. They opposed enclosures and demanded the throwing open of the commons—"that all grounds which anciently lay in common for the poor, and are now impropriate, enclosed and fenced in, may forthwith (in whose hands soever they are) be cast out and laid open again to the free and common use and benefit of the poor" (in Wolfe, 1944: 194)—and opposed primogeniture, which concentrated landed property (see also Hill, 1975). They demanded security of tenure for copyholders and the conversion of base tenures into freehold. In the cities they sought the abolition of monopolies, seeking protection instead for the rights of small shopkeepers to operate unfettered by restrictions on trade and the prohibitive excise taxes. "The Levellers saw the world as divided into rich and poor, strong and weak, rulers and ruled, those who eat their bread in the sweat of other men's brows and those who labored for their living with their own hands and sold the fruits of their labors" (Manning, 1976: 302, 306–7).

The Levellers also had some ideas about social reforms, grounded in legal changes that would eliminate the bicameral legal apparatus that allowed the nobility great latitude in political affairs. The Levellers insisted on equality before the law, trial by jury of one's peers, recodification and rationalization of the law, and the ousting of those lawyers who imposed an expensive and incomprehensible ritual between ordinary people and justice (Hill, 1972: 177). And, they demanded that all legal proceedings be in English:

> That all the laws of the land (locked up from common capacities in the Latin or French tongues) may be translated into the English tongue. And that all records, orders, processes, writs and other proceedings whatsoever may be all entered and issued forth in the English tongue . . . that so the meanest English commoner that can but read written hand in his own tongue may fully understand his own proceedings in the law. [Wolfe, 1944: 192]

The Levellers also proposed extension of the franchise, demanded the annual elections of officers and magistrates, and called for a representative convention to draft a constitution because the Civil War had "shattered the constitutional framework of the feudal society in which they were brought up. They had slid back into a state of nature" (Brailsford, 1961: 259). The state, they argued, was illegitimately constituted and required refounding; a new social contract was necessary. They argued for the abolition of the House of Lords, Privy Council, Star Chamber, and the privileges that accrued to the peerage (Hill, 1972: 129). Sovereignty was invested in the people, not in landowners, as Lilburne wrote in 1646 (in Wolfe, 1944: 14):

> The only and sole legislative law-making power is originally inherent in the people, and derivatively in their commissions chosen by themselves by common consent, and no other. In which the poorest that lives hath as true a right to give a vote as well as the richest and greatest.

The Levellers had developed a far-reaching political, economic, social, and religious vision based upon their alternative vision of social reconstruction, and they did so by organizing themselves into the "first genuine popular political movement in history," the "first political party" in English history (Hirst, 1986: 12, 273).[6] Had the changes they advocated been implemented, they would have dramatically transformed the structure of English society and refounded the state along very different lines.

The radical alternative remained only a tendency, an impossible dream in 1647, although others have followed the Leveller path. One reason that the Levellers were unsuccessful was the swift and decisive repression by Cromwell after the Putney debates in 1647 and the later clashes at Ware and Burford. To the moderate Parliamentarians who supported some version of the Cromwellian vision of the protectorate, the Levellers represented a significant threat: a spectre of the common people as fully sovereign. Further, the Levellers were divided internally into a moderate wing based in London and the more radical wing based among the regular soldiers of the New Model Army. "We were a heterogeneal body consisting of parts very diverse from one another settled upon principles inconsistent with one another," noted Leveller Henry Denne. The moderate wing envisioned a society based more along the lines of the New England town meeting; the radical wing envisioned something closer to the kibbutz; the division came primarily over the issue of the franchise. Radical Levellers, like Rainborough and Sexby, argued in *Light Shining in Buckinghamshire* that "all men being alike privileged by birth, so all men were to enjoy the creatures alike without property one more than another" (in Wolfe, 1944: 356). The moderates, like Lilburne, Petty, and Wildman, countered by repudiating "any idea of abolishing property, levelling estates or making all common" (in Wolfe, 1944: 374). We "never had it in our thoughts to level men's estates," they asserted in 1649, "it being the utmost of our aim that . . . every man with as much security as he be enjoy his property" (in Wolfe, 1944: 391).

Despite the division, the Levellers maintained a firm belief in the notions of individual freedom, political equality, and their inevitable connection. "All and every particular and individual man and woman that ever breathed in the world are by nature all equal and alike in their power, dignity, authority, and majesty, none of them having (by nature) any authority, dominion, or magesterial power one over or above another," wrote Lilburne in *The Free Man's Freedom Vindicated* (1646). And Richard Rumbold, condemned to death in 1683, remembered his days as a Leveller, declaring from the scaffold, "I am sure that there was no man born marked of God above another; for none comes into the world with a saddle on his back, neither any booted or spurred to ride him" (cited in Brailsford, 1961: 624).

The Levellers presented an alternative vision of the social order. Within the New Model Army, the radical wing of the movement developed this vision even more fully; there, in a "spontaneous outbreak of democracy" in 1647, the lesser officers proclaimed themselves a "peoples army which had pledged itself never to disband or divide until its democratic objectives were obtained" (Brailsford, 1961: 536; Hill, 1974: 56). Many in the rank and file "tried to make the Army as genuinely revolutionary in politics as it had been in religion. But in doing so they stripped away the facade of unity between the officers and the rank and file, and came up against the fears of the Grandees for their social pre-eminence" (Ellis, 1974: 41). Army Levellers pushed for a widening of the franchise, lest the goals of the revolution be utterly lost. As Sexby proclaimed at Putney in 1647 (cited in Ellis, 1974: 41),

> We have engaged in this kingdom and ventured our lives, and it was all for this: to recover our birthrights and privileges as Englishmen, and by the arguments urged there is none. There are many thousands of us soldiers that have ventured our lives; we have had little propriety in the kingdom as to our estates, yet we have our birthright. But it seems now except a man hath a fixed estate in the kingdom, he hath no right in this kingdom. I wonder we were so much deceived.

Although they might not have been deceived, the Levellers were certainly opposed by substantial numbers of the moderate Parliamentarians and the higher-level officers of the New Model Army. In the Putney debates Cromwell and Ireton made the moderate case against the Levellers; Cromwell declared that he had repulsed "this drive at a levelling and parity" (cited in Underdown, 1971: 87). In 1650 Marchmont Nedham's interesting pamphlet extended that line of reasoning. To Nedham, the Levellers were "zealous pretenders to liberty and freedom" but their vision was really "the ready road to all licentiousness, mischief, mere anarchy and confusion." But such a "democratic or popular form that puts the whole multitude into an equal exercise of the supreme authority, under the pretense of maintaining liberty, is . . . the greatest enemy of liberty" (Nedham, 1650: 110, 99).[7]

The Levellers in the New Model Army had laid their hopes of political transformation in the possibility of "influencing the Army leadership to broaden its vision of social reform rather than in contesting with it for power over the rank and file" (Kishlansky, 1982: 839). One Leveller journalist urged Fairfax to pay more attention to their demands, lest they "follow the example of those in Poland, who . . . have cut their landlords' throats because they would not regard their groans" (cited in Underdown, 1971: 191). "We the private soldiers," the pamphleteer continued, "represent the people and our offices the magistrate, whom we may as properly call to an account and alter and change them . . . as the people do their superiors and governors." By 1650, though, the Levellers had been crushed in both London and the New Model Army. The possibility of transforming the revolution of the saints into the revolution of the people by convincing the Parliamentarians and the generals of their moral vision had been dashed. The social revolution would not be accomplished by popular forces convincing the upper classes of its morality or efficacy.

No sooner did the army's Leveller faction find itself repressed, and the London Levellers find their organization dismantled by both army and Parliament, then a new revolutionary movement emerged in the English countryside, a new attempt to implement and extend the theories developed by the Levellers and others. It was the Diggers, or True Levellers, led by Gerald Winstanley, who developed a remarkable theory of primitive communism, presaging the more industrial collectivist theories of the mid-nineteenth century. His thought incorporated and surpassed many Leveller ideas, especially in his loathing of the idea of private property:

> In the beginning of time the great creator, Reason, made the earth to be a common treasury, to preserve beasts, birds, fishes and man, the lord that was to govern this creation. . . . Not one word was spoken in the beginning that one branch of mankind should rule over another. . . . But selfish imaginations . . . did set up one man to teach and rule over another. And thereby . . . man was brought into bondage, and became a great slave to such of his own kind than the beasts of the field were to him. And hereupon the earth . . . was hedged into enclosures by the teachers and rulers, and the others were made . . . slaves. And that earth that is within this creation made a common storehouse for all is bought and sold and kept in the hands of a few, thereby the great creator is mightily dishonoured, as if he were a respector of persons, delighting in the comfortable livelihood of some and rejoicing in the miserable poverty and straits of the others. From the beginning it was not so. [Hill, 1972: 106]

Winstanley extended the Leveller myth of origins of English servitude beyond the Norman Yoke to the Fall of Adam, and his goal was to restore "the pure law or righteousness before the Fall" (in Hill, 1972: 107). He also extended their notions of community and freedom. As Marchmont Nedham argued (1650: 109),

> From levelling they proceed to introduce an absolute community. And though neither the Athenian nor Roman levellers ever arrived to this high pitch of madness, yet we see there is a new faction started up out of ours known by the name of Diggers. Who, upon this ground that God is our common father, the earth our common mother, and that the original or [property] was men's pride and covetousness, have framed a new plea for a return of all men [to peasant cottages] that like the old Parthians, Sythian nomads, and other wild barbarians, we might renounce towns and cities, live as rovers, and enjoy all in common.

Winstanley held no illusions about convincing Parliament of the Diggers' position, and set about tearing down the enclosure fences and beginning to cultivate the wastelands collectively.[8] Like the Levellers, the Diggers were suppressed by the recharged New Model Army, which turned upon its popular supporters as soon as it had achieved its victory over the King's army. The popular classes had threatened the existing social order, but the proclamation of their victory was premature. They had supported Parliament during the political revolution but had failed to implement a social revolution that would have included them within the political nation. The political revolution succeeded, and the price of its success was the failure of the social revolution. As Bronterre O'Brien wrote in the *London Mercury* in 1837, on the eve of Chartism (cited in Hill and Dell, 1949: 477–78),

Political revolutions seldom go beyond the surface of society. They seldom amount to more than a mere transfer of power from one set of political chiefs to another. At best they only substitute one aristocratic form of government for another, and hence all political revolutions of which history makes mention have left the world pretty much as they found it—not wiser—not happier—not improved in any one essential particular. . . . Even the establishment of our "commonwealth" after the death of Charles I was a mere political revolution. It gave parliamentary privilege a temporary triumph over royal prerogative. It enabled a few thousand landowners to disenthrall themselves from the burdens of feudal services, and to throw upon the people at large the expenses of maintaining the government. . . . For the millions it did nothing.

The Successful Political Revolution in England

Despite its limitations the English Revolution must be counted as a successful political revolution, especially compared to the Fronde. The end of the Fronde was the beginning of the unbridled absolutist monarchy of Louis XIV, an absolutism based upon the political and economic subordination of all social groups that had earlier opposed the regency. But, the English Revolution succeeded at the political level. To be sure, Charles II assumed the throne in 1660, heralded as the only political leader capable of stabilizing trade and restoring order to the torn nation. Still, we must not mistake the restoration of a king for the restoration of a monarchy, unchanged by the political events of the Revolution. Just as we ought not to mistake immediate triggers of revolutionary events for their long-run structural causes, we ought not mistake the immediate historical results from the longer-run structural outcome of the revolution. In a sense the entire course of English history since that fateful day in 1649 when Charles was beheaded at Whitehall has been an attempt to define the relationship between the restored monarch and civil society, and to determine exactly the limits of the purview of each. The popular adage that in England "the king reigns but does not rule" contains an essential truth: the relationship between the king and society is radically different today from what it was before 1640, both in fact and in theory.

To explore the success of the English Revolution, two related issues must be addressed. We should demonstrate the success of the Revolution itself, for there is by no means unanimity on this issue. Trevor-Roper writes that the Revolution failed decisively (1966: 198), and many revisionist historians agree with Howell (1982: 87), who claims that a focus on the localities reveals that "the older political structures of the towns showed a remarkable capacity to absorb the Revolution, and by the process of accommodation, they managed to preserve against various forms of outside pressure a high degree of inherited privilege.'' Others suggest with McInnes (1982: 390) that the decisive transformative moment came not in the 1640s or even 1660 but in the 1680s and 1690s, during the reign of William III. I believe that arguments such as these mistake the trees for the forest: if the roots of a particular tree remain unscathed in a disastrous forest fire, the argument implies that one should conclude that nothing essential was changed, even if the entire landscape had been laid waste.

We should also account for the success of the English Revolution, especially as compared with the Fronde. Again, we will examine the unity among the various component elements of the coalition of political opposition and the administrative strength of the state to absorb, deflect, or defeat challenges. I will argue that the coalition of opposition was more unified in England because of the salience of religious ideologies in generating ideological cohesion despite differing economic interests, and because of the perception by coalition members of the enormous general threat posed by the radicalized and mobilized popular classes, who pressed for more sweeping social changes. In addition, the English monarchy was far less able to absorb political contenders because of its smaller administrative structure and the traditions of autonomous local administration.

After the Revolution England was a dramatically changed society, even if it was not immediately apparent to contemporaries. Parliament controlled taxation and therefore policy. On the local level rich landlords consolidated their powers, and the justices of the peace administered in accordance with their conception of local needs. The agrarian revolution that had been "continuing in spasms for a couple of centuries . . . now [went] forward in great waves, engulfing in its progress the open-field system, the self-governing village and often the peasant proprietors, the 'ancient and godly yeomen of England' " (Tate, 1967: 79). The Revolution "facilitated the conversion of rural society into a three-tiered structure of big landlords, substantial tenant leaseholders with reasonable security of tenure, and landless laborers" (Stone, 1980: 93). No longer does one hear arguments about the efficacy of enclosure, engrossing, or the conversion of the peasant proprietor into a wage-earning laborer. As Moore notes (1966: 19), the "English Civil War swept away the main barrier to the enclosing landlord and simultaneously prepared England for rule by a 'committee of landlords.' " There was "little fear that the state would upset an influential class by interfering with the economic activities of its members" (Tate, 1967: 78–79). The new programs for disafforestation, drainage of the fens, and capitalist investment in agricultural land and production began in earnest, as did new enclosures (Hill, 1972: 290). Landlords gained absolute rights to their estates, institutionalizing primogeniture, with the effect of maintaining the stability of large estates. The result was an ever-increasing concentration of land in the hands of the large landowners and the rapid growth, unfettered by political restrictions, of a pool of wage laborers, paving the way for the agricultural revolution of the eighteenth century and for the industrial revolution in the century that followed.

The dramatic changes in agrarian relations facilitated by the Revolution had important social consequences. As John Locke wrote of the enclosures in his *Second Treatise on Government* (1967: 312):

> He who appropriates land to himself by his labor does not lessen but increase the common stock of mankind. For the provisions serving to support of human life, produced by one acre of inclosed and cultivated land are . . . ten times more than those which are yielded by an acre of land of an equal richness lying waste in common. And therefore, he that incloses land and has a greater plenty of the conveniences of life from ten acres than he could have from a hundred left to nature, may truly be said to give ninety acres to mankind.

Though Locke's strictly economic calculations, themselves the product of the Revolution, decontextualize the notion of property and detach the economic functions of the land from the social functions of the common, he expresses a shift in the constituting principle of the local community, the bonds of which were dramatically altered by the Revolution. The "erosion of the cooperative, communally-organized open-field village" provoked both the Revolution and one of its chief products, and the suppression of the popular forces promoting social revolution finalized the disintegration of the moral economy of the traditional English village (Underdown, 1986: 284).

The English Revolution resulted in enormous changes in trade, as well as in colonial and foreign policy. Government policy became aggressively protectionist, and sources of policy shifted. "Before 1640," wrote Tawney (1935: 145), mercantilism "had been imposed by the government on business interests; after it, it became, to an increasing degree, a policy imposed by business interests on government." Although English society was dominated by merchants and an aristocracy that declared they disliked warfare as a means of conducting trade policy, three Dutch wars established English dominance over the Dutch, and won for the English the lucrative slave and Far Eastern trades. The Navigation Acts closed the British Empire to foreign shipping and established a monopoly area of privilege for English merchants, a victory of national trading interests over regional separatist interests. Trade had become "the life of the state," as Beattie had called it in 1645 (cited in Appleby, 1978: 121). Financial reorganization that culminated in the founding of the Bank of England in 1694 had a significant impact. The bank established "a structure of public credit through which England's trading wealth could be invested in the security and stability of government and give that government the power to engage successfully in long range war for political commercial ends" (Pocock, 1980: 14); it was this public credit that made England a world power (Pocock, 1980: 14). In industry, the Revolution removed the obstacles to free production. The new government rid itself of industrial monopolies and stopped the efforts to provide work for the unemployed, for fear that this might compete with private enterprise. Regulations over the labor market were also removed by a weakening of the guild system and rules of apprenticeship, which gave employers greater freedom to exploit juvenile labor. Coal and almost every other industry grew dramatically in the years after the Revolution (Langton, 1978: 178). The combined effect of the nation's new ambitious commercial policy, the powerful navy, and the revolution in agrarian relations "transformed England from a corn-importing to a corn-exporting country" (Hill, 1986: 54).

Politically, parliamentary control of the state meant that the old royal bureaucracy was decisively destroyed, which Hill called (1967: 76) the "most decisive single event in the whole of British history." The Revolution had been cast as a resistance to royal absolutism, and the consolidation of its victory "successfully prevented either Charles II or James II from creating in England a European-style royal absolutism" (Stone, 1980: 92). After the Revolution "the old state was not restored . . . only its trappings. The prerogative courts did not return, and so the sovereignty of Parliament and common law remained. The Privy Council henceforth had no effective control over local government" (Hill, 1967: 106). The administrative institutions that had retarded capitalist development most—the Star Chamber, High Commission, Court of Wards, for example—had been eliminated.[9] It was clear that "the king ruled for the convenience of the political nation rather than by divine authority," and that the political nation consisted of the great landlords who had been installed "at the heart of government, both central and local, and had made their power as great as their ambitions" (Thomas, 1978: 58; Tawney, 1912: 404). The new formula was "synthetic monarchy" controlled politically by "aristocratic parliamentarianism" (Hill, 1972: 285; Pocock, 1980: 10). Perhaps this new balance was expressed best by the French ambassador to the court of Charles II, who wrote to his king (cited in Hill, 1972: 107) that "if Aristotle were to come again to the world he could not find words to explain the manner of this government. It has a monarchical appearance, and there is a King, but it is very far from being a monarchy."

Socially, the Revolution facilitated the development of a class society in which classes were constituted through their relationship to the means of production and not their relation to political and social privileges. "The defeat of the radicals during the revolution thus helped to harden the formation of England into two nations," writes Hill (1972: 114). "Before 1640 the major social division had been between privileged and underprivileged; now it was between rich and poor, free and unfree, the armigerous and the disarmed . . . those paying for those subject to the Poor Law." The Revolution was a victory of one class over the other, seen through the telescope of historical and sociological time:

> The cultural divide between the respectable and the poor was deepened and consolidated in the century after 1660: by the continued expansion of commerce, producing a larger, more self-assured and sometimes even gentrified urban middle class; by the further inroads of agricultural capitalism, producing a rural society even more clearly stratified into the three tiers of landlords, tenant farmers, and laboring poor. [Underdown, 1986: 281–82]

The most celebrated legacy of the English Revolution was in the realm of ideas. For the first time "there came onto the stage of history a group of men proclaiming the ideas of liberty not liberties, equality not privilege, fraternity not deference" (Stone, 1972: 146). Although the problem for the Parliamentarian revolutionaries was how to utilize that liberty "to transfer control from the King and his personal advisors to the men of property, without also sharing this liberty with the middling sort of people," there survived, after the Revolution, ideas about religious toleration, limitations of the powers of the propertied, and popular consent to government (Stone, 1980: 36). Out of the English Revolution came the founding ideas of liberalism of Thomas Hobbes and John Locke, theorists of the rational contractual foundations of society. Here was "the victory of the interests over the passions," and the end to the age of fanaticism in English history (Stone, 1980: 98).

The most significant intellectual legacy of the English Revolution was the articulation of classical economic theory: Adam Smith is a direct descendant of the intellectual tradition expressed by Cromwell and Ireton at Putney. The theory of the individual's primacy over and above the demands of society is the cornerstone of liberal political and economic theory, and its origins were institutionalized in the aftermath of the Revolution. There remained "tensions between the interests of the whole and the individual, but the concept of a social goal greater than the sum of a private one appeared less an eternal verity and more as a vestigial notion," writes Appleby (1978:22). "To every individual in nature is given an individual property by nature, not to be invaded or usurped by any; for everyone as he is himself, so he hath a self-property, else he could not be himself"—so wrote moderate Leveller Richard Overton in his political pamphlet *An Arrow Against All Tyrants* in 1646. "For by natural birth," he continued, "all men are equally and alike born to like propriety, liberty, and freedom." Such a sentiment was echoed eighty years later by Jonathan Swift, who wrote in a letter to Alexander Pope in September 1725 that "I have ever hated all national, professions and communities, and my love is toward all individuals."

It is for this reason, the first clear articulation of the concept of individualism as the individual's inalienable rights, that many historians have interpreted the Parliamentary victory as a victory for human freedom. The political solution "established the sacred rights of property, gave political power to the propertied, and removed all impediments to the triumph of the ideology of the men of property—the protestant ethic" (Hill, 1972: 12). The English Revolution was a success, then, but our understanding of this history of English society does not permit unbridled enthusiasm for the triumph of human freedom. English society remained dominated by landowning and commercial gentry who, over the centuries, had successfully defeated the claims of the crown and the peasantry to develop the principles of property ownership. Property was at the disposal of the owner, and there were no competing rights over its use. This left thousands of small landowners and wage laborers defenseless, and with the erosion of the moral economy of the English village, at the mercy of the rich and powerful. Similarly, it would be an error to romanticize the monarchy's role in English history, yet the monarchy had provided some protection for all its subjects. With the victory of private interests, all this changed. The new society was crucially different from the old, not just in its conception of property and government, but also in its conception of human beings. By the eighteenth century, one's place in the social order was almost entirely determined by the amount and kind of one's property.

In the form and structure of government, the relationship between state and society, individual and society, economy and state, individual and state, and the relationships among individuals, the events of the English Revolution left a lasting impact. The Revolution swept away the economic, political, social, and ideological fetters that retarded the industrial and commercial development of the nation, laying the "foundations for a later bourgeois triumph" in which industrial development would be based upon capitalist principles and wage labor (Jenkins, 1983: 276). The English Revolution was a successful political revolution, based upon a failed social revolution; it removed the obstacles to a relatively peaceful social change that penetrated to the very foundations of English society, and was later to spread to every corner of the globe.

For these reasons—the administrative strength of the French and English monarchies and their respective capacities to absorb potential contenders and resist demands for reform; the level of unity and the strength of the coalition of opposition that challenged the monarchies; the presence or absence of an ideology capable of holding together the disparate constituent elements of the political coalition—the outcomes of the English Revolution and the Fronde were so strikingly divergent. The fiscal crisis of the old regime state had generated political opposition, which gradually developed into a revolutionary coalition in each country. In each, the first moves toward the expression of that opposition came from the lesser nobility lodged in the parliaments. But, the organizational structure of the parliaments and the longer-run structural preconditions of revolution—the society's position in the international economic and geopolitical system; the structure of domestic class relations; and the organizational structure of the state—proved ultimately decisive in producing different trajectories for the revolutionary coalitions.

The political coalition failed in France because the French state was stronger than the forces of opposition that were arrayed against it; because it was also stronger than either the agricultural or the commercial economies were in generating social change from below; because of the divergence of the various groups that formed the coalition; because there was no ideological unity to hold the coalition together; and because all privileged groups that had revolted against the crown feared revolt from the nonprivileged social classes more than they feared capitulation with the monarchy. The Frondeurs could not transform their opposition from a specific resistance to fiscal expedients to a challenge to the fiscal structure of absolute monarchy, from a weak and ineffective challenge to a regency government to a challenge to monarchy in general. The French monarchy was strong enough to withstand the onslaught of the Fronde, which provided the rationale for continued exclusion of some social groups and the domination and subordination of all potential pockets of resistance. The ability of the monarchy to weather this, the most serious political challenge of the old regime, generated a smug arrogance, for the crown believed it could weather any challenge without instituting reforms. When the pressure from domestic social opposition and international economic and geopolitical competition again intensified in the late eighteenth century and the French state did attempt to reform its social foundations, it was too little too late. The Bourbon monarchy was consumed in a powerful cataclysmic event that united political and social revolution.

The English monarchy was too weak to weather these challenges. The pressures on the state

were more various, the number of alienated more considerable. There was a growing movement toward economic individualism, both in commerce and on the land—struggling in the former case against the relics of state control and state-supported monopoly, and in the latter against the surviving customary restrictions on the utilization of the soil. Free trade was the slogan of one movement; enclosure of the other. [Beloff, 1962: 174]

Both movements, the movement for free trade and the movement for enclosures, were united in opposition to the weak absolutism of the early Stuarts. Unified by a radical religious ideology that forestalled the serious fissures that might have developed, these groups sustained, through a national representative institution and through a nationally organized military force, a profound and successful challenge to the absolute monarchy. And, though a Stuart king was restored in 1660, the balance between king and political nation was reorganized by 1688 along the lines first articulated in the years of the Revolution. The failure of the social revolution allowed the consolidation of the gains made by the moderates. Attempts at social transformation by the Levellers, Diggers, and other radical popular movements were suppressed by a strengthened Parliament and army, which further cemented the political unity of the political coalition (excluding the popular classes from the coalition) and increased the administrative capacity of the state to weather such challenges in the future. In France, the revolt of Parliament, which had earlier registered modest successes, was followed instead by a revolt of the high nobility, which wanted nothing more than the restoration of centrifugal, particularistic, and conservative political arrangements. The English Revolution built a successful political revolution on the suppression of the social revolution, while the degeneration of the political revolution into internecine strife in France precluded either political or social transformation.

The fiscal crisis of the old regime state provides an analytic linchpin in a theoretical model of the causes of revolution, and the longer-range structural variables and the relative balances of these forces help to explain revolutionary outcomes. The fiscal crisis of the state is a "middle-range" variable because it can be used to explain causes but not consequences. We come to view the state at the moment of collapse, and the development of the revolutionary coalition that will contend with the state for political power. The fiscal crisis empirically links the longer-run structural causes; it is the moment when these tensions become a political crisis, a crisis of legitimacy, setting up the potential for revolutionary activity. Thus, the analysis of fiscal crisis is the link between the longer-run structural preconditions of revolution and the immediate historical events that trigger its outbreak.

The different historical outcomes of the English Revolution and the Fronde have continued to mark the historical development of England and France. In each the solutions sought by the state to its endemic fiscal crisis alienated the social groups among which the monarchy had originally found its support, until state activity generated a significant and broad-based coalition of political opposition. The solutions sought by any political administration to fiscal crisis are a highly charged political decision, and they are likely to result in some voicing of political opposition. This is an important lesson, theoretically and empirically. It requires the refocusing of our analytic attention on the state in the generation of political opposition, and on the international economic and geopolitical systems and domestic class arrangements as the structural preconditions that set the parameters for state action. Empirically, it is important to remember the lessons of mid-seventeenth-century efforts to construct absolutist states, to centralize state power. As local and national leaders in the late twentieth century struggle to generate sufficient revenues, we can be sure that their policies will also generate new forms of resistance.

Notes

1. See also *Lettre des Jurats et Habitans de la Ville de Bordeaux* and *Réponse des Bourgeois et Habitans de Paris à Messieurs les Jurats et Habitans de la ville de Bordeaux*, Stadsbib. Antwerpen, K-49215, for exchanges between Orméeists and the Parisian Frondeurs.
2. Years later even those who preached funeral sermons over individuals who had been active during the Fronde often skipped over that period. The bishop of Amiens, for example, remarked in his funeral oration over Queen Anne in 1666, "I do not want to enter into the shadows of those times of confusion and of disorders nor to recall them to your memory. . . . It is better to draw a veil over these occurrences in our history" (cited in Knachel, 1967: 262).
3. Perhaps the most devastating testimony of the popular antipathy felt toward Louis XIV is this epitaph, noted in 1715 by a simple parish priest in Saint-Suplice, a small village near Blois (cited in Briggs, 1977: 164–65):
   Louis XIV, King of France and Navarre, died on September 1st of this year, scarcely regretted by his whole kingdom, on account of the exorbitant sums and heavy taxes he levied on all his subjects. He is said to have died 1,700,000,000 livres in debt. These debts were so great that the Regent has not been able to lift those taxes which the King promised to remove three months after the peace, the *capitation* and the *dixième* on all property. It is not permissible to repeat all the verses, all the songs, or all the unfavorable comments which have been written or said against his memory. During his life he was so absolute, that he passed above all the laws to do his will. The princes and the nobility were oppressed, the parlements had no more power; it was obligatory to receive and register all edicts, whatever they were, since the King was so powerful and so absolute. The clergy were shamefully servile in doing the King's will; he had hardly to request a grant to be given more than he asked. The clergy has become horribly indebted; other bodies were at peace, living joyfully with all the money of the kingdom in their possession.

4. One Fifth Monarchist wrote (cited in Hill and Dell, 1949: 321):

   Let not men despite [women] or wrong them of their liberty of voting and speaking in common affairs. To women I say, I wish ye be not too forward and yet not too backward, but hold fast your liberty; keep your ground, which Christ hath got and won for you, maintain your rights, defend your liberties even to the life. . . . Ye ought not by your silence to betray your liberty, trouble your consciences, lose your privileges and rights, or see the truth taken away or suffer before your eyes.

5. This theoretical tradition remains a relatively unexplored vein in social and political theory, noted by, among others, Pocock (1966), Wolin (1964), and Weintraub (1979). I develop the application of the Republican Virtue tradition among the Levellers and sans-culottes in my article (Kimmel, 1984).

6. For a detailed analysis of Leveller organization, and its relationship to the Leveller vision it prefigured, see Kimmel, 1984.

7. The Levellers have not fared so well among contemporary historians either. Jordan (1942: 203–4) suggests that their ideas ranged from "the impracticable dreams of the visionary to the disordered gropings of the demented"; specifically, their economic ideas were "quite as divorced from the economic realities of the age as [they were] from the political necessities of the period." Thus, he concludes that the Levellers were "so detached from the trend of English development as to be without great significance for the period." For a further elaboration of these hostile historians, who resist viewing the Leveller's failed vision as an important "road not taken" in the English Revolution, and, in fact, a condition for the consolidation of the political revolution above them, see Kimmel, 1984.

8. They planted carrots, parsnips, and beans on St. George's Hill in Surrey, which represented an interesting departure in crop selection. They wanted to keep the cattle alive during the winter to fertilize the land.

9. Ashton echoes this theme, arguing that the revolution facilitated "the further progress of capitalism [which] had become impossible without the overthrow of a regime which cramped and stifled it at every turn" (Ashton, 1970: 94). He points out that "although politics remained dominated by a class of landowners . . . the fundamental economic outlook of this ruling class changed, and can more or less be equated with that of those landowners who had opposed the Crown in 1642" (1970: 101).

Bibliography

Abbreviations

A.N., Archives Nationales, Paris
B. Maz., Bibliothèque Mazarine, Paris
B.N., Bibliothèque Nationale, Paris
Brit. Mus., British Museum, London
P.R.O., Public Record Office, London
Stadsbib. Ant., Stadsbibliotheek, Antwerp

General Works

Anderson, Perry
1974   *Lineages of the Absolutist State*. London.
Appleby, Joyce
1984   *Capitalism and a New Social Order: The Republican Vision of the 1790s*. New York.
Ardant, Gabriel
1975   "Financial Policy and Economic Infrastructure of Modern States and Nations" in *The Formation of National States in Western Europe* (C. Tilly, ed.). Princeton.
Asher, Eugene
1960   *Resistance to the Maritime Classes*. Berkeley.
Aya, Roderick
1979   "Theories of Revolution Reconsidered" in *Theory and Society*, 8(1).
Barker, Ernest
1946   *The Development of Public Services in Western Europe, 1660–1930*. London.
Behrens, C. B. A.
1967   *The Ancien Régime*. New York.
Bendix, Reinhard
1964   *Nation-Building and Citizenship*. New York.
1978   *Kings or People*. Berkeley.

Birnbaum, Norman
1953   "Conflicting Interpretations of the Rise of Capitalism: Marx or Weber"
        in *British Journal of Sociology,* 4.
Bloch, Marc
1967   *Land and Work in Medieval Europe.* New York.
Braudel, Fernand
1973   *Capitalism and Material Life, 1400–1800.* New York.
1975   *The Mediterranean and the Mediterranean World in the Age of Philip
        II,* 2 vol. New York.
Braun, Rudolf
1975   "Taxation, Sociopolitical Structure, and State-Building: Great Britain
        and Germany" in *The Formation of National States in Western Europe*
        (C. Tilly, ed.). Princeton.
Brenner, Robert
1976   "Agrarian Class Structure and Economic Development in Pre-Industrial
        Europe" in *Past and Present,* 70.
1977   "The Origins of Capitalist Development: A Critique of neo-Smithian
        Marxism" in *New Left Review,* 104.
Brinton, Crane
1965   *Anatomy of Revolution.* New York.
Brustein, William
1985   "Class Conflict and Class Collaboration in Regional Rebellions, 1500 to
        1700" in *Theory and Society,* 14.
———, and Margaret Levi
1987   "The Geography of Rebellion: Rulers, Rebels, and Regions, 1500–
        1700." *Theory and Society,* 16.
Burke, Peter
1978   *Popular Culture in Early Modern Europe.* New York.
Cahnman, Werner, and Alvin Boskoff, eds.
1964   *Sociology and History.* New York.
Chance, James
1981   "Insolvent America" in *New York Review of Books,* March 19.
Chaunu, Pierre
1959   *Seville et l'Atlantique, 1504–1650, VIII* (1). Paris.
Cipolla, Carlo
1976   *Before the Industrial Revolution: European Society and Economy,
        1000–1700.* New York.
Clark, G. N.
1927   "War, Trade, and Trade War, 1701–1713" in *Economic History Review*
        (series 1), 1.
Cooper, J. P.
1970   "The Fall of the Stuart Monarchy" in *New Cambridge Modern History,*
        vol. 4, Cambridge.
Crouzet, François
1966   "Angleterre et France au XVIIe siècle: essai d'analyse comparée de
        déux croissances économiques" in *Annales, E.S.C.,* 2.
Dahrendorf, Ralf
1959   *Class and Class Conflict in Industrial Society.* Stanford.

Davies, C. S. L.
 1973   "Peasant Revolt in France and England: A Comparison" in *Agricultural History Review*, XXI.
Davies, James C.
 1962   "Toward a Theory of Revolution" in *American Sociological Review*, 27(1).
Davies, R. Trevor
 1957   *Spain in Decline, 1621–1700*. New York.
 1961   *The Golden Century of Spain, 1501–1621*. New York.
Dobb, Maurice
 1971   *Studies in the Development of Capitalism*. New York.
Edwards, Lyford.
 1927   *The Natural History of Revolution*. Chicago.
Eisenstadt, S. N.
 1978   *Revolution and the Transformation of Societies*. New York.
Elias, Norbert
 1982   *Power and Civility*, New York.
Elliot, J. H.
 1961   "The Decline of Spain" in *Past and Present*, 20.
 1963   *The Revolt of the Catalans*. Cambridge.
 1969   "Revolution and Continuity in Early Modern Europe" in *Past and Present*, 42.
 1974   "Revolts of the Spanish Monarchy" in *Precondition of Revolution in Early Modern Europe* (R. Foster and J. Greene, eds.). Baltimore.
 1977   *Imperial Spain, 1469–1715*. New York.
 1984   *Richelieu and Olivares*. New York.
Engels, Frederick
 1970   *The Origin of the Family, Private Property, and the State*. New York.
 1971   *Anti-Dühring*. New York.
Finer, Samuel E.
 1975   "State and Nation-Building in Europe: The Role of the Military" in *The Formation of National States in Western Europe* (C. Tilly, ed.). Princeton.
Forster, Robert, and Greene, Jack, eds.
 1974   *Precondition of Revolution in Early Modern Europe*. Baltimore.
Gardiner, S. R.
 1912   *The Thirty Years War, 1618–48*. London.
Gindeley, Anton.
 1884   *History of the Thirty Years War*. New York.
Gold, David and Lo, Clarence Y. H., and Wright, Erik Olin
 1975   "Recent Developments in Marxist Theories of the Capitalist State" in *Monthly Review*.
Goldfrank, Walter
 1975   "World-System, State Structure, and the Onset of the Mexican Revolution" in *Politics and Society*.
 1979   "Theories of Revolution and Revolution without Theory: The Case of Mexico" in *Theory and Society*, 7(4).
Gottschalk, L.
 1944   "Causes of Revolution" in *American Journal of Sociology*, 50(1).

Gurr, Ted Robert
1971   *Why Men Rebel*. Princeton.
Hamilton, E. J.
1929   "American Treasure and the Rise of Capitalism" in *Economics*, IX.
1960   "The History of Prices Before 1750" in *XIe Congrès International des Sciences Historiques—Rapports*. Stockholm.
Hilton, Rodney, ed.
1976   *The Transition from Feudalism to Capitalism*. London.
Hintze, Otto
1964   "The Emergence of the Democratic Nation-State" in *The Development of the Modern State* (H. Lubasz, ed.). New York.
1975   *The Historical Essays of Otto Hintze* (Felix Hilbert, ed.). New York.
Hobsbawm, E. J.
1954   "The Crisis of the Seventeenth Century" in *Past and Present*, 5–6.
1958   "Seventeenth Century Revolutions" in *Past and Present*, 13.
1960   "The Seventeenth Century in the Development of Capitalism" in *Science and Society*, 24(2).
1962   *The Age of Revolution*. New York.
1975   "Revolution," paper presented to the 14th International Congress of Historical Sciences. San Francisco.
Holt, Robert T., and Turner, John E., eds.
1970   *The Methodology of Comparative Research*. New York.
Huntington, Samuel P.
1968   *Political Order in Changing Societies*. New Haven.
Hurstfield, Joel, ed.
1965   *The Reformation Crisis*. New York.
Johnson, Chalmers
1966   *Revolutionary Change*. Boston.
Kamen, Henry
1977   *The Iron Century*. New York.
Kiernan, V. G.
1957   "Foreign Mercenaries and Absolute Monarchy" in *Past and Present*, 11.
1980   *State and Society in Europe, 1550–1650*. New York.
Kimmel, Michael
1977   "Wallerstein's World System: A Review Essay" in *Contemporary Crises*, 1(2).
1977   Review of R. Hilton, ed., *The Transition from Feudalism to Capitalism* in *American Journal of Sociology*, July.
1979   "Absolutism in Crisis: The English Civil War and the Fronde" in *The World System of Capitalism: Past and Present* (W. Goldfrank, ed.). Beverly Hills, CA.
1984   "War, State Finance and Revolution: Foreign Policy and Domestic Opposition in the 17th Century World-Economy" in *Foreign Policy and the World System* (C. Kegley and P. McGowan, eds). Beverly Hills, CA.
Knachel, Paul
1967   *England and the Fronde*. Ithaca.
Koenigsberger, H. G.
1971a.   *Estates and Revolutions*. Ithaca.
1971b.   *The Habsburgs and Europe, 1516–1600*. Ithaca.

1972   "Revolutionary Conclusions" in *History* 57(191).
1978   "Monarchies and Parliaments in Early Modern Europe" in *Theory and Society*, 5(2).
Krejci, Jaroslav
1983   *Great Revolutions Compared: The Search for a Theory*. New York.
Lenin, V. I.
1929   *Letters on Tactics* in *Collected Works*, vol. 20. New York.
Linz, Juan J.
1972   "Intellectual Roles in Sixteenth and Seventeenth Century Spain" in *Daedalus*, Summer.
Lis, C. and H. Soly
1979   *Poverty and Capitalism in Pre-Industrial Europe*. Atlantic Highlands.
Lubasz, Heinz, ed.
1964   *The Development of the Modern State*. New York.
1966   *Revolutionaries in Modern European History*. New York.
Lukàcs, Georg
1971   *History and Class Consciousness*. Cambridge, Mass.
Marx, Karl
1967   *Capital*, 3 vol. New York.
Moore, Barrington, Jr.
1962   *Political Power and Social Theory*. New York.
1966   *The Social Origins of Dictatorship and Democracy*. Boston.
Moote, A. Lloyd
1973   "The Preconditions of Revolutions in Early Modern Europe: Did They Really Exist?" in *Canadian Journal of History*, 8.
Mousnier, Roland
1954   *Les 16e et 17e siècles*. Paris.
1960   "Trevor-Roper's General Crisis" in *Past and Present*, 18.
Nef, John U.
1942   "War and Economic Progress, 1540–1640" in *Economic Historical Review*, ser. 1, v. 12.
1967   *The Conquest of the Material World: Essays on the Coming of Industrialism*. Cleveland.
Noonan, J. T.
1957   *The Scholastic Analysis of Usury*. Cambridge, Mass.
North, Douglass C., and Robert Paul Thomas
1973   *The Rise of the Western World*. Cambridge.
O'Connor, James
1973   *The Fiscal Crisis of the State*. New York.
Oestereicher, Emil
1978   "Marx's Comparative Historical Sociology" in *Dialectical Anthropology*, 3.
Pagès, Georges
1972   *The Thirty Years War, 1618–1648*. New York.
Parker, Geoffrey, and Lesley Smith, eds.
1978   *The General Crisis of the Seventeenth Century*. London.
Parsons, Talcott
1955   *The Social System*. New York.

Pirenne, Henri
  1914   "The Stages in the Social History of Capitalism" in *American Historical Review*, 19(3).
  1946   *Medieval Cities*. Princeton.
Polanyi, Karl
  1971   *The Great Transformation*. New York.
Polisensky, J. V.
  1954   "The Thirty Years War" in *Past and Present*, 6.
  1978   *War and Society in Europe, 1618-1648*. New York.
Porter, R., and C. R. Whittaker
  1976   "States and Estates: Review Essay on Anderson" in *Social History*, 3.
Rabb, Theodore K.
  1975   *The Struggle for Stability in Early Modern Europe*. New York.
Ritter, Gerhard
  1964   "Origins of the Modern State" in *The Development of the Modern State*. Heinz Lubasz, ed. New York.
Romano, Ruggiero
  1964   "Encore la crise de 1619-1622" in *Annales E.S.C.*
Schoffer, Ivo
  1978   "Did Holland's Golden Age Coincide with a Period of Crisis?" in Parker and Smith, eds. *The General Crisis of the Seventeenth Century*. London.
Schumpeter, J.
  1954   "The Crisis of the Tax State" in *International Economic Papers*, 4.
Seaver, Henry L.
  1966   *The Great Revolt in Castille*. New York.
Skocpol, Theda
  1973   "A Critical Review of B. Moore's *Social Origins of Dictatorship and Democracy*" in *Politics and Society*, Fall.
  1976   "France, Russian China: A Structural Analysis of Social Revolution" in *Comparative Studies in Society and History*, 18(2).
  1976   "Old Regime Legacies and Communist Revolutions in Russia and China" in *Social Forces*, 55(2).
  1976   "Explaining Revolutions: In Quest of a Social-Structural Approach" in *The Uses of Controversy in Sociology* (L. Coser, ed.). New York.
  1977   "Wallerstein's World System: A Critical Review" in *American Journal of Sociology*.
  1979   *States and Social Revolution*. Cambridge.
Skocpol, Theda and Ellen Kay Trimberger
  1978   "Revolutions in the World Historical Development of Capitalism" in *Berkeley Journal of Sociology*, 22.
Smelser, Neil J.
  1976   *Comparative Methods in the Social Sciences*. Englewood Cliffs.
Strayer, Joseph R.
  1970   *On the Medieval Origins of the Modern State*. Princeton.
Steinberg, S. H.
  1966   *The Thirty Years War and the Conflict for European Hegemony, 1600-1660*. New York.
Stinchcombe, Arthur
  1978   *Theoretical Methods in Social History*. New York.

Stone, Lawrence
  1966   "Century of Crisis" in *New York Review of Books*, 12 February.
  1987   "The Century of Revolution" in *New York Review of Books*, 26 February.
Swart, K. W.
  1949   *Sale of Offices in the 17th Century*. Netherlands.
Symcox, Geoffrey
  1974   *War Diplomacy and Imperialism, 1618–1763*. New York.
Tawney, R. H.
  1941   "Harrington's Interpretation of His Age" in *Proceedings of the British Academy*, 28.
Taylor, George
  1966–7 "Noncapitalist Wealth and the Origins of the French Revolution" in *American Historical Review*, 72.
  1964   "Types of Capitalism in Eighteenth Century France" in *English Historical Review*, 79.
Tilly, Charles
  1975   *The Formation of National States in Western Europe* (ed.). Princeton.
  1978   *From Mobilization to Revolution*. Reading, Mass.
  1981   *As Sociology Meets History*. New York.
  1985   *Big Structures, Large Processes, Huge Comparisons*. New York.
Trevor-Roper, H. R.
  1959   "The General Crisis of the Seventeenth Century" in *Past and Present*, 16.
Vilar, Pierre
  1979   "On Nations and Nationalism" in *Marxist Perspectives*, 2(1).
Wallerstein, Immanuel
  1972   "Three Paths of National Development in Sixteenth Century Europe" in *Studies in Comparative International Development*, 7(2).
  1974   *The Modern World System*, vol. 1. New York.
  1979   *The Capitalist World Economy*. New York.
  1980   *The Modern World System*, vol. 2. New York.
Weber, Max
  1964   *General Economic History*. New York.
  1971   *The Protestant Ethic and the Spirit of Capitalism*. New York.
  1978   *Economy and Society*, 2 vol. Berkeley.
Zagorin, Perez
  1982   *Rebels and Rulers, 1500–1660*. 2 vol. New York.

France

Primary Sources

Published Sources and Collections

Comptes de la Prévôté de l'Hôtel de Ville de Paris. A.N. KK 97
Comptes de l'Hôtel de Ville de Paris. A.N. KK 93
Comptes de ventes sur l'Hôtel de Ville. B.N. Ms. français 17335
Estats généraux des officiers de la maison du roi, 1643–1647. A.N. Z^{1a}473
Evénements arrivés en France de 1612 à 1649. B. Maz. Ms 2117
Gages de la Prévôté de l'Hôtel, A.N. KK 99

Gages des officiers du roi, A.N. KK 98

Histoire abrégée du Parlement durant les troubles du commencement du regne de Louis XIV. Rennes, 1762.

Histoire du temps ou le véritable récit de ce qui s'est passé dans le Parlement depuis le mois d'août 1647 jusque'au mois de novembre 1647. Paris, 1839.

Journal de ce qui s'est fait au Parlement de Rouen en 1649. B.N. Ms Français 18940.

Registres de l'Hôtel de Ville de Paris pendant la Fronde (Le Roux de Linay and Douet D'Arcy, eds.). 3 vols. Paris, 1846.

Memoirs and Letters

Anon. *Mémoire sur l'état des finances depuis 1616 jusqu'en 1644.* Paris, 18381.

de Boislisle, A. M.
1874   *Correspondence des controleurs généraux.* vol. 1. Paris.

Dubuisson-Aubenay, François-Nicolas Baudant, Seigneur de. *Journal des Guerres Civiles, 1648–1652.* 2 vol. Paris, 1883–1885.

Feillet, Alphonse. *Relation véritable de ce qui c'est passé de plus remarquable en la sédition arrivée à Paris (26 août 1648).* Paris, 1866. B. Maz. 40563A⁹ᵉ.

Mazarin, Jules. *Lettres du Cardinal Mazarin pendant son ministère.* (Cheruel and d'Avenal, eds.), 9 vol. Paris, 1872–1906.

Molé, Mathieu. *Mémoires* (Chambollion-Figeac, ed.), 4 vol. Paris, 1855.

Montglat, François de Paule de Clermont, Marquis de. *Mémoires* (in Michaud-Poujoulat, 3rd series, V). Paris, 1838.

De Monville, Alexandre Bigot. *Mémoires du Président Alexandre Bigot de Monville: le Parlement de Rouen, 1640–43* (Madelaine Foisil, ed.). Paris, 1976.

Ormesson, Olivier Lefevre de. *Journal* (A. Cheruel, ed.), 2 vol. Paris, 1860–1.

Pasquier, Etienne. *Lettres Historiques, 1556–1594* (D. Thickett, ed.). Geneva, 1966.

Patin, Guy. *Lettres du Temps de la Fronde* (A. Therive, ed.). Paris, 1921.

Retz, François Paul de Gondi, Cardinal de. *Mémoires* (Michaud-Poujoulat, eds.), 3rd series, I. Paris, 1837.

Saint-Simon, Henri duc de. *The Age of Magnificence.* New York, 1963.

Séguier, Chancelier P. *Lettres de Mémoires adressés au Chancelier Séguier 1633–1649,* 2 vol. (Roland Mousnier, ed.). Paris, 1964.

Séguier, P. *Lettres et Mémoires adressés au Chancelier P. Séguier, 1633–1649.* (A. Lublinskaya, ed.) Moscow, 1966.

de Sevigné, Mme. *Lettres de Madame de Sevigné.* Paris, 1953.

Talon, Omer. *Mémoires* (in Michaud-Poujoulat, eds.), 3rd series, VI. Paris, 1838.

de Verthamont, François. *Daire ou journal du voyage du chancelier Séguier en Normandie après la sédition des nu-pieds, 1639–1640.* Rouen, 1842 (Reprinted Geneva, 1975).

de Wicquefort, Abraham. *Chronique discontinue de la Fronde* (Robert Mandrou, ed.). Paris, 1978.

Political Pamphlets (all publications are Paris, unless otherwise noted)

A Tous les Evèques, Prestres et Enfans de l'Eglise (1660). B. Maz. M 10,005.

Advis aux Partisans Maltotien, Monopoleurs, et Ferniers de ce Royaume, trouvé dans le Cabinet de d'Emery après sa mort (1650). B. Maz. 10633 fol 605–623.

Advis Salutaires aux Citoyens et Peuple de la Ville de Paris (1649). B. Maz. 17648 fol 30.

Apologie des Frondeurs (1650). B. Maz. 10633 fol 248–273.

Apologie pour Messieurs les Princes envoyée par Madame de Longueville à Messieurs du Parlement de Paris (1650). B. Maz. 16033 fol 315–358.

Arrêts de la Cour de Parlement, 2 janvier 1649. B. Maz. 13982 fol 1–2.

Arrêts de la Cour de Parlement, 6 janvier 1649. B. Maz. 13982 fol 3–4.

Arrêts de la Cour de Parlement donné toutes les chambres assemblées de 6ème janvier 1649. B. Maz. 17648 fol 11.

Arrêt de la Cour de Parlement, 30 décembre 1650 (1651). B. Maz. 10633.

Bon advis sur plusieurs mauvais advis (1650). B. Maz. 10633 fol. 238–251.

Cathécisme des Courtisans de la Cour de Mazarin (1649). B. Maz. M 12620.

Cathéchisme des Partisans, ou résolutions théologiques touchant l'Impositions, levées et employ des Finances (1649). B. Maz. 17648 fol 39.

Choix des Mazarinades, 2 vol. (c. Moreau, ed.) 1853.

Contract de Marriage du Parlement avec la ville de Paris (1649). B. Maz. 17648 fol 29.

Décision de la Question du Temps à la Reyne Régente (1649). B. Maz. A 10666 fol 29.

Déclaration du Roy contre les sieurs duc de Bouillon, Mareschaux de Brezé de Turenne et de Marillac (1650). B. Mazarin 16033, fol 122–127.

Déclaration du Roy contre Madame la Duchesse de Longueville, les sieurs Duc de Bouillon, Marchel de Turenne, Prince de Marillac et leurs adherans (1650). B. Maz. 16033 fol 128–35.

Déclaration du Roy portant abolition générale de ce qui s'est passé en la ville de Paris l'onzième décembre dernier mil six cents quarante-neuf (1650). B. Maz. 10633, fols 92–95.

Discours sur la Députation du Parlement à M. le Prince de Condé (1650). B. Maz. 10633 fol 96–102.

Estat de la valeur des finances du roy pour l'année 1567. Brit. Mus. Ms Cott, Cal E VI, fol 27–8.

Factum pour Messieurs les Princes (1650). B. Maz. 10633, fol 244–292.

Factum servant au Procès Criminel fait au Cardinal Mazarin touchant ses intelligences avec éstrangers, ennemis de l'Estat (1649). B. Maz. 17648, fol 23.

Haranges faites à la Reyne Régente par Monsieur le Premier Président du Parlement (1650). B. Maz. 17648 fol 8.

Harangue faite à Monsieur le Duc d'Orleans par Monsieur Nicolai, Premier Président en la Chambre des Comptes (1649). B. Maz. 17648 fol 9.

Histoire des dernières guerres civiles en France (1660). B. Maz. 81490.

Histoire véritable de tout ce qui s'est fait et passé en Guienne pendant la guerre de Bordeaux (1651). B. Maz. 17641 fol 1.

Instructions sur le gaict des finances et Chambre des Comptes (1582). B. Maz. 27383.

La France Desolée aux Pieds du Roy (1649). B. Maz. 17648 fol 52.

La Fronde Royale (1650). Stadsbib, Antwerp. K-49215.

La Guyenne aux pieds du Roy (1649). B. Maz. 17641 fol 15.

La Liberté de France et l'Anéantissement des ministres étrangers (1645). B. Maz. 17648 fol 76.

La Politique du Temps: Discours pangirique du gouvernement, contenant plusieurs belles maximes d'Estat (1642). B. Maz. A 12668.

La politique étrangère ou les intrigues de Jules Mazarin (1649). B. Maz. 17648 fol 20.

La vérité découverte ou l'innocence reconnue (1650). B. Maz. 10633, fol 541.

La Voix du Peuple à Monsieur le Duc de Beaufort, pair de France (1649). B. Maz. 17641, fol 4.

Le Manifeste pour la Justice des Armes des Princes de la Paix (1641). B. Maz. A 12668.

Le Roy des Frondeurs, et comme cette dignité est la plus glorieuse de toutes les dignitéz de la Terre (1649). B. Maz. 17641, fol 42.

Le Sécret de la Paix à la Reyne (1649). B. Maz. 17648 fol 55.

Le Théologien d'Etat à la Ryene pour faire desboucher Paris (1649). B. Maz. 17648 fol 17.

Les Alarmes de la Fronde et l'insensibilité des Parisiens sur les approches du Cardinal Mazarin (1650). B. Maz. 17641 fol 36.

Les Emblèmes Politiques Presentés à son éminence (1649). B. Maz. 17641 fol 38.

Les Gabelles espuisées à Monsieur le Duc de Beaufort (1649). B. Maz. 17641 fol 7.

Les Impietéz sanglantes du Prince de Condé (1650). B. Maz. 17641 fol 9.

Les Motifs de la Tyrannie du Cardinal Mazarin (1649). B. Maz. 17648 fol 25.

Les Raisons ou les motifs véritables de la défense du Parlement et des Habitans de Paris (1649). B. Maz. 17648 fol 19.

Lettre contenant de qui s'est passé en l'assemblée du Parlement depuis 14–15 mars 1649, sur le sujet des articles signées à Reuil (1649). B. Maz. A 10666 fol 21.

Lettre des Jurats et Habitans de la ville de Bordeaux (Bordeaux, 1650). Stadsbib, Antwerp K-49215.

L' Infidelité du Prince (1650). B. Maz. 16033 fol 141–5.

L'Ombre du Grand Armand, Cardinal duc le Richelieu parlant à Jules Mazarin (1649). B. Maz. 17648 fol 47.

L'Union ou Association des Princes sur l'injuste Détention du Prince de Condé, Conty et Duc de Longueville (Bordeaux, 1650). B. Maz. 17641 fol 33.

Manifeste ou raisonnement sur les Affaires de Catalogne contre les intrigues du Cardinal Mazarin (1649). B. Maz. A 15669 fol 7.

Panégyrique à Msr. le Cardinal de Richelieu sur ce qui s'est passé aux derniers troubles de la France (1629). B. Maz. A 12668.

Récit véritable de tout ce que s'est fait et passé tant dedans la ville de Bordeaux qu'aux environs de la ville (Bordeaux, 1649). B. Maz. 17641 fol 17.

Règlement que le Roy veut Estre observé pour les subsistences de ses Armées (1638). B. Maz. A 15939.

Règlements au fait des finances. B. N. Ms francais 4222.

Relation de ce qui s'est passé à St. Germain et la députation de la Cour des Aydes (1649). B. Maz. 17648 fol 12.

Relation de l'Estat présent des soulèvements de Rouèrgue (1642). B.N. Ms. français 15621 fol 247–8.

Relation véritable de tout ce qui s'est fait et passé au barricades de Paris le 26, 27 et 28 août 1648 (1648). B. Maz. 17648 fol 5.

Rémonstrance du Roy à la Reyne Régente sur l'obligation qu'ont leurs Majestés de cesser en bref le siège de Paris (1649). B. Maz. 17648 fol 49.

Rémonstrances sur les Abus des Intendans de Justice et de la cruauté de l'Exaction des derniers Royaux à Main Armée (1649). B. Maz. 17648 fol 37.
Rémonstrances Faites au Roy en son conseil d'Estat pour la cour des monnaies (1651). B. Maz. A 10666 fol 33.
Réponse de Messieures les Princes aux Calomnies et Impostures du Mazarin (1650). B. Maz. 16033 fol 293–314.
Répose des Bourgeois et Habitans de Paris à Messieurs les Jurats et Habitans de la Ville de Bordeaux (1650). Stadsbib. Antwerp K-49215.
Suite du Vray des Assemblés du Parlement (1651). B. Maz. M 12038.
Testament de Monsieur le Cardinal de Richelieu (1642). B. Maz. A 12668.

Secondary Works

Adam, Antoine
1972   *Grandeur and Illusion*. New York.
André, Louis
1906   *Michael LeTellier et l'organization de l'armée monarchique*. Montpellier.
Antoine, Michel
1981   "Le régalement des tailles, 1623–1625" in *Revue Historique*, 265(537).
Arriaza, Armand
1980   "Mousnier and Barber: The Theoretical Underpinnings of the 'Society of Orders' in Early Modern Europe" in *Past and Present*, 89.
Asher, Eugene
1966   *Resistance to the Maritime Classes*. Berkeley.
Ashley, Maurice
1970   *Louis XIV and the Greatness of France*. New York.
Audiat, Louis
1866   *La Fronde en Saintogne*. La Rochelle.
1867   *La Reforme et la Fronde en Bourbonnais*. Moulins.
d'Avenal, Vicomte G.
1895   *Richelieu et la Monarchie Absolue*. 4 vol. Paris.
1901   *La noblesse française sous Richelieu*. Paris.
Baulant, Micheline, and Meuvret, Jean
1962   *Prix des céréales extraits de la mercuriale de Paris*, 2 vol. Paris.
Baxter, Douglas Clark
1976   *Servants of the Sword: French Intendants of the Army, 1630–1670*. Urbana, Ill.
Beik, William
1974   "Magistrates and Popular Uprisings in France before the Fronde: the Case of Toulouse" in *Journal of Modern History*, 46.
1974   "Two Intendants Face a Popular Revolt: Social Unrest and the Structure of Absolutism in 1645" in *Canadian Journal of History*, 9(3).
1985   *Absolutism and Society in Seventeenth Century France: State Power and Provincial Aristocracy in Languedoc*. New York.
Beloff, Max
1962   *The Age of Absolutism*. New York.
Benedict, Philip
1975   *Rouen during the Wars of Religion: Popular Disorder, Public Order and the Confessional Struggle*. Ph.D. diss., Princeton University.

Bercé, Yves M.
1974   *Croquants et Nu-pieds*. Paris.
1974   *Histoire des croquants: les soulèvements dans le sud-ouest de la France du XVIe et XVIIe siècles*, 2 vol. Paris.
1976   *Fête et révolte*. Paris.
Bergin, Joseph
1985   *Cardinal Richelieu: Power and the Pursuit of Wealth*. New Haven.
Bien, David and Raymond Grew
1978   "France" in *Crises of Political Development in Europe and the United States* (R. Grew, ed.). Princeton.
Bitton, Davis
1973   *The French Nobility in Crisis*. Stanford.
Bluche, F.
1960   *Les magistrats du Parlement de Paris au XVIIIe siècle*. Paris.
Bois, Paul
1960   *Paysans de l'Quest: Des structures économiques et sociales aux options politiques depuis l'époque révolutionnaire*. Paris.
Boissonade, P.
1909   "L'Etat, l'organization et la crise de l'industrie" in *Annales du Midi*.
1927   *Industrie et classes industrielles en France pendant les deux premièrs siècles de l'ère moderne, 1453–1661*. Paris.
Bondois, Paul
1924   "La première Fronde à Pont Audemar" in *Bulletin de la société des antiquaires de Normandie*, 35.
Bonney, Richard
1978a   *Political Change in France under Richelieu and Mazarin*. Oxford.
1978b   "The French Civil Wars" in *European Studies Review*, 12.
1979   "The Failure of the French Revenue Farms, 1600–60" in *Economic Historical Review*, (2nd series) 32.
1981   *The King's Debts: Finance and Politics in France, 1589–1661*. Oxford.
de Bourgneuf, Patas
1745   *Mémoires sur les privilèges et fonctions des trésoriers généraux de Franch*. Orleans.
Bourgeon, Jean-Louis
1962   L'Ile de la Cité pendant la Fronde: Structure sociale" in *Paris et Ile de France. Memories*. 13.
Bridges, John H.
1912   *France under Richelieu and Colbert*. London.
Briggs, Robin
1977   *Early Modern France, 1560–1715*. Oxford.
Brown, Bernard
1969   "The French Experience of Modernization" in *World Politics*, 21(3).
Brown, W. E.
1971   *France under the Bourbons*. London.
Brown, Walter
1973   *French Provincial Opinions at the Time of the Fronde*. Ph.D. diss. Emory University.
Buisseret, David
1966   "A Stage in the Development of the French Intendants: the Reign of Henry IV" in *Historical Journal*, 9(1).

1968   *Sully*. London
Burkhardt, Carl J.
1971   *Richelieu and his Age*. 3 vol. London.
Caillard, P.
1963   "Recherches sur les soulèvements populaires en Basse-Normandie, 1620–1640" in *Cahiers des Annales de Normandie*, 3.
Caillet, J.
1861   *L'Administration en France sous le ministère de Cardinal de Richelieu*. Paris.
Caraman, P.
1920   "La Fronde à Bordeaux d'après le registre sécret du parlement de Guyenne" in *Archives Historiques de la Gironde*, 53.
        Pt. 2   *Idem*. 54, 1921–2
        Pt. 3   *Idem*. 56, 1925–6
        Pt. 4   *Idem*. 57, 1927–8
Cans, A.
1909   *L'Organisation financière du clergé de France*. Paris.
Cauwès, P.
1895   "Les commencements du crédit publique en France: les rentes sur l'Hôtel de Ville au XVIe siècle" in *Revue d'Économie Politique*.
Charmeil, Jean-Paul
1964   *Les Trésoriers de France à l'Epoque de la Fronde*. Paris.
Chartrier, Roger
1974   "L'Ormée de Bordeaux" in *Revue d'Histoire Moderne et Contemporaine*, 21.
Chaleur, Andrée
1964   "Le rôle des traitants dans l'administration financière de la France de 1643 à 1653" in *XVIIᵉ siècle*, 65.
Cheruel, A.
1879   *Histoire de France pendant la minorité de Louis XIV*, 4 vol. Paris.
1882   *Histoire de France sous le ministère de Mazarin*. 3 vol. Paris.
Church, William
1961   "Cardinal Richelieu and the Social Estates of the Realm" in *Album: Helen Maud Cam*, 24. Louvain.
1972   *Richelieu and Reason of State*. Princeton.
Coquelle, P.
1908   "La Sédition de Montpellier en 1645 d'après des documents inédits des archives des affaires etrangères" in *Annales du Midi*, 20(77).
Courtelant, Henri
1930   *La Fronde à Paris*.
Couton, Georges
1951   *Corneille et la Fronde*. Paris.
Couyba, L.
1903   *Etudes sur la Fronde en Agenais et ses origines*. 3 vol. Villeneuve.
Coveney, P. J. ed.
1977   *France in Crisis, 1625–1675*. Totowa, N.J.
Davies, C. S. L.
1969   "Les Révoltes populaires en Angleterre, 1500–1700" in *Annales, E. S. C.*, 24.

Debidour, A.
1877   *La Fronde Angevine*. Paris.
Degarne, Monique
1962   "Etudes sur les soulèvements provinciaux en France avant la Fronde" in *XVIIe siècle*, 56.
Denis, M. J.
1892   *Littérature politique de la Fronde*. Caen.
Dent, Julian
1967   "An Aspect of the Crisis of the 17th Century: the Collapse of the Financial Administration of the French Monarchy (1653–1661)" in *Economic History Review*, 20(2).
1874   *Crisis in France: Crown, Financiers, and Society in 17th Century France*. New York.
Dessert, Daniel
1984   *Argent, pouvoir et société au Grand Siècle*. Paris.
Dethan, George
1977   *The Young Mazarin*. London.
Dwarld, Johnathan
1980   *The Formation of a Provincial Nobility*. Princeton.
Deyon, Pierre
1967   *Amiens, capitale provinciale*. Paris.
Doolin, Paul R.
1936   *The Fronde*. Cambridge, Mass.
Doucet, Roger
1920   "L'Etat des finances de 1523" in *Bulletin Philologique et Historique*.
1926   "L'Etat des Finances de 1567" in *Bulletin Philologique et Historique*.
Dumont, François
1960   "Recherches sur les ordres dans l'opinion française sous l'Ancien Régime" in *Album: Helen Maud Cam*, 23. Louvain.
1963   "Royauté française et monarchie absolue au XVIIe siècle;; in *XVIIe siècle*, 58.
1965   *Les assemblées de la noblesse de France au 17e et 18e siècles*. Paris.
Esmousin, Edmund
1915   *La Taille en Normandie au Temps de Colbert (1661–1683)*. Paris.
1935   "La suppression des intendants pendant la Fronde et leur rétablissement" in *Bulletin de la Société d'Histoire Moderne*.
1964   *Etudes sur la France des XVIIIe et XVIIIe siècles*. Paris.
Feillet, Alphonse
1862   *La misère au temps de la Fronde et St. Vincent de Paul*. Paris.
Fitch, Nancy
1978   "The Demographic and Economic Effects of 17th century Wars: The Case of the Bourbonnais France" in *The Review*, 2(2).
Floquet, A.
1842   *Hisstoire du Parlement de Normandie*, v. 4–6. Rouen.
Foisil, Madelaine
1956   "Les biens d'un receveur general des finances à Paris" in *XVIIe siècle*, 33.
1970   *La révolte des Nu-pieds et les révoltes normandes de 1639*. Paris.

Forbonnais, François Veron Duverger de
1758   *Recherches et considérations sur les finances de France depuis 1595 jusqu'en 1721*, 5 vol. Liège.
Fox, Edward W.
1971   *History in Georgraphic Perspective*. New York.
Franklin, Julian, ed.
1969   *Constitutionalism and Resistance in the Sixteenth Century*. New York.
Gaffaret, Paul
1877   "La Fronde en Provence" in *Revue Historique*, 2.
Gately, Michael, A. Lloyd Moote, and John Wills
1979   "Seventeenth Century Peasant Furies: Some Problems in Comparative History" in *Past and Present*, 51.
Germain-Martin, Louis, and Marcel Bezancon
1913   *L'Histoire du crédit en France sous le régime de Louis XIV*. v. 1. Parks.
Giesey, Ralph
1983   "State Building in Early Modern France: The Role of Royal Officialdom" in *Journal of Modern History*, 55.
Golden, Richard
1978   "The Mentality of Opposition: The Jansenism of the Parisian *Curés* During the Religious Fronde" in *Catholic Historical Review*, 64(4).
1979   "Religious Extremism in the Mid-17th Century: The Parisian *Illuminés*" in *European Studies Review*, 9(2).
1981   *The Godly Rebellion: Parisian Curés and the Religious Fronde, 1652–1662*. Chapel Hill, NC.
Gordon, D.
n.d.   *The Fronde*. London.
Goubert, Pierre
1958   "Ernst Kossman et l'énigme de la Fronde" in *Annales E. S. C.*, 1.
1959   "Les officiers royaux des Presideiaux, Baillages et Elections dans la société française au XVIIe siècle" in *XVIIe siècle*, 42–3.
1960   *Beauvais et le Beauvasis*. Paris.
1973   *Louis XIV and the Twenty Million Frenchmen*. New York.
1973a.   *The Ancien Régime*. (v. 1.: Society) New York.
1973b.   *L'Ancien Régime*. (v. 2: Les Pouvoirs) Paris.
Grand-Mesnil, Marie-Noele
1967   *Mazarin, la Fronde et la Presse, 1647–9*. Paris.
Griffet, H.
1758   *Histoire du regne de Louis XIII*, 3rd. Paris.
Grimaldi, Charles, and Jacques Gaufridy
1870   *Mémoire pour servir à l'histoire de la Fronde en Provence*. Aix-en-Provence.
Guery, A.
1978   "Les finances de la Monarchie française sous l'Ancien Régime" in *Annales E. S. C.*, 33.
Hamscher, Albert
1977   *The Parlement of Paris After the Fronde, 1653–1673*. Pittsburgh.
Hanley, Sarah
1983   *The Lit de Justice of the Kings of France: Constitutional Ideology in Legend, Ritual, and Discourse*. Princeton.

Harding, Robert
1978   *Anatomy of a Power Elite*. New Haven.
1981   "Revolution and Reform in the Holy League: Angers, Rennes, Nantes" in *Journal of Modern History*, 53.
Hatton, Ragnhild, ed.
1976a.   *Louis XIV and Absolutism*. London.
1976b.   *Louis XIV and Europe*. London.
Hayden, J. Michael
1974   *France and the Estates-General of 1614–1615*. Cambridge.
Henry, D. M. J.
1855   "Toulon pendant les troubles de la Fronde, 1649–1653" in *Bulletin semestriel de la société des sciences, belles-lettres et arts du département du Var*, 22.
Hinker, François
1971   *Les Français devant l'impôt sous l'Ancien Régime*. Paris.
Jacquart, Jean
1960   "La Fronde des princes dans la région parisienne et ses conséquences materielles" in *Révue d'Histoire Moderne et Contemporaine*, 7.
1974   *La Crise rurale en Ile de France (1550–1670)*. Paris.
de Jouvencal, Henri
1901   *Le Controleur général des finances sous l'Ancien Régime*. Paris.
Jouhaud, Christian
1983   "Ecriture et action au XVIIᵉ siècle: sur un corpus de mazarinades" in *Annales E. S. C.*, 38.
Keohane, Nannerl O.
1980   *Philosophy and the State in France*. Princeton.
Kettering, Sharon
1978   *Judicial Politics and Urban Revolt in Seventeenth Century France*. Princeton.
Kevder, Calgar
1978   "The Transition to Capitalism in 17th Century France" unpublished. Binghamton.
Klaits, Joseph
1976   *Printed Propaganda under Louis XIV*. Princeton.
1982   "Witchcraft Trials and Absolute Monarchy in Alsace" in *Church, State and Society Under the Bourbon Kings* (Richard Golden, ed.). Lawrence, KS.
Kleinmann, Ruth
1965   "The Unquiet Truth: An Exploration of Catholic Feeling against the Huguenots in France, 1646–1664" in *French Historical Studies*, 4(2).
1968   "Gratitude Revisited: The Declaration of Saint-Germain, 1652" in *French Historical Studies*, 5(3).
Knecht, R. J.
1975   "The Fronde" in *Appreciations in History*, v. 5. London.
Koenigsberger, H. G.
1955   "The organization of Revolutionary Parties in France and the Netherlands during the Sixteenth Century" in *Journal of Modern History*, 27.
Kossman, Ernest
1954   *La Fronde*. Leiden.

Labatut, Jean-Pierre.
1958   "Situation sociale de quartier du Marais pendant la Fronde parlemen-
        taire 1648–49" in *XVIIe siècle*, 38.
1972   *Les ducs et pairs de France au XVIIe siècle.* Paris.

Lassaigne, Jean-Dominique
1960   "Les revendications de la Noblesse pendant la Fronde" in *Album:
        Helen Maud Cam* 23. Louvain.

Lavisse, Ernest
1911   *Histoire de France depuis les origines jusqu'à la révolution*, 9 vol. Paris.

Leceste, Leon
1913   *Les Mazarinades.* Paris.

Lecocq, G.
1881   *Lutte entre la ville d'Amiens et le Duc de Chaulnes, gouverneur de
        Picardie en 1636.* Amiens.

Leguai, Andre
1965   "Les émotions et séditions populaires dans la généralité de Moulins au
        XVIIe et XVIIIe siècles" in *Revue d'Histoire Economique et Sociale*,
        43(1).

Lemarchand, Guy
1967   *"Crises économiques et atmosphére sociale en milieu urbain sous Louix
        XIV"* in *Révue d'Histoire Moderne et Contemporaine*, 14.

Le Roux de Lincy et Douet d'Arcy
1846   *Régistres de l'Hôtel de Ville de Paris pendant la Fronde.* 3 vol. Paris.

Le Roy Ladurie, Emmanuel
1974   *The Peasants of Languedoc.* Urbana, Ill.
1980a. *Carnival in Romans.* New York.
1980b. *Territory of the Historian.* Chicago.

Lewis, W. H.
1964   *The splendid Century.* New York.

Ligou, Daniel
1964   "Les soulèvements populaires en France de 1623 à 1648" in *Révue
        d'Histoire Economique et Sociale* 42(3).

Lloyd, Howell A.
1983   *The State, France and the Sixteenth Century.* London.

Locke, John
1953   *Travels in France, 1675–79* (John Lough, ed.). Cambridge.

Logié, Paul
1951-2 *La Fronde en Normandie.* Amiens.

Lorris, Pierre-Georges
1956   *Le Cardinal de Retz.* Paris.
1963   *La Fronde.* Paris.

Lossky, Andrew
1975   "Popular Uprisings and the System in Europe in Mid-Seventeenth
        Century" in *Reviews in European History*, 11(2).

Lublinskaya, Alexandra
1960   "Les Etats généraux de 1614–1615 en France" in *Album: Helen Maud
        Cam 23.* Louvain.
1967   *French Absolutism: The Crucial Phase.* Cambridge.

Luria, Keith
  1977   "Territories of Grace: Popular Religion, the Counter-Reformation and the Growth of the State in 17th Century France" unpublished. Berkeley.
Luthy, Herbert
  1959   *La Banque protestante en France: de la révocation de l'édit de Nantes à la Révolution.* 2 vol. Paris.
Lynn, John
  1980   "The Growth of the French Army during the 17th century" in *Armed Forces and Society*, 6(4).
Madelin, Louis
  1931   *La Fronde.* Paris.
Magné, Alfred
  1876   *Quelques Lettres relatives à l'histoire de la Fronde en Perigord.* Perigeux.
Major, J. Russell
  1960   *Representative Institutions in Renaissance France, 1421–1559.* Madison.
  1962   "The French Renaissance Monarchy as Seen Through the Estates-General" in *Studies in the Renaissance*, 9.
  1966   "Henry IV and Guyenne: A study Concerning Origins of Royal Absolutism: in *French Historical Studies*, 4.
Mandrou, Robert
  1959   "Les soulèvements populaires dns la société française." in *Annales E.S.C.*, 22.
  1963   *Classes et lutte des classes dans la premièrr moitié du XVIIIe siècle.* Florence.
  1968   *Magistrats et sorciers en France au XVIIe siècle.* Paris.
  1969   "Vingt ans après, où en direction de recherches fécondes: les révoltes populaires en France au XVIIe siècle" in *Revue Historique*, 491.
  1976   *An Introduction to Modern France.* New York.
  1977   *L'Europe Absolutiste.* Paris.
Marion, Marcel
  1910   *Les Impôts directs sous l'Ancien Régime, principalement au XVIIIe siècle.* Paris.
  1927   *Histoire Financière de la France*, 3 vol. Paris.
Merriman, George
  1938   *Six Contemporaneous Revolutions.* New York.
Mettam, Roger, ed.
  1977   *Government and Society in Louis XIV's France.* Toronto.
Methevier, Hubert
  1977   "A Century of Conflict: the Economic and Social Disorders of the Grand Siecle: in P. J. Coveny, ed. *France in Crisis: 1620–1670.* Totowa, N.J.
Meuvret, Jean
  1955   "Comment les Français voyaient l'impôt" in *XVIIe siècle*, 25–6.
Meyer, Jean
  1973   *Noblesse et Pouvoir dnas l'Europe d'Ancien Régime.* Paris.
Michaud, Claude
  1977   "Notariat et sociologie de la rente à Paris au XVIIIe siècle: l'emprunt du clergé de 1690" in *Annales E.S.C., 32(6).*

1981   "Finances et guerres de réligion en France" in *Revue d'Histoire Moderne et Contemporaine*, 28.

Molnar, Erik
1965   "Les Fondements économiques et sociaux de l'absolutisme" in *XIIe International Congress of Historical Sciences*, 12.

Moote, A. Lloyd
1962   "The Parlementary Fronde and 17th Century Robe Solidarity" in *French Historical Studies* 2(3).
1964   "The French Crown versus its Judicial and Financial Officials" in *Journal of Modern History* 34.
1972   *The Revolt of the Judges*, Princeton.

Mousnier, Roland
n.d.   *Etat et société sous François Ier et pendant le gouvernement personnel de Louis XIV*. Paris.
1948   *La vénalité des offices sous Henri IV et Louis XIII*. Rouen.
1949   "Quelques raisons de la Fronde: les causes des journées révolutionnaires parisiennes de 1648" in *XVIIe siècle*.
1951   "L'Evolution des finances publiques en France et en Angleterre" in *Revue Historique*, 205.
1952   "Etudes sur la population de la France au XVIIe siècle" in *XVII siècle*, 16.
1956   "Monarchie contre Aristocratie dans la France du XVIIe siècle" in *XVIIe siècle*, 31.
1962   "Note sue les rapports entre les gouverneurs de provinces et les intendants dans la première moitié du XVIIe siècle" in *Revue Historique*, 227.
1969a. *Paris au XVIIe siècle*. (Collection of Sorbonne lectures). Paris.
1969b. *Les Hierarchies sociales de 1450 à nos jours*. Paris.
1970a. "The Fronde" in *The Preconditions of Revolution in Early Modern Europe* (R. Forster and J. Greene, eds.). Baltimore.
1970b. *Le Conseil du roi de Louis XIII à la Révolution*. Paris.
1970c. *La Plume, la faucille et le marteau*. Paris.
1970d. *Pleasant Uprisings in Seventeenth Century France, Russia and China*. New York.
1971   *Social Hierarchies, Past and Present*. London.
1973   *The Assassination of Henry IV*. London.
1975   "Les Droits de l'Homme," paper presented to the XIV International Congress of Historical Sciences, San Francisco.
1978   *Paris, capitale au temps de Richelieu et Mazarin*. Paris.
1979   "La Fonction publique en France du début du 16e siècle à la fin du dix-huitième siècle" in *Revue Historique*, 261(2).
1980   *The Institutions of France under the Absolutist Monarchy*. vol. I. Chicago.
1984   *The Institutions of France Under the Absolute Monarchy, 1598–1789*, vol. II. Chicago.

Necker, Jacques
1784   *L'Administration des finances en France*, 3 vol. Paris.

Normand, Claude
1906   *La bourgeoisie française au XVIIe siècle*. Paris.

Olivier-Martin, Fr.
1938   *L'Organisation corporative de la France d'ancien régime.* Paris.
Pagès, Georges
1938   *Etudes sur l'histoire administrative et sociale de l'ancien régime.* Paris.
1948   *Naissance du Grand Siècle.* Paris.
1952   *La Monarchie d'Ancien Régime en France de Henri IC à Louis XIV.* Paris.
1962   *Les Institutions monarchiques sous Louis XIII et Louis XIV.* Paris.
Palm, Franklin Charles
1928   *The Establishment of French Absolutism.* New York.
Parker, David.
1971   "The Social Foundaiton of French Absolutism 1610–1630" in *Past and Present,* 53.
1978   "The Huguenots in Seventeenth Century France" in *Minorities in History* (A. C. Hepburn, ed.). London.
1980   *La Rochelle and the French Monarchy.* London.
1983   *The Making of French Absolutism.* New York.
Perkins, James B.
1886   *France under Mazarin.* 2 vol. New York.
Permezel, Jacques
1935   *La Politique financière de Sully dans la généralité de Lyon.* Lyon.
Perrers, F. T.
1872   *L'Eglise et l'état en France sous le règne de Henri IV et la régence de Marie de Médicis.* 2 vol. Paris.
Pillorget, René.
1975   *Les mouvements insurrectionnels de Provence entre 1596 et 1715.* Paris.
Porchnev, Boris
1963   *Les soulèvements populaires en France, 1623–1648.* Paris.
Prestwich, Menna
1957   "The Making of Absolute Monarchy" in J. M. Wallace-Hadrill and John McMannes, eds. *France: Government and Society.* (J. M. Wallace-Hadrill and J. McMannes, ed.). London.
Priestly, Herbert Ingram
1939   *France Overseas through the Old Regime.* New York.
Ranum, Orest
1963   *Richelieu and the Councillors of Louis XIII.* Oxford.
1963   "Richelieu and the Great Nobility: Some Aspects of Early Modern Political Motives" in *French Historical Studies,* 3(2).
1972   *Paris in the Age of Absolutism.* New York.
1980a.   "Courtesy, Absolutism and the Rise of the French State, 1630–1660" in *Journal of Modern History,* 52.
1980b.   *Artisans of Glory: Writers and Historical Thought in Seventeenth Century France.* Chapel Hill.
Regusse, Charles de Grimaldi de
1870   *Mémoires pour servir à l'histoire de la Fronde en Provence.* Aix-en-Provence.
Richet, Denis
1968   "Croissance et blocage en France du XVe au XVIIIe siècles" in *Annales, E.S.C.,* 4.
1973   *La France moderne: l'esprit des institutions.* Paris.

Rothkrug, Lionel
1965 *Opposition to Loius XIV: The Political and Social Origins of the French Enlightenment*. Princeton.
Rothbeck, George A.
1960 "The French Crown and the Estates-General of 1614" in *French Historical Studies*, 1(3).
Roux, Pierre
1916 *Les fermes d'impôts sous l'ancien régime*. Paris.
Rowen, Herbert
1961 "L'état c'est moi: Louis XIV and the state" in *French Historical Studies*, 2(1).
Rule, John ed.
1969 *Louis XIV and the Craft of Kingship*. Columbus, Ohio.
Saint-Aulaire, Comte de
1827 *Histoire de la Fronde*. 3 vol. Paris.
Salmon, J. H. M.
1959 *The French Religious Wars in English Political Thought*. Oxford.
1967 "Venality of Office and Popular Sedition in 17th Century France" in *Past and Present*, 37.
1972a. *Cardinal de Retz*. New York.
1972b. "The Paris Sixteen, 1584–94: The Social Analysis of a Revolutionary Movement" in *Journal of Modern History*, 44(4).
1976 "French Government and Society in the Religious Wars" (Forum Series). St. Louis.
1979 "Peasant Revolt in Vivarais, 1575–1580" in *French Historical Studies*, 2(1).
Schnapper, Bernard
1957 *Les Rentes au XVI siècle: histoire d'un instrument de crédit*. Paris.
1965 "Les Rentes chez les théologiens et les canonistes du XIIIe au XIVe siècles" in *Etudes d'histoire du droit canonique*. Paris.
Schneider, Robert A.
1984 "Swordplay and Statemaking: Aspects of the Campaign against the Duel in Early Modern France" in *Statemaking and Social Movements: Essays in History and Theory* (C. Bright and S. Harding, eds.) Ann Arbor, MI.
Shennan, J. H.
1976 *Government and Society in France*. Boston.
1968 *The Parlement of Paris*. Ithaca, NY
Socard, M. Emile
1876 *Supplément à la Bibliographie des Mazarinade*. Paris.
Solomon, Henry
1889 "La Fronde en Bretagne in *Revue Historique*, 11.
Sosnowski, Thomas
1975 *The French Church at Mid-Century: An Analysis of religious attitudes in the popular literature of the Fronde*. Ph.D. dissertation, Kent State University.
Spooner, F. C.
1956 *L'éconmie mondiale et les frappes monétaires en France, 1493–1680*. Paris.

Stankiewicz, W. J.
   1960   *Politics and Religion in Seventeenth Century France.* Berkeley.
Sturdy, D. J.
   1976   "Tax Evasion, the Faux Nobles and State Fiscalism: The Example of the Généralité of Caen, 1634–35" in *French Historical Studies*, 9(4).
Sutherland, N. M.
   1973   *The Massacre of St. Bartholomew and the European Conflict.* 1559–1572. London.
   1980   *The Huguenot Struggle for Recognition.* New Haven.
Tapié, Victor
   1959   "Les officiers seigneuriaux dans la société française du XVIIe siècle" in *XVIIe siècle*, 42–3.
   1974   *France in the Age of Louis XIII and Richelieu.* London.
Temple, Nora
   1966   "The Control and Exploitation of French Towns during the Ancien Regime" in *History.*
Thomson, J. K. J.
   1982   *Clermont-de-Lodève, 1633–1789.* Cambridge.
Tilley, Charles
   1986   *The Contentious French.* Cambridge, MA.
Todière, M.
   1852   *La Fronde et Mazarin.* Tours.
Treasure, G. R. R.
   1972   *Cardinal Richelieu and the Development of Absolutism.* New York.
Westrich, Saul A.
   1972   *The Ormée of Bordeaux.* Baltimore.
Wolfe, Martin
   1972   *The Fiscal System of Renaissance France.* New Haven.
Wolf, John P.
   1970   *Louis XIV.* New York.
Zeller, Gaston
   1947   "L'administration monarchique avant less intendants: parlements et gouveneurs" in *Revie Historique*, 197.
   1964   *Aspects de la politique française sous l'Ancien Régime.* Paris.

England

Primary Sources

Manuscript Collections

Calendar of State Papers, Domestic. P.R.O., London.
Harleian manuscripts. Brit. Mus., London.
Sackville manuscripts, Brit. Mus., London.

Published Works

Bonsey, Carol G. and J. G. Jenkins, eds.
   1965   *Ship Money Papers,* Buckingham Record Society.
Gardiner, S. R., ed.
   1861   *Commons Debates in 1610,* London.

1958   *The Constitutional Documents of the Puritan Revolution, 1625–1660.* Oxford.
Hinds. A. B. ed.
1911   *Calendar of State Papers, Venetian. V. 27, London.*
Prothero, G. W., ed.
1954   *Select Statutes and Other Constitutional Documents Illustrative of The Reigns of Elizabeth and James I. Oxford.*
Tanner, J. R. ed.
1961   *Constitutional Documents of the Reign of James I, 1603–1625.* Cambridge.
Woodhouse, A. S. P. ed.
1938   *Puritanaism and Liberty.* London.

Secondary Sources

Adair, John
1976   *A Life of John Hampden: The Patriot.* London.
Allan, D. G. C.
1952   "The Rising in the West, 1628–31" in *Economic History Review* (2nd series), 5.
Alexander, H. G.
1968   *Religion in England, 1558–1662.* London.
Alsop, J. D.
1982   "The Theory and Practice of Tudor Taxation" in *English Historical Review,* 97 (382).
1986   "The Structure of Early Tudor Finance, c.1509–1558" in *Revolution Reassessed* (C. Coleman and D. Starkey, eds.) Oxford.
Appleby, Joyce O.
1978   *Economic Thought and Ideology in 17th Century England.* Princeton.
Ashton, Robert
1960   *The Crown and the Money Market.* Oxford.
1978   *The English Civil War.* New York.
1979   *The City and the Court.* Cambridge
1980   "Tradition and Innovation and the Great Rebellion" in *Three British Revolutions, 1641, 1688, 1776* (J.G.A. Pocock, ed.), Princeton.
Aylmer, G. E.
1961   *The King's Servants.* New York: Columbia U.
1963   *The Struggle for the Constitution.* London.
1965   "Officeholding" in *Social Change and Revolution in England, 1540–1640,* (L. Stone, ed.). London.
1972   The Interregnum: The Quest for Settlement, 1646–1660.
1973   *The State's Servants.* London.
1980   "Crisis and Regrouping in the Political Elites: England from the 1630s to the 1660s" in *Three British Revolutions, 1641, 1688, 1776* (J.G.A. Pocock, ed.). Princeton.
Barbour, Hugh
1964   *The Quakers in Puritan England.* New Haven.

Bard, N. P.
1977   "The Ship Money Case and William Fiennes, Viscount Saye and Sele" in *Bulletin of the Institute of Historical Research*, 50.
Barnes, Thomas, G.
1961   *Somerset, 1625–1640: A County's Government During the "Personal Rule"*. Oxford.
Bernard, G. W.
1986   *War, Taxation and Rebellion in Early Tudor England: Henry VIII, Wolsey and the Amicable Grant of 1525*. New York.
Bernstein, Edward
1963   *Cromwell and Communism*. New York.
Bindoff, S. T.
1950   *Tudor England*. Baltimore.
et al. eds.
1961   *Elizabethan Government and Society* London.
Black, J. B.
1936   *The Reign of Elizabeth, 1558–1603*. Oxford.
Bowden, Peter J.
1962   *The Wool Trade in Tudor and Stuart England*. London.
Brailsford, H. N.
1961   *The Levellers and the English Revolution*. Stanford.
Brenner, Robert
1973   "The Civil War Politics of London's Merchant Community" in *Past and Present*, 58.
1976   "Agrarian Clan Structure and Economic Development in Pre-Industrial Europe" in *Past and Present;* 70.
Butlin, R. A.
1982   *The Transformation of Rural England, c. 1580–1800: A Study in Historical Geography*, Oxford.
Campbell, Mildred
1960   *The English Yeoman*. New York.
Capp, B. S.
1972   *The Fifth Monarchy Men*. London.
Carlin, Norah
1984   "Leveller Organization in London" in *Historical Journal*, 27(4).
Carlton, Charles
1980   "Three British Revolutions and the Personality of Kingship" in *Three British Revolutions, 1641, 1688, 1776* (J. G. A. Pocock, ed.). Princeton.
Clark, Peter and Paul Stock, eds.
1976   *English Towns in Transition, 1500–1700*. London.
Clarkson, L. A.
1971   *The Pre-Industrial Economy in England, 1500–1750*. London.
Clifford, C. A.
1982   "Ship Money in Hampshire: Collection and Collapse" in *Southern History*, 4.
Coleman, Christopher and David Starkey, eds.
1986   *Revolution Reassessed: Revisions in the History of Tudor Government and Administration*. Oxford.
Cooper, J. P.
1963   "A Revolution in Tudor History?" in *Past and Present*, 26.

Coward B.
  1982   "A 'Crisis of the Aristocracy' in the 16th and early 17th Centuries? The
          Case of the Stanleys, Earls of Derby, 1504–1642" in *Northern History*,
          18.
Davies, Godfrey
  1959   *The Early Stuarts 1603–1660*. Oxford.
de Salmonet, Robert Monteith
  1735   *History of the Troubles of Great Britain*. London.
Dickens, A. G.
  1939   "Some Popular Reactions to the Edwardian Reformation in Yorkshire"
          in *Yorkshire Archaeological Journal*. 34.
  1972   *The English Reformation*. New York.
Dietz, Frederick
  1928   "The Receipts and Issues of the Exchequer during the Reign of James I
          and Charles I" in *Smith College Studies in History*, 13(4).
  1964   *English Public Finance 1558–1641*. New York.
Durston, C. G.
  1981   "London and the Provinces: The Associations between the Capital and
          the Berkshire County Gentry of the early 17th Century" in *Southern
          History*, 3.
Ellis, John
  1974   *Armies in Revolution*. New York, Oxford.
Elton, G. R.
  1963   *Reformation Europe, 1517–1559*. London.
  1964   "The Tudor Revolution: A Reply" in *Past and Present*, 29.
  1966   *Tudor Revolution in Government*. London.
  1974   *Reform and Renewal*. London.
  1974   *Studies in Tudor and Stuart Politics and Government*. 2 vol. Cambridge.
  1977   *England Under the Tudors*. London.
Eusden, John
  1958   *Puritan Lawyers and Politics in Early 17th Century England*. New
          Haven.
Evans, John Y.
  1979   *Seventeenth Century Norwich*. Oxford.
Everitt, Alan
  1966   "Social Mobility in Early Modern England" in *Past and Present, 33*.
  1969   *The Local Community and the Great Rebellion*. London.
Farnell, J. E.
  1977   "The Social and Intellectual Basis of London Politics in the English
          Civil War" in *Journal of Modern History*, 49.
Firth, C. H.
  1926   "London during the Civil War" in *History*, 2.
Fletcher, A.
  1968   *Tudor Rebellions*. London.
  1983   "Parliament and People in Seventeenth Century England" in *Past and
          Present*, 98.
Fox, H. S. A. and Butlin, R. A.
  1979   *Change in the Countryside: Essays on Rural England*. London.

Fullbrook, Mary
1982   "The English Revolution and the Revisionist Revolt" in *Social History*, 7.
Gentles, Ian
1980   "Politics, Religion and the New Model Army" in *Canadian Journal of History*, 15(3).
George, C. H.
1976   "Hill's Century: Fragments of a Lost Revolution" in *Science and Society*, 40(4).
Goldstone, Jack A.
1986   "State Breakdown in the English Revolution: A New Synthesis" in *American Journal of Sociology*, 92(2).
Gordon, M. D.
1910   "The Collection of Ship Money in the Reign of Charles I" in *Transactions of the Royal Historical Society* (3rd series), 4.
Habakuk, H. J.
1940   "English Landownership, 1680–1740" in *Economic History Review* 10(1).
1965   "La disparition du paysan anglais" in *Annales E.S.C.*, 20(4).
Harriss, G. L.
1963   "Medieval Government and Statecraft" in *Past and Present*, 25.
——— and Penry Williams
1963   "A Revolution in Tudor History?" in *Past and Present*, 25.
1965   "A Revolution in Tudor History?" in *Past and Present*, 31.
Hechter, Michael
1975   *Internal Colonialism*. Berkeley.
Hexter, J. H.
1961   *Reappraisals in History*. New York.
Hibbard, Caroline
1983   *Charles and the Popish Plot*. Chapel Hill, NC.
Hill, Christopher
1940   *The English Revolution, 1640*. London.
1948   "The English Civil War Interpreted by Marx and Engels" in *Science and Society*, 12(1).
1949   "The English Revolution and the State" in *Modern Quarterly*, 4.
1956   *Economic Problems of the Church*. Oxford.
1958   "Oliver Cromwell, 1658–1958," London.
1964   *Puritanism and Revolution*. New York.
✓ 1966   *The Century of Revolution, 1603–1714*. New York.
1967a.   *Reformation to Industrial Revolution*. London.
1967b.   *Society and Puritanism in Pre-Revolutionary England*. New York.
1970   *God's Englishman*. New York.
1972   *The World Turned Upside Down*. New York.
1975   *Change and Continuity in 17th Century England*. Cambridge, Ma.
1978a.   *Milton and the English Revolution*. New York.
1978b.   "The Religion of Gerrard Winstanley" in *Past and Present*, Supplement 5.
1980   "A Bourgeois Revolution?" in *Three British Revolutions, 1641, 1688, 1776* (J. G. A. Pocock, ed.). Princeton.

1983   "Religion and Democracy in the Puritan Revolution" in *democracy*, 2(2).

1985a   "Popular Religion and the English Revolution" in *Religion Rebellion, Revolution* (Bruce Lincoln, ed). New York.

1985b   *The Collected Essays of Christopher Hill* Vol. I: Writing and Revolution in 17th Century England. Amherst.

1986a   *The Collected Essays of Christopher Hill*, vol II: Religion and Politics in 17th Century England. Amherst.

1986b   *The Collected Essays of Christopher Hill*, vol. III: People and Ideas in 17th Century England. Amherst.

Hinton, R. W. K.

1957   "The Decline of Parliamentary Government under Elizabeth T and the Early Stuarts" in *Cambridge Historical Journal*, 13.

Hirst, Derek

1978   "Court, Country and Politics before 1629" in *Faction and Parliament*, (K. Sharpe, ed). Oxford.

1986   *Authority and Conflict in England, 1603–1658*. Cambridge.

Hochberg, Leonard

1984   "The English Civil War in Geographical Perspective" in *Journal of Interdisciplinary History*, 14(4).

Holorenshaw, Henry

1939   *The Levellers and the English Revolution*. London.

Hoskins, W. G.

1968   "Harvest Fluctuation and English Economic History, 1620–1759" in *Agricultural History Review*, 16(1).

Howat, G. M. D.

1974   *Stuart and Cromwellian Foreign Policy*. New York.

Howell, Roger

1982   "Neutralism, Conservatism and Political Alignment in the English Revolution: The Case of the Towns, 1642–9" in *Reactions to the English Civil War, 1642–1649* (J. Morrill, ed). New York.

Hurstfield, Joel

1966   *The Reformation Crisis*. New York.

1979   *The Illusion of Power in Tudor Politics*. London.

Ives, E. W.

1971   *The English Revolution, 1600–1660*. New York.

Jones, J. R.

1966   *Britain and Europe in the 17th Century*. New York.

Jordan, W. K.

1942   *Men of Substance: A Study of the Thought of Two English Revolutionaries, Henry Parker and Henry Robinson*. Chicago.

1959   *A History of Philosophy in England*. London.

1968   *Edward VII: The Young King*. London.

Keeler, M. F.

1954   *The Long Parliament, 1640–1*. Philadelphia.

Kenyan, J. P.

1966   *The Stuart Constitution*. Cambridge.

1970   *The Stuarts*. London.

1978   *Stuart England*. London.

Kerridge, Eric
1953   "The Movement of Rent" in *Economic History Review*, 6.
1957   "The Revolts in Wiltshire against Charles T" in *The Wiltshire Archaeo-logical and Natural History Magazine*, 57.
Kishlansky, Mark
1979   *The Rise of the New Model Army*. Cambridge.
Lake, P.
1981   "The Collection of Ship Money in Cheshire During the 1630's: A Case Study of the Relations Between Central and Local Government" in *Northern History*, 17.
Lane, F. C.
1958   "The Economic Consequences of Organized Violence" in *Journal of Economic History*, 18(4).
Lang, R. G.
1974   "Social Origins and Social Aspiration of Jacobean London Merchants" in *Economic History Review* (series 2), 27.
Langton, J.
1978   "Industry and Towns, 1500–1730" in *An Historical Geography of England and Wales* (R. A. Dodgson and R. A. Butlin, eds.). London.
Laslett, Peter
1965   *The World We Have Lost*. New York.
Leonard, E. M.
1905   "The Inclosure of Common Fields in the 17th Century" in *Transactions of the Royal Historical Society*, 19.
Locke, John
1967   *Two Treatises on Government*, Cambridge.
Lockyer, R.
1964   *Tudor and Stuart Britain*. New York.
MacCaffrey, W. T.
1963   "Elizabethan Politics: The First Decade, 1558–1568" in *Past and Present*, 24.
Macfarlane, K. B.
1965   "The English Nobility in the Later Middle Ages" in *XII International Congress of Historical Sciences*, Vienna.
MacPherson, C. B.
1962   *The Political Theory of Possessive Individualism*. Oxford.
Mann, Michael
1980   "State and Society, 1130–1815: An Analysis of English State Finances" in *Political Power and Social Theory*, 1.
Manning, Brian
1966   "The Nobles, the People and the Constitution" in Trevor Aston, ed. *Crisis in Europe, 1560–1660*. New York.
1968   "The Levellers" in *The English Revolution, 1660–1660*, (E. W. Ives, ed.). New York.
1975   "The Peasantry and the English Revolution" in *Journal of Peasant Studies*, 2(2).
1976   *The English People and the English Revolution*. London.
        "Review Essay of Brunton and Pennington's *The Long Parliament*" in *Past and Present*, 12.
1984   "What was the English Revolution?" in *History Today*, 34.

Mattingly, Garrett
1964   *Renaissance Diplomacy.* London.
McIlwain, C. H.
1940   *Constitutionalism Ancient and Modern.* Ithaca.
Meyer, Arnold O.
1967   *England and the Catholic Church under Queen Elizabeth.* London.
Mingay, G. E.
1976   *The Gentry: The Rise and Fall of a Ruling Class.* London.
Morrill, John
1982   *Reactions to the English Civil War, 1642–1649.* New York.
1984a   "What Was the English Revolution?" in *History Today,* 34.
1984b   "The Religious Context of the English Civil War" in *Transactions of the Royal Historical Society* (5th series), 34.
Morton, A. L.
1970   *The World of the Ranters: Religious Radicalism in the English Revolution.* London.
Neale, J. E.
1949   *The Elizabethan House of Commons.* London.
Nedham, Marchamont
1650   *The Case of the Commonwealth of England, Stated.*
(1969) reprint: Charlottesville, VA.
New, John F. H.
1964   *Anglicanism and Puritanism: The Basis of their Opposition, 1558–1640.* Stanford.
Pearce, Brian
1942   "Elizabethan Food Policy and the Armed Forces" in *Economic History Review* (series 1), 12.
Pearl, Valerie
1961   *London and the Outbreak of the Puritan Revolution.* London.
1966   "Oliver St. John and the 'Middle Group' in the Long Parliament. August 1643–May 1644", in *English Historical Review,* 81.
Pennington, Donald and Keith Thomas, eds.
1978   *Puritans and Revolutionaries.* Oxford.
Plumb, J. H.
1969   *The Origins of Political Stability: England 1675–1725.* New York.
Pollard, A. F.
1920   *The Evolution of Parliament.* London.
Prestwich, Menna
1966   *Cranfield, Politics and Profits Under the Early Stuarts.* Oxford.
Price, William Hyde
1906   *The English Patents of Monopoly.* Boston.
Ramsay, G. D.
1943   *The Wiltshire Woolen Industry in the 16th and 17th Centuries.* Oxford.
Renmuth, Howard ed.
1970   *Early Stuart Studies.* Minneapolis.
Richardson, W. C.
1954   "Some Financial Expedients of Henry VIII" in *Economic History Review* (series 2), 7.
Roberts, Clayton
1966   *The Growth of Responsible Government in Stuart England.* Cambridge.

Roots, Ivan, ed.
1973   *Cromwell: a Profile.* New York.
Rowse, A. L.
1965   *The Expansion of Elizabethan England.* New York.
Russell, C. R.
1967   "Arguments for religious unity in England, 1530–1650" in *Journal of Ecclesiastical History,* 18.
1971   *The Crisis of Parliaments.* Oxford.
1973   "Parliament and the King's Finances" *The Origins of the English Civil War,* (C. Russell, ed.). London.
1979   *Parliaments and English Politics, 1621–1629.* Oxford.
Scarisbrick, J. J.
1969   *Henry VIII.* Berkeley.
Seaver, Paul ed.
1976   *Seventeenth Century England.* New York.
Sharpe, Kevin ed.
1978   *Faction and Parliament.* Oxford.
Shaw, Howard
1968   *The Levellers.* London.
Smith, Alan G. R.
1967   *The Government of Elizabethan England.* New York.
ed.
1973   *The Reign of James VI and I.* New York.
Smith, R. B.
1970   *Land and Politics in the England of Henry VIII.* Oxford.
Stone, Lawrence
1947   "State Control in 16th Century England: in *Economic History Review* (series 1), 17.
1949   "Elizabethan Overseas Trade" in *Economic History Review* (series 2), 2.
1965   *Social Change and Revolution in England, 1540–1640.* New York.
1966   *The Crisis of the Aristocracy.* London.
1972   *The Causes of the English Revolution.* New York.
1977   *The Family, Sex and Marriage in England, 1500–1800.* New York.
1980   "The Result of the English Revolutions of the Seventeenth Century" in *Three British Revolutions,* 1641, 1688, 1776 (J.G.A. Pocock, ed.). Princeton.
Supple, B. E.
1959   *Commercial Crisis and Change in England, 1600–1642.* Cambridge.
Swales, R. J. W.
1977   "The Ship Money Levy of 1628" in *Bulletin of the Institute of Historical Research,* 50(122).
Tanner, J. R.
1966   *English Constitutional Conflicts of the 17th Century.* Cambridge.
Tate, W. E.
1967   *The Enclosure Movement.* New York.
Tawney, R. H.
1912   *The Agrarian Problem in the Sixteenth Century.* London.
1935   "Review" in *Economic History Review,* 5.
1958   *Business and Politics Under James I.* Cambridge.

Thirsk, Joan
   1967   *The Agrarian History of England and Wales, 1500–1640.* Cambridge.
Thomas, Keith
   1971   *Religion and the Decline of Magic.* New York.
   1972   "The Levellers and the Franchise" in *The Interregnum: The Quest for Settlement, 1646–1660,* (G. E. Aylmer, ed.) Hamden, Conn.
   1978   "The United Kingdom" in *Crises of Political Development in Europe and the United States* (R. Grew, ed.). Princeton.
Trevelyan, G. M.
   1953   *History of England.* 2 vol. New York.
   1965   *England Under the Stuarts.* London.
Trevor-Roper, H. R.
   1966   *Historical Essays.* New York.
   1969   *The European Witch Craze of the 16th and 17th Centuries and Other Essays.* New York.
Underdown, David
   1971   *Pride's Purge: Politics in the Puritan Revolution.* Oxford.
   1981   "The Problem of Popular Allegience in the English Civil War" in *Transactions of the Royal Historical Society,* 31.
   1984   "What was the English Revolution?" in *History Today,* 34.
   1985   "The Taming of the Scold: the Enforcement of Patriarchal Authority in Early Modern England" in *Order and Disorder in Early Modern England* (A. Fletcher and J. Stevenson, eds.). Cambridge.
   1986   *Revel, Riot and Rebellion: Popular Politics and Culture in England, 1603–1660.* New York.
Unwin, George
   1927   "The Merchant Adventurers Company in the Reign of Elizabeth" in *Economic History Review* (ser. 1), 1.
Walzer, Michael
   1974   *The Revolution of the Saints.* New York.
Wernham, R. B.
   1966   *Before the Armada.* New York.
   1980   *The Making of Elizabethan Foreign Policy, 1558–1603.* Berkeley.
Williams, Penry
   1963   "The Tudor State" in *Past and Present,* 24.
   1979   *The Tudor Regime.* Oxford.
Yelling, J. A.
   1978   "Agriculture, 1500–1730" in *An Historical Geography of England and Wales* (R. A. Dodgson and R. A. Butlin, eds). London.
Zagorin, Perez
   1971   *The Court and the Country.* New York.
Zaller, Robert
   1971   *The Parliament of 1621.* Berkeley.

Index